I0815446

RECKONING WITH THE DEVIL

RECKONING WITH THE DEVIL

COURT CARNEY

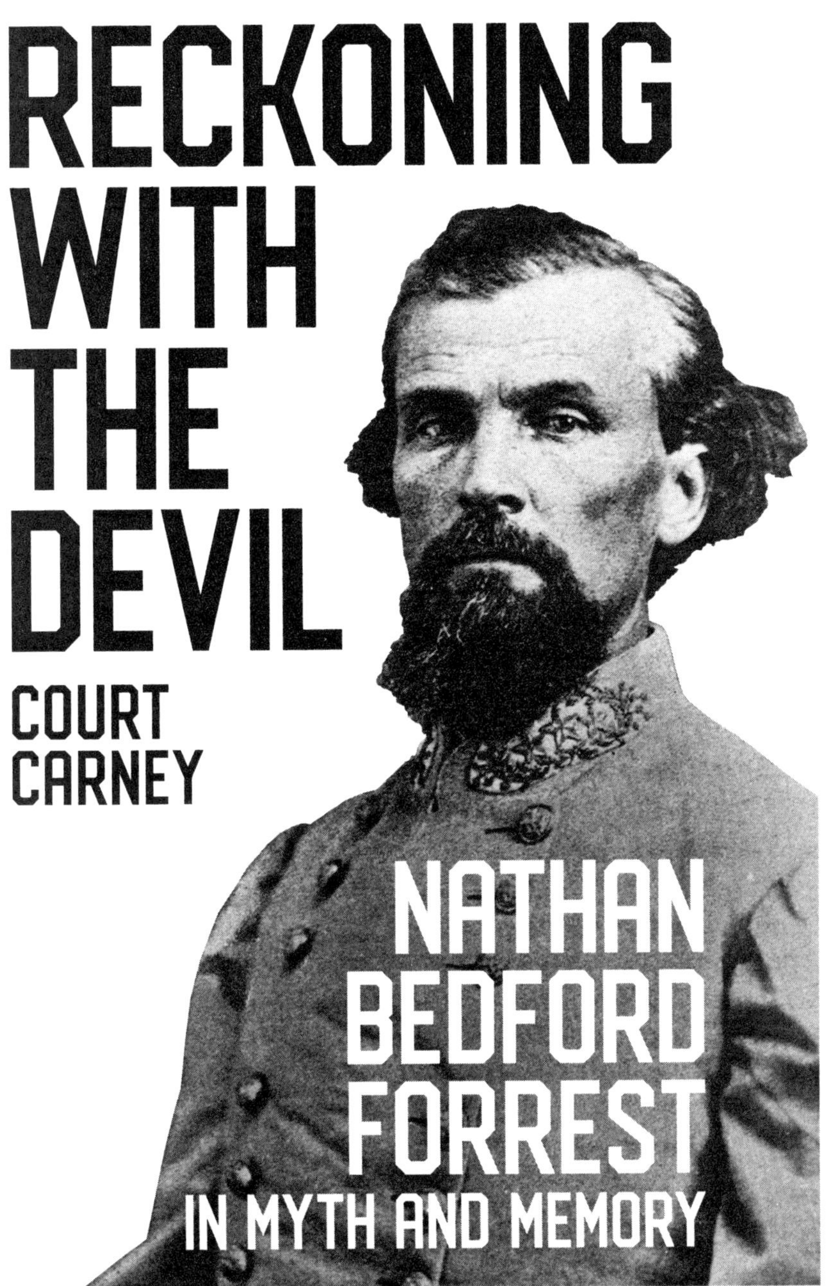

NATHAN BEDFORD FORREST IN MYTH AND MEMORY

LOUISIANA STATE UNIVERSITY PRESS BATON ROUGE

Published by Louisiana State University Press
lsupress.org

Manufactured in the United States of America
First printing

DESIGNER: Michelle A. Neustrom
TYPEFACES: Calluna, text; Areno, display
PRINTER AND BINDER: Sheridan Books, Inc.

JACKET PHOTOGRAPH: Nathan Bedford Forrest, ca. 1864. Carte de visite by Bingham & Brother's Gallery, Memphis, TN.

Portions of this book first appeared, in somewhat different form, in "The Contested Image of Nathan Bedford Forrest," *Journal of Southern History* 67, no. 3 (Aug. 2001): 601–630.

LIBRARY OF CONGRESS CATALOGING-IN-PUBLICATION DATA
Names: Carney, Court, author.
Title: Reckoning with the devil : Nathan Bedford Forrest in myth and memory / Court Carney.
Other titles: Nathan Bedford Forrest in myth and memory
Description: Baton Rouge : Louisiana State University Press, [2024] | Includes bibliographical references and index.
Identifiers: LCCN 2024009650 (print) | LCCN 2024009651 (ebook) | ISBN 978-0-8071-7153-0 (cloth) | ISBN 978-0-8071-8308-3 (epub) | ISBN 978-0-8071-8309-0 (pdf)
Subjects: LCSH: Forrest, Nathan Bedford, 1821–1877. | Collective memory—United States. | Generals—Mythology—Confederate States of America. | United States—Race relations—History.
Classification: LCC E467.1.F72 C37 2024 (print) | LCC E467.1.F72 (ebook) | DDC 973.7/13089—dc23/eng/20240314
LC record available at https://lccn.loc.gov/2024009650
LC ebook record available at https://lccn.loc.gov/2024009651

In memory of Strauss, the cat,
who will be forever missed

><

There will never be peace in Tennessee till Forrest is dead.

—WILLIAM TECUMSEH SHERMAN

CONTENTS

ACKNOWLEDGMENTS

This book has endured a long gestation period. The upside of this protracted process is that many people had an impact on the book in various ways and at various times. I want to thank:

In Nacogdoches, Charity Rakestraw, Christine Broussard, Arye Chakravartty, Hunter Hampton, David Kimling and Amy Sanford, Suparna Chakraborty and Arhaan Chakravartty, Jeff and Angie Brewer, Jimmy Crow, Jim Neal, Robert Allen, Mark Barringer, Randi Cox, Andrew Lannen, Dianne Dentice, John McDermott, Jeana Paul-Urena, and Jerry Wilson.

In Memphis, Charles Hughes, Tami Sawyer, Van Turner, Tim Huebner, Willie Bearden, Kim Bearden, Wayne Dowdy, and Tad Pierson.

In Houston, Holly and David Smith, Stephen Mills, William Tayar, Angelina Lopez and Peter Lundquist, Gabriel Lundquist, and Ana Lehrhaupt.

In cities near and far, Preston Lauterbach, David Hajdu, John David Smith, Elaine Frantz, Colin Snider, Anne Dean and Hayes Dotson, John Sacher, Gaines Foster, Bob Gudmenstead, Jason Tebbe, Colin Woodward, Chip Dawson, Eralda Lameborshi, Amy King, Jessica Dauterive, Chuck Shindo, Megan Boccardi, Michael Louderback and Jared Kahler, Nicole Greenwald, Steph and Matt Tigert, Adam and Collette Bishop, Nichole Staab, Susie Knight McNabb, Ben Cloyd, Matt Reonas, Julie Henderson, Tracey Kimbrell, Andrew Brininstool, Amy Ashford, Heather Morrison, Ava Daniels, Chris Leahy, Chad and Trishelle Edwards, Mark Boulton, Alisa Plant, Mike Parrish, and Stan Ivester.

My friends in the Woody Guthrie Teaching Collective: Aimee Zoeller, Michele Fazio, Mark Fernandez, and Gus Stadler.

My Bob Dylan crew: Erin Callahan, Graley Herren, Rob Reginio, Jim Salvucci, Nina Goss, Laura Tenschert, Jeff Fallis, and Harold Lepidus.

For their research assistance, Sarah Shade, Able Habte, and Stuart Priest.

The staff at the following libraries and archives: Laura Talley at the Memphis and Shelby County Room at Benjamin L. Hooks Public Library, Teresa Grey at the Special Collections and University Archives at Vanderbilt University, Kevin Cason at the Tennessee State Library and Archives, Bryan Cheeseboro at the National Archives, Jennifer M. Cole and Jana Meyer at the Filson Historical Society, and Marc Brodsky at the Special Collections at Virginia Tech.

Several people have played outsized roles in the years shadowed by the writing of this book. I want to thank Phil Johnson for his letters and his specific brand of inspiration. In ways large and small, this book would simply not exist without Rand Dotson's direction and patience. My parents, Rosemary and Pat, have been steadfast in their support and encouragement. My grandfather, too, was a fierce advocate for me and my work. Finally, Ashlee Knight ensured, in all the best ways, that I would finish this book. This book is for her.

Finally, special shout-outs to Blackwing pencils, Leuchtturm1917 notebooks, Java Jacks Coffee, Black Hole Coffee, Agnes Café, Herkimer Coffee, and easily two dozen other coffee shops, bars, and public spaces.

RECKONING WITH THE DEVIL

INTRODUCTION
WHY NATHAN BEDFORD FORREST MATTERS

> I have been lying like a gentleman.
>
> —NATHAN BEDFORD FORREST

The image of Nathan Bedford Forrest—slave trader, Confederate general, Klansman—reflects and refracts infinite reactions and responses. A century and a half after his death, Forrest continues to portend violence and mayhem, a battered icon representing the totality of the southern past. Forrest skulks across the southern memorial landscape with the uneasy gait of a ghost hobbled by the relentless shifts of time and perception. The Forrest image underscores how omissions and erasures continuously recast history and memory into an endless loop of transformation. Forrest collapses the distance between past and present so utterly that examining any particular moment, 2017, say, or 1998, or 1958, or 1905, sets off a reverberation that ripples backward and forward. Burnished by a century of making/unmaking and a gradual unmooring from historical context, Forrest represents any number of ideological perspectives throughout the twentieth century: the southern antihero, the archetype of self-made military genius, the What Could Have Been, the What Should Be. Forrest forces us to confront the distortions of history to make sense of the relationship between the past and the present and the desire, perhaps, to wrench new meaning out of the complicated nexus of history, memory, and a contested past. Ultimately, Forrest speaks (loudly, sometimes; quietly, sometimes) to the brutality and unpredictability of the southern past and American present.

Born in 1821 near Chapel Hill, Tennessee, Nathan Bedford Forrest grew up in a secluded patch of land in Middle Tennessee. A dearth of records and an excess of fables obscure much of Forrest's early life. In 1842, acting as head of household after his father's death, he moved to Hernando, Mississippi, where he farmed and traded and eventually helped build a successful mercantile business. He speculated. He schemed. Venture upon venture piled up. None of these endeavors made Forrest unique or remarkable within the milieu of white southern strivers. Still, he began to display a striking presence. Forrest built a persona in Hernando by fusing frontier resilience with a particularly violent and explosive temper. Hernando made Forrest. Much of what followed in his life stemmed primarily from these early forays into adulthood. The bluff, the gaze, the audacity—these elements that served Forrest well in the war found their origins in this hardscrabble town in northwestern Mississippi. In Hernando, Forrest used violence to avenge familial death. In Hernando, Forrest used intimidation to pursue his business matters. In Hernando, he met his wife, Mary Ann Montgomery, a Presbyterian minister's daughter. And in Hernando, Forrest instigated his first association with slavery as he inherited enslaved Black laborers following the murder of his uncle.[1]

The land, money, and power Forrest began to acquire in Hernando sparked in him a hunger for more. Slavery was the key, and the lucrative economic world of the trafficking of Black men, women, and children helped push Forrest up the white southern social hierarchy. This change in focus required a more extensive base than small Hernando, so in 1852, Forrest relocated his family to Memphis. There, Forrest quickly worked to expand his slave trade connections. Forrest traveled throughout the early 1850s to broaden the geography of his business. During this period, he purchased the first of several lots on Adams Street in Memphis and soon expanded his business to include his brothers and various business partners. By his mid-thirties, Forrest had emerged as one of the larger dealers in enslaved Black laborers in the area and cut a formidable shadow across Memphis society. Forrest parlayed his financial successes into a political seat as he ran for and won the position of alderman for Memphis's Third Ward—a role he kept for most of the late 1850s. The connections between business and politics afforded him a great deal of latitude in polite and impolite society. With a complex tapestry of deals related to enslaved Black laborers and real estate ventures, Forrest had amassed quite a fortune (most biographers place his wealth in terms of slavery between $50,000 and $90,000, which would sit over $1,000,000 in modern money) as well as a good deal of local power. At forty, Forrest had wealth, connections, and an extensive network of slave trade contacts that would come in handy as Tennessee moved toward secession.

In June 1861, Forrest enlisted as a private in a unit connected with the Seventh Tennessee Cavalry. He soon rose to lieutenant colonel and, by October, had command of his first regiment. Forrest's first year in the military set the pattern for much of the war: a skilled raider who fought in a handful of more significant battles. Many of these encounters, regardless of tactical or logistical importance, featured moments of electricity—Forrest slashing away at Union soldiers with his saber or having his horse(s) shot out from under him, or his battle wounds—that would help propel his name forward by contemporary and latter-day supporters. This combination of restlessness and determination made Forrest a gifted warrior on the ground and a challenging subordinate in terms of command. These same traits would also make him an indelible icon for the Confederacy: unschooled, untrained, and ferocious. By early May 1865—almost a month after Robert E. Lee surrendered to Ulysses S. Grant—Forrest began dismantling his command. For a brief moment, another path opened as Forrest considered taking the fight to Texas and perhaps Mexico. Whether or not Forrest seriously considered taking the war to Texas and beyond, it represents the ultimate Lost Cause fantasy: Forrest never surrenders and forever continues the fight. Yet Forrest did, in fact, relinquish his command. "Whatever your responsibilities may be to the government, to society, or to individuals," Forrest said in his farewell message, "meet them like men."[2]

Forrest spent the summer after the war looking into the abyss of his economic and business future. Much of the following years would serve as the template for the remaining years of his life: struggling to find that next workable financial scheme (lumber, maybe, or railroads, or cotton, or insurance, or railroads again) while negotiating the lingering questions of his actions in the Civil War. Forrest also stepped directly into state and national politics and attempted to use his fame or notoriety to influence the Democratic Party. All of these different areas of his life collided in the turbulent year of 1868 as Forrest's connection to a newly formed anti-Black organization, the Ku Klux Klan, dovetailed with his business interests as well as his political affiliations and motivations. Forrest's introduction to the Klan remains murky—a difficulty made more challenging through persistent yet spurious claims of him forming the group. Forrest represented a great asset to the group, and they soon approached him to play a more overt role in the Klan. His notoriety and fame went a long way, as did his political and business contacts, and eventually, Forrest would play a leadership role in the Klan.[3] Across Reconstruction, Forrest represented a microcosm of New South labor schemes—sharecropping, wage labor, renting, convict labor, and encouraging Chinese laborers to immigrate—in all manner of jobs: brickyards, sawmills, insurance, railroads, and all sorts of more minor speculations. Still, the Klan loomed large by the early 1870s, especially after a congressional inquiry called Forrest to testify on his knowledge of the organization. In a lengthy testimony, Forrest both edified the aims of the Ku Klux Klan and argued he had no direct connection with it. When members of Congress pushed him on various points, Forrest hedged and dissembled in an almost comical subterfuge.

Until his death in 1877, Forrest mainly confronted his legacy and position within Memphis society. These final years signified a whirlwind of upended expectations as he publicly supported Black Tennesseans after a murder at a barbeque; honored Union war dead at a cemetery ceremony; professed a newfound Christian faith; and perhaps most infamously, spoke in openly reconciliatory terms to a group of Black Memphians. Combined, these moments complicate Forrest's image across multiple vectors, then and now. These speeches, actions, and events recast his connection to Memphis even if his sincerity remains an impossible-to-solve mystery—and Forrest was nothing if not pragmatic. In other words, Forrest's status in Memphis reflected a kaleidoscopic array of infinite interactions with the city. He was a military hero for white Memphians, to be sure, but also someone who had complicated relationships throughout the city. Most of these interactions likely fell under the umbrella of Forrest desperately trying anything to rebuild his career and wealth. Yet, in his final years, Forrest suffered setback after setback. Forrest's prospects, one biographer has written of this period, "were bleak."[4]

Three central pillars—the slave trade, the massacre at Fort Pillow, and the Ku Klux Klan—represent fundamental elements of Forrest's image to his admirers and his detractors. These pieces also underscore how race and racism made Forrest a usable symbol. As much as his supporters emphasize his military accomplishments, the gnarled roots of racism and white supremacy provide the larger context of his actions and the more considerable significance of his legacy. For example, one of the keys to Forrest's success as a raider in the Civil War was his reliance on connections made through his career in the slave trade. This network of landowners sprawled across Tennessee, Mississippi, and Kentucky and allowed Forrest and his men to acquire supplies and resources. What gives energy to these points, too, is their fluidity. Although detractors claim that each of these elements of his life proves Forrest's inexcusable racial views, enough ambiguity—in definitions, sources, and a lack of sources—exists to cast doubt on every piece of this narrative.

Regarding the slave trade, to which Forrest was unquestionably connected, there are dubious claims that he avoided separating families and went to considerable lengths to provide for the enslaved men, women, and children he bought and sold. Although hardly true, the tales provided cover for people wanting to absolve Forrest of the cruelest of antebellum occupations. Forrest's connection to Fort Pillow also contained enough narrative holes and questions of definitions to allow for plausible deniability. Defenders of the general could point to the lack of direct orders—and the fact that Forrest arrived at the battlefield after the fighting had commenced—to suggest that the massacre occurred outside of his control. Not to mention, supporters have claimed, how does one even measure a "massacre"? By fighting a war of semantics on the one hand and a fine-toothed combing of the historical record on the other, defenders could argue that even one of the most egregious events in the war was not attributable to Forrest. The connection between Forrest and the first Ku Klux Klan is even more nebulous as a lack of sources related to the origins and early leadership of the "secret" society provides even more room to prevaricate. The commentators who concede that Forrest perhaps played at least some leadership role in the organization quickly added that the general moved fast to tamp down the racially motivated violence, again pointing to comments made well after the time. Of course, there are many defenders under no such illusion. They honor and support Forrest and his legacy precisely *because* he was involved in these activities.

Far from weakening the Forrest image, the fluid and ambiguous nature of these three central signifiers provides the general with authority and white cultural stability. Forrest could (and did) represent practically any element of the Civil War memorial landscape: autodidactic military genius, the cruel embodiment of violent racism, self-made millionaire, the hardened visage of the unreconstructed rebel. Forrest's image grew in power within this gnarled matrix of fact, fiction, and partisan narratives. And yet, to understand the Forrest story's potency, one must confront the realities of race, racism, and white supremacy and how these themes define the broad strata of southern and American society and culture. Without racism, Forrest becomes a vapor, another neglected southern marker of the past. Unlike other significant figures of the Confederacy (Robert E. Lee, as the best example), none of the war's broader politics connected to Forrest. Forrest was not a symbol of the principles of secession, the philosophies of states' rights, nor existential questions of the nature of sovereignty. Forrest, in life and death, operated outside of this theoretical framework. Instead, his image rests on a pedestal shaped and warped by violence and racism. Not just a farmer and enslaver before the war, Forrest operated as a slave trader known explicitly for his brutality. Not merely a warrior for Tennessee and the Confederacy, Forrest acted as the commanding battlefield officer in the uncompromising death of Black soldiers at Fort Pillow. Not just a former Confederate officer working to rebuild his life and career after the war, Forrest helped lead and shape the first iteration of the Ku Klux Klan. Ultimately, however, fluidity defined the Forrest image, and his significance shifted greatly depending on the context, and the groups engaged most directly with his memory at any particular moment. Thus, Forrest could serve as rebel, antihero, populist, and warrior while simultaneously—certainly by the late 1990s—functioning as a critical symbol of the racist and violent southern past and present.

To understand Forrest, one must first understand Memphis. Conversely, to understand contemporary Memphis, one must also confront the realities, myths, and fictions of Forrest and his place within the city's history and historical identity. The Forrest story is also the American story. The local, regional, and national threads to the Forrest story play a significant role in this book, though teasing out these stories requires nuance. Throughout the nineteenth century, Forrest connected most explicitly to the region of Tennessee, Kentucky, Mississippi, and Alabama. White southerners to the east and west of this area would no doubt know his name to varying degrees. However, Forrest's southern fame could be centered on Memphis, with concentric fading circles of fame radiating into neighboring states. In some ways, Forrest's name might have been better known in the North as the 1864 coverage of Fort Pillow spread through Chicago and New York papers. Forrest may not have pushed Robert E. Lee, "Stonewall" Jackson, or even John Mosby from newspaper coverage in Virginia. Still, by the war's end, many northerners would have had passing knowledge of Forrest via media coverage of various atrocities. By the end of the twentieth century, however, Forrest's name had much wider currency. White Tennesseans, who played such a central role in the creation of the Forrest myth, certainly saw themselves as representing the white South. Forrest's legacy played less loudly in the areas outside of where he lived and fought, but his image incorporated all of the tropes of the white South. For clarity and general consistency, I refer to "white southerners," not to infer that all white southerners knew Forrest in equal measures nor to ignore the regional divisions involved. Instead, this shorthand denotes a regional and racial categorization that helps highlight where Forrest's myth would most likely adhere. The jumbled filaments of regionalism, shifting public memory, the Lost Cause, the politics of reconciliation, and an expanding national media helped magnify Forrest's appeal by the 1990s.

When I first became interested in the Forrest memorialization story, it seemed couched within the culture wars of the late twentieth century, which served as the context for my first forays into this discussion in the late 1990s and early 2000s.[5] However, the 1990s and the fights over memorialization are a melted glacial age away from the deep, frenzied capitulation to the baser, darker natures of the American experiment of the racialized chaos of the 2010s. In some ways, the 1990s represented the crested apotheosis of the Lost Cause narrative as popular and academic sources alike pointed toward the magnetic north of reconciliation. Throughout the debates regarding memorializing the Civil War, tensions generally moved through the discourse without erupting into violence—or any real change. However, this consensus broke down by the 2010s as ideologies disconnected from the Lost Cause narrative began to define the conversation surrounding monuments and the ultimate meaning of the Civil War. The white supremacist violence in Charlottesville in 2017 capped off the tensions brewing underneath these years. With chants of "blood and soil" and violence roiling beneath mute bronze memorials to the past, Civil War statuary at once seemed hopelessly antique and at the center of the collapsing identity of the United States. The 2010s witnessed the replacement of the rather staid dialogue related to a diminished version of the Lost Cause by a furious clash of ideologies battling in the streets to the ultimate significance of this shattered American moment.[6]

This book comes from this context. I have lived with the Forrest story for a long time. The primal tendrils of the book reach back to the mid-1990s when I wrote my master's thesis on the Forrest image. This piece tended to see Forrest as ascendant, especially considering the erection of the Jack Kershaw statue outside of Nashville. At the time, the field of Civil War memory was just beginning to cohere, with the few studies that existed tending toward two critical books from the 1980s: *Baptized in Blood* (1980) by Charles Reagan Wilson and *Ghosts of the Confederacy* (1987) by Gaines Foster, who directed my thesis. In 2001, I published "The Contested Image of Nathan Bedford Forrest" in the *Journal of Southern History,* stemming from the thesis research. This article represented the first academic study of the Forrest myth, though with both the Memphis and the Nashville statues standing, it again implied a certain plateauing of his public memory. In 2005, Paul Ashdown and Edward Caudill published *The Myth of Nathan Bedford Forrest,* the first book-length examination of the Forrest image. These authors capably build a story of Forrest's legacy, especially in terms of Civil War media, though we differ in analysis, argument, and focus. Since the 2000s, several fundamental changes transformed the Forrest myth. The removal of both noteworthy Forrest statues in the late 2010s and early 2020s helped draft a different, less ambiguous punctuation mark to a 150-year-old story.

The chapters that follow trace the various clusters of Forrestphilia in roughly chronological order, spanning the way he invented a mythic persona during his life, to the construction of a Memphis statue honoring him decades after his death, to the way historiography shaped understanding of his life in the twentieth century, to the gendered and sexual elements embedded in his image, and finally to the process of monument removals in the twenty-first century that capped off a generation of protests. Chapter 1, "The Butcher," examines how Forrest curated and cultivated an image of violence. He played well with the press (North and South), and newspapers appreciated his mythic exploits. Forrest thus loomed large in the press, which helped craft his outsized legacy. Fort Pillow outlined Forrest to a national audience during the war more than any other element of his life. After the war, in 1868, Forrest served as a delegate-at-large from Tennessee at the Democratic National Convention held in New York City. His presence at the convention created much consternation within the northern press, and this chapter examines the various media portrayals that helped establish his national image. Much of this identity framing came from the cartoons of Thomas Nast. For Nast, Forrest spoke to multiple points and functioned as shorthand for the brutality of the former Confederacy, the racism of the white South, and, more important to his current readership, the casual cruelty of the Democratic Party. This chapter concludes with a discussion of Forrest's role with the Ku Klux Klan as he worked to recapture his power and position in the white South.

Focused primarily on the Forrest statue in Memphis, chapter 2, "Memphis, 1905," establishes the memorial landscape of the general and its local power. As Memphis sought to reclaim its space within the southern urban landscape in the early twentieth century, the city unveiled an expensive statue honoring Forrest. By 1905, the Klan served as a straightforward part of Forrest's image, and many of his white supporters saw this KKK as a crucial part of his importance. Later writers sympathetic to the general would attempt to distance Forrest from the Klan. Still, his late-nineteenth and early twentieth-century supporters voiced fewer questions or qualms regarding the organization. To many white Memphians, the Grand Wizard aspect of the Forrest myth signified a vital part of the civic story. Tracing how these narratives connect to Forrest allows for a unique perspective on how race and racism played essential and crucial roles in establishing and diffusing the Forrest image.

In 1931, Andrew Nelson Lytle published *Bedford Forrest and His Critter Company.* A member of the Southern Agrarians—the eccentric assemblage of Vanderbilt poets and writers—Lytle wrestled openly with the meaning of southern history and identity. The first half of chapter 3, "Forrest as History, Forrest as Fiction," thus focuses on Lytle's biography to explore the extant historiography of Forrest to that point. Lytle's book—routinely dismissed by academic writers as too factually fuzzy—remains a crucial aspect of the Forrest myth narrative. On one level, the biography works more as a symbolic manifesto than a traditional profile. Lytle largely fuses his philosophy with Forrest to craft a workable hero for the present South. In the early 1950s, Shelby Foote added to the Lytle narrative through his novel *Shiloh.* Forrest plays a prominent role in the book, and Foote soon materializes as the proxy voice for the general throughout the next fifty years. *Shiloh* sold well, and Random House asked Foote to craft a history of the Civil War that would appeal to a mainstream readership. This project culminated in a massive three-volume history of the war. In the 1980s, as documentarian Ken Burns began working on his Civil War series for PBS, he tapped Foote as an on-screen participant. Through Foote's ingratiating depictions, Forrest came through to viewers as a major player in the war. Interest in the general skyrocketed, and Forrest-themed books, including two full-scale biographies—were popular throughout the 1990s, just as the culture wars over history and its presentation began to play out in American politics and culture. Foote played a considerable role in this resurgence, and this chapter shows how Forrestphilia took off during the 1990s. Forrest transcended the racism of his core elements to serve as an all-purpose symbol of southern whiteness and masculinity.

Chapter 4, "The Most Man in the World," focuses on how gender, gendered expectations, and sexual elements contoured Forrest's iconography. Only a handful of photographs exist of Forrest, but this absence of sources provides a unique power to the ones that get reprinted. In addition to these photos, numerous descriptions of Forrest focused on his physicality and constructed an image defined by a fundamental eroticism. Sexuality and gender animate much of this discussion. Artists and writers often imbued Forrest with a particular form of swagger—an off-the-cuff volatility that shapes much of the retelling of his military exploits. By examining photographs, cartoons, pulp magazines, and novels, this chapter highlights how race and sexuality fueled much of the Forrest image. Beyond the battlefield, beyond the Confederacy, beyond contemporary politics, the general maintained a grip on white imagination in ways both blatant and surreptitious.

The final chapter, "Removal(s)," outlines how race and racism came to define the public memory of the general in specific and essential terms. As southern heritage organizations sprouted up alongside various militia groups across the country, Forrest spoke to the militarism and masculinity these groups desired. The enigmatic nature of Forrest appealed to these multiple organizations, and they could bob and weave claims that they were racist, all while claiming to be proud southerners. In the 2010s, as more and more cities began to confront—or were forced into confronting—their memorial landscapes, Kershaw's Forrest statue reemerged in the news as coy pundits used it as an example of what was at stake in this debate. Between the Charleston shooting at the Emanuel African Methodist Episcopal Church in the summer of 2015 and the white nationalist protests in Charlottesville in the summer of 2017, various activist groups attacked Confederate monuments. Also, a series of high-profile police shootings (and resultant acquittals or non-indictment decisions) led to the creation of Black Lives Matter. Within this context, the Memphis statue once again made headlines. The final section of the chapter, then, centers once again on Memphis and uses the eventual removal of the Forrest statue to examine the various perspectives embedded in a contentious series of decisions. The police shootings ultimately inspired a group of activists in Memphis to create Take 'Em Down 901, an organization focused on removing the Forrest statue—along with a smaller Jefferson Davis statue erected in the 1960s. Unlike other high-profile memorial removals, such as in New Orleans, the Memphis narrative stemmed almost exclusively from the grassroots level. In December 2017, as a crane removed the bronze statue from its pedestal, lawsuits regarding the legality of the process filtered through the court system.

Why, ultimately, does Forrest matter? He matters, of course, to some degree to the story of the Confederacy and the history of Memphis. Forrest exists within a void matrix of historical knowing and unknowing, cynical posturing, and uncritical disinterest. Distortions exist on the side of denunciation, too. For many, on either side of the Forrest debate, he served mainly as an abstraction—something that lit up political ideologies at various times, rarely consistently and rarely entirely rooted in fact. An understanding of his legacy, though, relates little to historical actions. Forrest's military exploits are mostly unknown outside a subset of Civil War enthusiasts. Still, he maintained a civic power through the more amorphous elements of his legacy. One central irony of his public image is that many of his advocates and detractors share an imprecise and often distorted understanding of his life and activities. He matters despite these historical warps and biases. Forrest matters because, at numerous times throughout the twentieth and twenty-first centuries, people have looked to him as a signifier of a particular version of the white southern past and imagined future. Two broad perspectives—he was a hero and a villain—encompassed countless more nuanced iterations of his importance.

One reason the fights over his memory sparked so much tension was because no group of people saw Forrest in precisely the same way. Admirers might focus on his military acumen, southern virility, Memphian symbolism, or white supremacy. He could mean all of these things or just a jumble of bits and pieces. Detractors, on the other hand, might share more opinions in common, but none of them corresponded directly with the issues that electrified his devotees. Erasures meant to edify Forrest are sometimes met with exaggerations intended to condemn. Fabrications abound concerning actions at Fort Pillow beyond the historical record, for example, or that Forrest initiated the Klan. Commitments to alternative and incompatible perspectives created fiction and stalled debates over the removal of monuments. But they also underscored the relative power of these arguments. Unlike tracing the significance of Ida B. Wells, say, or any number of Black Memphians—where one can see political activism connected to the expansion of the human understanding of connection—Forrest's impact and consequence reach into bleaker recesses of American history.

Forrest matters because, through a study of his image, we can view the compression of time from such an angle that the various trajectories of memory emerge as arcs across chronologies. In myth and memory, Forrest speaks to the power of the past, however imagined, to shape present-minded perceptions of the future. Tracing these debates and disputes helps explain the alternative history of the Civil War—one where winners and losers matter less than contemporary struggles over power, representation, and the implications of the past. And yet, a thread of nihilism runs through the Forrest memorial narrative. Not merely because he somehow began to represent everything and nothing, as cognitive dissonance reframed the memorial landscape and recast Confederates as both unrepentant rebels *and* patriotic Americans, but also, more crucially, at the core of his memorialization was the basic tenet of destruction, of bloodshed, of violence, of historical obliteration. Forrest matters as an illustration of the way public memory has shaped our understanding of the Civil War through a flattening of history. Forrest matters as an example of the way memorialization unmakes and demolishes any imaginable consciousness of a shared past. And Forrest matters precisely because these tensions—of construction and destruction, of building and erasure—define the ever-shifting connection between the bewilderment of the past and the disorientation of the present.

1

THE BUTCHER

> The picture of Forrest in command of a Confederate Army is about as plausible as a picture of Robert E. Lee beating his subordinates with his fists and threatening to kill Jefferson Davis.
>
> —CHARLES ROYSTER

> And at Pillow! God have mercy
> On the deeds committed there.
>
> —PAUL LAURENCE DUNBAR

War made Nathan Bedford Forrest. More precisely, *the* war—the American Civil War—conceived Forrest. Forrest's actions during the Civil War, especially when they slid across the spectrum between the unverifiable and the exaggerated, existed within the realm of myth even as he was slashing his way across furrowed and bloodied fields. The prewar slave trade made Forrest wealthy and notorious, but dozens of other white southern men held similar jobs and had similar trajectories. The Reconstruction leadership of the Ku Klux Klan made Forrest a symbol of white supremacy, but many other white southern men held similar convictions and remained nameless. The war was a hinge between Forrest's antebellum infamy and postwar notoriety. The slave trade and the Ku Klux Klan played essential roles within the Forrest mythology, but the war made him a celebrated icon in large parts of the South. However, Forrest was not a typical war hero, even within the context of the Confederate search for solace within the ravaged landscape of loss confronting the region.

A look, then, at Forrest's actions during the war, explicitly emphasizing the fragments that would cohere into the rich, flexible lore in the twentieth century, offers a good starting point to understanding Forrest as man and as myth. His creation and use of a specific and volatile image is vital to understanding his career during and after the Civil War. During the war, it allowed him notoriety and fearsomeness on the battlefield, which he used to his advantage when facing superior enemy numbers or in less advantageous positions. Fabrications, uncertainties, and exaggerations formed the nexus of his public persona. Forrest capitalized on this malleability to achieve his various means, be it outwitting Union troops, business opponents, or political rivals. After the war and his death, this plasticity defined the general's image as he could reflect many different positions. Sometimes martial, sometimes civic, Forrest could evolve and change with the times. This fluidity defined his public persona throughout the Civil War and his public memory since his death.

On one level, a parade of astonishing skirmishes, feats of fancy, improvised tactics, and broadcast bravado provided Forrest with newspaper coverage both regionally and occasionally nationally. Early biographers of the general would routinely posit these tales (sometimes losing detail, sometimes gaining) as evidence of Forrest's preternatural talent. On another level, however, specific battles and actions took on larger dimensions, moments that developed unique gravities, bending time and significance. For example, the 1864 massacre of Black soldiers at Fort Pillow shifted from a murky combination of tragedies into an essential measure of all that Forrest represented. Fort Pillow looms large across the Forrest myth. It defined Forrest more than any other military action by the late twentieth century. Opponents of the general, in particular, saw it as a crucible of violence and racism that should speak to all that Forrest symbolized. The battle and massacre came to shape Forrest more than any other issue. As crucial as the slave trade and Klan were in delineating the contours of Forrest's life and significance, the stories of battlefield trickery, ferocity, and brashness gave the myth unending power. The war made Forrest.

Forrest enlisted in the Confederate Army on June 14, 1861, one month shy of forty. He entered the war as a private. Untrained in warfare, Forrest used his intuition and wide-ranging enmity toward adversaries to good effect as he proved a particular aptitude for fighting and military life. His wealth, too, served him well as he caught the attention of his superior officers intrigued by his voluntary low rank. For much of his first year in the war, Forrest exhibited the early personal and martial values and traits that would carry him through battles large and small over the next three years. He rose in rank quickly, and within four months he commanded a regiment—the Third Tennessee Cavalry—as a lieutenant colonel. Forrest acquitted himself well in early skirmishes and, throughout the fall of 1861, he worked to build a fighting force. Much of his early training and forays in cavalry fighting took place in the heavily contested landscape of western Kentucky, where both Federal and Confederate regiments recruited and trained. Here, in the days following Christmas, Forrest stumbled upon a Union force roughly twice the size of his 150–200 cavalrymen. Although a small engagement, Sacramento established a template for many of Forrest's later encounters, especially when he commanded his own corps. At Sacramento, Forrest divided his men against a larger Union cavalry force, a tactic he would continue to use throughout the war. Speed and audacity made up for numbers, and Forrest successfully routed the Union troops.

Two battles in the spring of 1862 underscore Forrest's quickly emerging martial style, his combative relationship with his superiors, and his impulsive decision-making. In these battles, Forrest quickly studied tactics and battlefield improvisation. At the same time, these more extensive engagements placed him in a subordinate position, compelling Forrest to fight under commanders he generally found lacking in battlefield aggression. Both battles ended in Confederate losses, but Forrest's staving off greater defeat led to a growing reputation for risk-taking and brashness. Two months after Sacramento, in February, Forrest fought in a much larger battle as he led cavalry forces attached to the Army of Central Kentucky (later organized as the Army of Tennessee) to protect the Confederate-held Fort Donelson on the Cumberland River. At Fort Donelson, after several days of concentrated fighting on Forrest's part, Confederate commanders considered a surrender—an option that angered the cavalry commander. He soon led his cavalry, numbering approximately 700, out of the fort and across a shallow creek toward Nashville. The Confederate army surrendered the following day. A similar set of circumstances played out in April 1862, when Forrest fought at Shiloh, near the Tennessee-Mississippi border—an area that Forrest knew well. In the tumultuous wake of the main battle, Forrest and his cavalry worked to protect the rearguard of the Confederate army near a place called Fallen Timbers. Union Brigadier General William T. Sherman and his soldiers crashed into Forrest's cavalry. Forrest charged and immediately outran his soldiers and found himself surrounded by Union troops. A Union soldier aimed his rifle point-blank at Forrest and shot him in the pelvis. Then, in myth, if not reality, Forrest hoisted a Union soldier (sometimes implied to be the shooter) onto the back of his horse to serve as a human shield and rode off to safety. Even as the Confederacy suffered defeat, Forrest emerged as an intuitive, charismatic, and compelling warrior.

For much of the eighteen months after Shiloh, Forrest expanded on his pattern of commanding raids with small- to medium-sized forces, working in more specific constraints as an attachment to larger forces in more significant battles and bristling with most of the command structure directly over him. He also stabbed a subordinate to death. Brash, quick to anger, spontaneous, and instinctual, Forrest, in the first years of the war, transferred his lifetime of skills in the slave trade, farming, and politics into the dexterities of an emerging military talent. Untrained and uneducated, Forrest made his name through military actions audacious in their creativity and resourcefulness. Too often, however, biographers and enthusiasts often detach Forrest's military career from his prewar—and postwar—activities. His early battlefield successes notwithstanding, Forrest's military achievements stemmed from his ability to recruit soldiers and equip his troops with horses, guns, boots, and food. Working as an experienced horseman with solid, if unprofessional, fighting skills may not have set Forrest apart from many other white southern men who farmed or planted in the nineteenth century, but Forrest's prewar occupation certainly did. Slavery generally and the slave trade specifically made Forrest. His prewar career in the buying, selling, and trading of Black men, women, and children afforded him social and political power that resonated far outside Memphis. Forrest's slave-trading territory ranged across Tennessee into northern Mississippi, northern Alabama, and western Kentucky, where he fostered a network of slaving contacts in the years running up to the Civil War. Writers have long characterized these connections as "business" associates, but Forrest clearly took advantage of his slave-trade contacts to equip his cavalry and extend his recruiting range.[1] His actions in this area gave him a profound knowledge of the landscape and terrain of these states, and most of Forrest's military career can be placed along this map of slave-trade connectors. Many of his successes came through "scouts," some of them surely civilians he had worked with before the war. Through euphemisms and understatements, writers have distorted the power the slave trade afforded Forrest: giving him contacts that he used during the entirety of the war, providing him with deep pockets of resources not available to other forces in the area, a wide range of recruiting opportunities—especially given his access to boots and guns, and an intimate knowledge of how slavery and Black people undergirded the landscape. Forrest's early success in the Civil War—not to mention the culmination of horrors at Fort Pillow—stems directly from his position in the slave trade in the 1850s.

Several significant pieces of the Forrest myth came together during the period of late 1862 into late 1863, often connected to relatively inconsequential skirmishes. On New Year's Eve, 1862, Forrest engaged several Union infantry regiments near Parker's Crossroads in West Tennessee. After a day of fighting and demanding "unconditional surrender," Forrest gained momentum, a tactic he would use throughout the war. The Union commander refused. Without warning, Forrest realized that Federal forces had started moving in from the opposite direction. "Charge 'em both ways," Forrest allegedly yelled, bringing the battle to a dramatic draw and providing apocryphal fodder for his military legacy. Despite the disputed victory and small stakes, Parker's Crossroads plays a role within the Forrest image as biographers and military historians use the battle to show his emerging aptitude for using aggressive tactics on the fly. "Notwithstanding Forrest's complete surprise and defeat here," one of his earliest biographers wrote, "the careful student of his military career will not find better evidence of his remarkable genius than the fight at Parker's Crossroads."[2]

Several months later, in April 1863, another series of small-force movements culminated in a days-long slog of near-constant skirmishing against a Union force led by Abel Streight. Forrest and Streight traded advantages and disadvantages as they crawled through northern Alabama. Civilians in the area assisted Forrest throughout the ordeal, including Emma Sansom, a sixteen-year-old girl who helped guide the Confederate army across Black Creek near Gadsden, Alabama. Forrest's men eventually wore down the Union forces, and after a dramatic deception, making the northern commander believe he was hopelessly outnumbered, Streight surrendered to Forrest. However, the small victory mattered little as Streight was a diversion to Grant's move on Vicksburg. Still, the ordeal kept Forrest occupied for weeks. In the process, Forrest lost two cannons to Streight's men—who later spiked them after they ran out of ammunition. The destruction of these cannons led to a heated confrontation between Forrest and Andrew Gould, the lieutenant who had lost the artillery pieces during an ambush. The two men met soon after the battle, and Gould, feeling as if Forrest had dishonored him, pulled a gun and fired. Forrest, hit in the hip, stabbed Gould between the ribs with a knife he had been using to pick his teeth. Gould fled, and according to legend, Forrest shouted for him to stop: "No damned man kills me and lives." Later stories portray Forrest deep in grief over his actions as he visited Gould on his deathbed, where he "wept like a child."[3]

The other significant encounter between Forrest and a fellow Confederate occurred in September of 1863 after Chickamauga—another large battle, with approximately 120,000 combatants, where Forrest played a minor role. Forrest had sparred with Bragg since early 1862, annoyed by what he saw as the general's unwillingness to fight with sufficient aggressiveness. In the aftermath of Chickamauga, as Forrest moved against Union forces in East Tennessee, the cavalry commander erroneously believed that Bragg had given command of his brigades to Joe Wheeler, another Confederate officer with whom Forrest harbored a sour relationship. Incensed, Forrest confronted Bragg with an angry monologue, culminating with, "You may as well not issue any more orders to me, for I will not obey them, and I will hold you personally responsible for any further indignities you endeavor to inflict upon me." "If you ever again try to interfere with me or cross my path," Forrest told Bragg, "it will be at the peril of your life."[4] This argument, central to the Forrest myth, falls apart upon closer inspection—certainly regarding the specifics. Still, the Forrest-Bragg confrontation and its continued resonance speaks to Forrest's role in Civil War mythology. Bumbling, wavering, quick-to-anger Bragg is an easy target, and Forrest represents a useful foil with his irritability painted as virtuous and his aggression defined as necessary. The untrained cavalry commander once more got the upper hand of the West Point–trained general. By December 1863, Bragg had relinquished control of the Army of Tennessee, and Forrest wore the stars of a major general.

The most important year of Forrest's career, 1864, began quietly. Gone were the large, ground-shattering battles and relentless flanking attacks. Instead, Forrest devoted most of his energies to small-scale raids and expeditions. Moving into Kentucky in March, Forrest worked to secure Union supplies and weapons. He also aimed to pick up Confederate stragglers. Kentucky and Tennessee represented hotly contested and divided territories, and as the war dragged on, both sides confronted deserters and low morale. The introduction of Black Union soldiers also added to the thorny knot, and a region long divided by politics, secession, and varying loyalties now had an additional pressure point. On March 25, Forrest seized Union-controlled Paducah, Kentucky. The Federal forces in the area regrouped in a nearby fort and began shelling Forrest's soldiers. Forrest pushed back and eventually sent a note demanding surrender with a caveat of "no quarter." Forrest had used similar bluffs throughout his career. The Union commander rejected the proposition, and as Federal forces remained in the fort, Forrest's men stole or torched the supplies left behind. After a brief assault on the stronghold, the Confederates moved on with a small-stakes victory. Despite its relative insignificance, the battle at Paducah introduced a new element to Forrest's military landscape: armed Black soldiers.

By the spring of 1864, when Forrest first encountered Black Union troops, the move to build what would be known as the United States Colored Troops (USCT) was almost two years old in terms of policy but entwined with the central issues since the very beginning of the war. Union trepidation—at turns political (Abraham Lincoln feared losing the border states over the matter) and racist (not a few white northerners saw Black soldiers as inferior fighters)—delayed action, though Black men volunteered for service once fighting started. By the war's end, Black soldiers represented roughly 10 percent of the Union Army. In 1862, the U.S. Congress passed two acts that would, in conjunction with the Emancipation Proclamation, allow Black men to enter the Union Army and Navy. In 1863, after several minor engagements, Black regiments began fighting in more significant battles, including at Port Hudson, Louisiana, that May; Milliken's Bend in Tennessee that June; and most famously at Fort Wagner, South Carolina, in July. These efforts led to more Black recruits and growing acceptance by white commanders, though discrimination—in pay, treatment, and command—defined USCT units throughout the war. By 1864, the number of white volunteers had fallen appreciably, and USCT units began to see more battlefield action.

The arming of Black soldiers struck at the existential issues, North and South, that led to the eruption of the Civil War in the first place. As uniformed and armed Black regiments spread out into Kentucky and Tennessee, their appearance frayed the already taut lines crisscrossing the area. For three months, starting with Paducah, Forrest encountered more and more Black combatants. Looking back, it seems easy to mark how these military interactions played out. Still, the various ways Black soldiers represented the deep divisions within places like West Tennessee often get lost. Once Forrest left Paducah and headed south to Jackson, Tennessee, he reentered his home territory, the area he knew most intimately and which was most connected to his slavery business. In 1861, the plantation economy and culture centered on large numbers of enslaved people, and West Tennessee led the region to support secession (in opposition to the eastern part of the state). After 1862, however, most of the area fell under Union control. In some ways, Federal forces changed little the dynamics in West Tennessee as Union soldiers, especially near the Mississippi River, ran smuggling operations and often had no interest in undermining the system of slavery that had defined the region for generations.

Forrest's first encounter with Black soldiers at Paducah ended so ambivalently that few people commented. The appearance of the USCT in Kentucky and West Tennessee nevertheless prompted renewed anxieties in white Confederates. The spring of 1864 represented a low point in Confederate morale. Forrest kept busy during this period, capturing AWOL Confederates and amassing Union war goods. These tensions continued to ratchet up throughout the year until West Tennessee pulsed with dissension—not simply between "North" and "South" but also between southerner and southerner, Tennessean and Tennessean. The arming of uniformed Black soldiers only heightened pressures as many recently freed men volunteering for area regiments of the USCT came from local farms and plantations. Southern command structure refused to acknowledge these soldiers, and Confederate policy defined Black Union soldiers as escaped slaves; any Black Union soldiers captured would thus face enslavement or death. Forrest's men hardly needed policy to treat these Black soldiers differently from other Union troops. As more and more white Confederates engaged Black Union soldiers, the occurrence of a newly freed man fighting against a former overseer increased as rapidly as neighbors confronting neighbors. With people intimately connected across all dividing lines, the political merged with the personal, inflaming and intensifying an already contested and bloodied landscape. Paducah served as the low-voiced prologue to one of the most ignominious afternoons of the entire war.

On April 4, 1864, Forrest told his superiors that he had ordered some of his men (roughly two thousand soldiers as Forrest routinely split and divided his forces during this period) to move on Fort Pillow to capture supplies and horses. As with many infamous and terrible events, the paper trail looks exceedingly dull compared to the actions to come. The larger context of the Fort Pillow story illustrates the complexity of West Tennessee, of Border States, of divided loyalties, of Black southerners fighting for freedom on the land of their enslavement, and the bloodthirst of armies stretched to their limit, unsure and unaware of any end point. Fort Pillow occurred outside military orders because Confederate soldiers did not need orders to allow the consumptive fires of rage and racism to burn through their ranks. When Forrest and his men arrived at Fort Pillow, all the pieces were honed and placed on the board. For months, Forrest had tossed "unconditional" surrenders and "no quarter" declarations at Union lines, hoping to unnerve the enemy into bloodless submission. But Forrest also meant these words, and he was prepared to fight to the death. His men understood the tactic, and they understood the reality crouching behind whatever barricade they encountered. By the spring of 1864, Forrest's troops represented an efficient clique of horse soldiers able to fight in small, medium, or large combinations. They moved fast. They seized horses and supplies. They fought hard. They charged through Kentucky and Tennessee to wreak as much havoc as possible. Amid this frenzy of Forrest's creation emerged Black Union soldiers, many of whom were from neighboring areas, some of whom knew the Confederate general personally. All of whom were aware of his violent past and ferocious present.

Fort Pillow, located north of Memphis, began as a Confederate fort constructed in the heady days of the war in 1862. Built with slave labor on the First Chickasaw Bluff to protect Memphis, Fort Pillow—named for Confederate general Gideon Pillow—saw action as the Union Army worked to control the Mississippi River.[5] Abandoned in May 1862, Union soldiers took over Fort Pillow by that summer and maintained control throughout the next two years. Earthen fortifications and parapets constituted most of the fort, and Union soldiers had added a series of ditches to increase defensive protection. Fort Pillow saw little action during this period, and Union garrisons, which increased and decreased in size routinely through the war, occupied themselves through intermittent training, some carousing, and a good deal of smuggling as they operated around Cold Creek, which emptied into the Mississippi just north of the fort. For much of the fort's existence, soldiers from Indiana served as the garrison as well as a good example of the ambiguities of the Civil War. White Tennesseans resented the idea of Union troops in their area. Still, many of the actions of these particular Union soldiers mirrored what white locals had been doing for years. On the one hand, the Indianan-comprised garrison sheltered Confederate deserters, raided nearby farms and towns for supplies, and represented Federal occupation and control. On the other hand, the Indianan soldiers tended to have no strong feelings about emancipation and ended up much like other local farmers working in the illicit, sometimes ambiguous, world of covert trade. Far from a landscape of hard-fought ideologies and time-tested allegiances, West Tennessee slipped and skidded along more ephemeral lines as civilians sought their best advantage at any given time. The theft and pillage infuriated local civilians, and these stories of outrage made their way to Forrest once he entered the area after Paducah. The Indiana regiment had moved on by then, but the sore feelings, real and imagined, had seeped deep into the West Tennessee soil.

In the spring of 1864, Fort Pillow's garrison consisted of parts of two Black artillery units (commanded by Lionel Booth, who also served as the fort's commanding officer) and a regiment of white Union cavalry forces (commanded by William Bradford). The white cavalry troopers came primarily from Tennessee, and the problems first created by the Indiana soldiers only worsened in February and March as Bradford worked explicitly to build up his forces and counteract regular and irregular Confederate actions in the area. A divided region mirrored a divided command at Fort Pillow. Ostensibly in command, Booth had to confer with Bradford, his subordinate, on military decisions. This confusion in leadership only exacerbated an unstable garrison and led to confusion once fighting broke out. By late March, as Forrest fought at Paducah, the garrison at Fort Pillow numbered maybe 600. Once Forrest chose to hit the fort—having divided his forces—his men totaled 1,500–2,000. After a couple of years of quiet turmoil, Fort Pillow sat in the crosshairs of an army at once irritable, tired, and angry. Irate at Tennessee unionists and outraged by uniformed Black soldiers, Forrest's men crashed through forty miles of rough terrain in one night to reach Fort Pillow before sunrise on April 4.

The battle of Fort Pillow began in confusion and ended in chaos. Forrest's men (the general would not arrive until later in the morning) surprised the garrison as they tended to morning chores. The outer defenses of the fortification—a ragged "U" of trenches—fell quickly to the Confederates, and bleary Union soldiers recongregated in the central part of the fort. Confederate sharpshooters spent most of the morning picking off officers inside the fort, including Booth, whom they targeted and killed early in the battle. Bradford picked up complete command at that point but crucially ensured that the Confederacy remained unaware of Booth's death. Forrest arrived several hours into the action and quickly ordered an assault on the fort. Union forces stopped the attack, but Confederates gained favorable ground around the perimeter. The Union garrison had help from a gunboat, the *New Era,* but almost everything else failed them once they confronted actual fighting. The artillery in the fort could not be depressed far enough downward to have any effect against Forrest's troops below in the abandoned trenches and ravines. Furthermore, small arms fire could only work if Union soldiers exposed themselves on the under-protected parapets. Still, Forrest's troops contended with gunboat shelling and wide-open areas to cross if they were to surround the fort for a final assault. By midafternoon, after a Union rifleman killed Forrest's horse and knocked him hard to the ground, Forrest received word from one of his captains that "to all intents and purposes the fort was ours."[6] With this assurance, Forrest drafted a message for the Union commander, still assumed to be Booth. "I demand," Forrest wrote, "the unconditional surrender of this garrison, promising you that you shall be treated as prisoners of war." "Should my demand be refused," Forrest ended, "I cannot be responsible for the fate of your command."[7] This message echoed Forrest's standard practice for months, and he had been pushing bluffs since the war began; still, what followed would be debated for the next 150 years.

Although he held both the high ground and had superior numbers, Forrest feared Union reinforcements once another ship approached the fort. In response, and under the flag of truce, Forrest sent some of his men to the bluffs to shore up his defenses. Forrest's movements under a flag of truce would be crucial to the post-battle dialogue. Bradford, signing his name as Booth, had asked for more time to deliberate the surrender demand. Forrest saw this move as a delay tactic for reinforcements and responded that Bradford/"Booth" had only twenty minutes. The remaining Union command rejected Forrest's call for surrender, and the Confederate bugle call for "charge" resonated across the parapet and ravines. Confusion reigned as the battle swirled through the fort and down to the river. Based on extant records, congressional testimony, and later remembrances from both sides after the war, the fighting devolved once Forrest's men breached the parapet. Union artillery, filled with grapeshot, could hold off one advancing line, but Confederates swarmed up the sides of the fort before cannoneers could reload. Confederate sharpshooters continued to pick off easy targets on top of the walls. Once inside the fort, Forrest's men encountered pandemonium. Some Union soldiers fought to the death while others surrendered immediately. Some Union soldiers stayed at their positions in the fort while others rushed down the banks toward the river, hoping to make it to the gunboat. However, during the earlier surrender negotiations and unbeknownst to Bradford, the *New Era* had sailed away from the fort after exhausting its ammunition. In less than thirty minutes, almost 50 percent of the Union garrison lay dead, many of whom died after surrendering. "The River," Forrest later wrote, "was dyed with the blood of the slaughtered for 200 yards."[8] Confederate killed in action numbered fourteen.

Notwithstanding the unequal death rates in the aggregate, the racial breakdown offered starker statistics as Forrest's men killed over 60 percent of the Black soldiers at Fort Pillow. Throughout the twentieth century, various scholars worked to determine whether the battle was a massacre. Even stepping away from the "massacre" debate, the number of deaths and the wanton butchery post-surrender pushes Fort Pillow into the atrocity category. The sheer number of amplifying issues that compelled Forrest to move on Fort Pillow in the first place illustrates the tenuous situation. The presence of Black soldiers escalated the rage within Forrest's ranks and prodded them into outrageous acts of cruelty. The contradictions, gaps, and unknowns at Fort Pillow force a reckoning as to the brutality and meaning of warfare deep in the Civil War. Far from the vainglorious battles of masses of uniformed soldiers facing across broad fields, Fort Pillow countered gallantry with merciless, violent death and ruthless racial retribution. Forrest's report hints at something more extensive, too, as he writes: "It is hoped that these facts will demonstrate to the Northern people that negro soldiers cannot cope with Southerners."[9] Forrest may not have sought out specifically to attack Black soldiers, but once engaged, he allowed and condoned his men to slaughter at levels appreciably higher than in any earlier battle.

Later, supporters of Forrest pointed out that he never ordered a massacre, and once bloodshed continued to erupt, the general did all he could to stop the slaughter. But Forrest did not need to order a massacre. His men knew the game, and they knew the score. Fort Pillow stood at the apex as dozens of vectors crashed into each other—of race and racism and regional politics and fatigue, and the viscous ebbing of hope of a Confederate victory began to drain, perhaps imperceptibly, the morale of southern soldiers. The lofty ideals of secession and nation-building had dimmed in Forrest's men by this bloody moment in 1864. These men fought and camped and marched and bled on their home turf. They pursued supplies. They pursued deserters. They pursued Tennessee unionists. They pursued retaliation. And then, during these engagements, they collided with Black Union soldiers. A lack of a specific order tends to mollify supporters of the general. Yet, this absence leaves open the far more frightening idea of casual groupthink. Much of the Fort Pillow affair comes down to semantics and the parsing of definitions. What constitutes a massacre? What percentage dead equals "too much"? Which testimonials get believed? Which ones get dismissed as "propaganda"? The reality is much more straightforward: Forrest and his men killed way more combatants in more suspicious circumstances than in other similar-sized engagements. Forrest also never attempted to conceal or suppress what happened at Fort Pillow, and his reports tended toward the matter-of-fact. Forrest viewed Fort Pillow as just one more battle until it became a media story he could no longer avoid.

The repercussions of Fort Pillow played out for the next few weeks and months. News of the battle began to emerge two weeks after the battle. A Memphis newspaper broke the story on April 14, followed by an Associated Press report that set off northern reactions. The Fort Pillow massacre failed to reflect clear sectional lines as neatly as one might anticipate. While generally appalled at the news, a not small number of white northerners (including some military leaders) disagreed with enlisting and arming Black soldiers. Forrest's actions, disgusting as most northerners viewed them, stemmed in part from the presence of the USCT units. Forrest's own report several weeks after the battle made this situation his major point as he emphasized that the battle proved Black soldiers represented no threat to Confederate armies. Confederate reports eventually cohered to a position of "no massacre." Yet, the earliest pieces (out of Memphis and New Orleans) condemned the violence and undue bloodshed, with newspapers routinely calling it a "slaughter" of various proportions. Two points remain evident in this early coverage: news spread rapidly, with the national discourse on the battle growing to an uproar in just two to three weeks after the battle. Secondly, although perspectives on the idea of a massacre converged along regional lines eventually, the early reports represented a muddle of interpretations. Southern newspapers used the language of massacre before conforming to a latter stance of blaming northern newspapers for exaggerating all claims of gratuitous killing. For Forrest's part, he moved quickly on from Fort Pillow and entered Mississippi to resupply and gather reinforcements. The Confederate Congress praised Forrest and his soldiers "for their late brilliant and successful campaign."[10]

On May 4, 1864, the *Chicago Tribune* published an article (credited to correspondence with the *New York Tribune*) that connected Fort Pillow to the darker impulses that braced much of Forrest's life. "The news of the capture of Fort Pillow by Forrest," the writer began, "and the cowardly butchery which followed of blacks and whites alike, has produced a profound sensation here." Instead of summarizing the battle, the newspaper writer plunged into a detailed discussion of Forrest's connection to slavery and the slave trade. "They [Forrest and his brothers] accumulated large sums of money in their nefarious trade," the writer noted, and Forrest "won by that and other influences" promotion in the "women-whipping, baby-stealing Rebel Confederacy." Puncturing the self-made southern myth, the *Chicago Tribune* explicitly connected Fort Pillow to Forrest's slave business. The rest of the article detailed brutal accounts of torture and death of enslaved Black men and women at the hands of Forrest. One man, "whipped to death by Bedford . . . was secretly buried." The murder and burial were "known only to the slaves of the prison, who only dared to refer to the circumstance in whispers." A direct contrast to southern descriptions of Forrest (contemporary and later biographical interpretations), the Chicago article corrodes the myth while simultaneously bonding the horrors of the Adams Street slave pen to the terrors committed just north at Fort Pillow. Few other sources, certainly in the 1860s, even mentioned Forrest's occupation as a slave trader, yet this northern writer contextualized Forrest's actions at Fort Pillow with these earlier atrocities. "Such are," the article concludes, "the appropriate antecedents in the character of the monster who murdered in cold blood the gallant defenders of Fort Pillow."[11]

Irrelevant in terms of strategy, Fort Pillow played an important part in the growing conversation over morale, race, and prisoners of war. As the war slogged past the three-year mark, finding new ways to maintain resolve remained difficult, but the battle and massacre provided a new slogan of "Remember Fort Pillow" for Union forces. Despite some ambivalence of white northerners to take up the cause of Black soldiers, Fort Pillow also demonstrated that the members of the USCT fought bravely against a recalcitrant enemy. A critical element that connected these issues related to the thorny conversation surrounding the treatment of prisoners of war and the exchange of Union and Confederate captives. Race played a central role here as Confederate leadership refused to acknowledge the legitimacy of Black soldiers. Abraham Lincoln had a standing order condemning the Confederate position and pushed for retaliation against Confederate prisoners if any Black soldiers suffered mistreatment. Nothing came of these orders, and the Confederacy backed away from its position of labeling Black soldiers as enslaved insurrectionists even as Black soldiers continued to face brutal treatment throughout the war. In conjunction with media reports, these high-level discussions led to a congressional investigation into Forrest's actions at Fort Pillow. A subcommittee sought out testimony from as many sources as they could find. These witness accounts underscore the severity of the actions taken against Black soldiers by men under Forrest's command and stand as a sober reminder of the scale of atrocities committed that afternoon. Politics and racism shaped reactions to the massacre, but it bears notice just how quickly these accounts, testimonies, and responses transpired. Not a month had passed—deep within the Civil War, no less—before action and (re)reaction materialized on both sides. After Fort Pillow, after Forrest's name came to represent unforgiving violence and precipitous aggression after Forrest captured a new sobriquet of "The Butcher," William T. Sherman referred to Forrest in a dispatch as simply "the very devil" and wanted the Confederate cavalry leader's power checked. "There never will be peace in Tennessee," Sherman concluded, "till Forrest is dead."[12]

Fort Pillow represented something much more expansive than a matter of military policy or political maneuvering for Black soldiers. The desire to fight for the Union cause energized Black men throughout the country. Still, the fear of something like Fort Pillow drifted through the ranks from the very origins of the USCT. In West Tennessee, as formerly enslaved men donned Union uniforms and mustered near their captivity, the fears of reprisal rang even more forcefully. Still, they fought. For the next few months, if not throughout the final year of the war, Fort Pillow's shadow fell across every confrontation between Black soldiers and white Confederates. The cries for retaliation swelled, and an already fraying sense of order on both sides came close to snapping. At the battle of Brice's Crossroads, two months later in northeastern Mississippi, Black soldiers donned "Remember Fort Pillow" badges and armbands as they went into action. The handmade badges at Brice's Crossroads, the poems and lines of Black poets, and the violence-soaked memories of survivors and families led to a secret history of death, destruction, and loss that never came to the surface throughout much of the twentieth century. As the river shifted course away from the long-removed fort over the last 150 years, the battle site gives up even fewer of its mysteries. Tellingly, however, the most accessible aspects of the space for visitors today are the ditches and ravines that served as doomed defensive trenches and hastily made mass graves. Fort Pillow continues to challenge.

The media helped make Fort Pillow a story, but Forrest engaged with newspaper owners and journalists throughout his career. A central element of the Forrest myth relates to his untutored military understanding and rudimentary grasp of written English. Substantially true, these elements undervalue Forrest's use of the media to his own ends and his ability to push newspaper narratives and coverage. As with so many other components of his life, Forrest's manipulation of the media most likely originated during his time as a slave trader, where he used advertising and personal politics to shape public opinion. As a city alderman, Forrest understood the power of the Memphis press. An early example of Forrest's media shrewdness related to a less-covered incident in 1859 when he planted a story in the press advertising that his inventory of enslaved men and women included the daughter of Frederick Douglass. "She remembers," the article noted, "her 'parient' very vividly, having seen him" during a recent trip to North Carolina, her birthplace. "Fred," the article concludes, "is ample able to make the outlay he should either purchase his own flesh and blood from servitude, or cease his shrieks over an institution which possesses such untold horrors."[13] No doubt a sarcastic rejoinder to Douglass's national prominence, the article floated around southern newspapers and served as an attack on Douglass and an advertisement for Forrest's services—his crude humor connecting directly with white southerners in and adjacent to the slave trade.

During the Civil War, Forrest employed newspaper editors and writers on his staff as aides-de-camp, among other positions. Matthew Gallaway, a one-time owner of the *Memphis Avalanche,* served with Forrest at various times throughout the war. He also worked to get positive press for the general into regional newspapers and helped shape public opinion of Forrest.[14] George Adair, from Georgia, also worked with Forrest. A slave trader like Forrest, Adair owned an Atlanta-area newspaper and would later work on Forrest's staff. Later, Adair wrote affirmative pieces about Forrest's slave pens, which would significantly affect the way later historians would write about his business practices.[15] Henry Watterson also worked briefly on Forrest's staff and wrote for several newspapers throughout the war. Forrest's public image rested in considerable measure on the press reports written by his staff. These writers helped craft Forrest's image in real time as columns and articles emanated from encounter after encounter. This favorable press played off in various ways for Forrest as his minor raids made headlines even far from more significant battles. Staff writers also reframed lapses in judgment and battlefield losses. Readers, too, began to see Forrest as a personality to follow as these print pieces reached a larger audience.

Forrest's two early recruitment posters in Memphis newspapers underscore his use of journalists to get what he wanted and his growing sense of dramatic public flair. The first recruitment poster, no doubt written by Galloway, ran in the *Memphis Avalanche* in August 1861. "FOR ACTIVE SERVICE!" the notice proclaimed as Forrest sought out men to round out a mounted regiment. "Now, freemen!" the ad concluded, "rally to the defense of your liberties, your homes and your firesides!" Specific and appealing to protecting their land, Forrest's first published recruitment attempt had the hallmarks of journalist integrity, if not Forrest's voice. A year later, in the *Memphis Appeal,* Forrest once again pushed for recruits, asking for two hundred "able-bodied men . . . with good horse and gun" to join him in battle. This time, however, Forrest omitted the call to home and hearth. Instead, this announcement climaxed with "Come on, boys, if you want a heap of fun and to kill some Yankees."[16] Forrest rarely played into the pretense of superficial courteousness, and here, he dictated what he wanted to see in print. Nothing staid or conventional here. Forrest spoke the language he knew and anticipated it would reach the audience he wanted. Preternaturally aware of the power of harnessing community opinion and crafting a public persona, Forrest used these skills throughout the war to influence both civilian and martial arenas. His outsized reputation after the war rested considerably on how he manipulated and contorted his image as someone who saw warfare as one more piece of southern masculine fun. At the same time, aggression and violence exemplified the point, and Forrest demanded to be seen in the most fearsome light by northerners and southerners alike.

Four years after Fort Pillow, in 1868, the public connection of Forrest to the massacre hit a high note as the general moved more in the public eye than at any other time of his life. Basil Duke's train story and Andrew Lytle's spinster encounter transpired as Forrest went to New York City to attend the Democratic National Convention. These two stories illustrate how Fort Pillow continued to throb in the national consciousness. In 1868, as Forrest served as a delegate-at-large from Tennessee at the Democratic National Convention held at Tammany Hall in New York City, Fort Pillow signified everything. His presence at the convention created much consternation within the northern press, and media portrayals established his *national* image. Much of this identity framing came from the pen of Thomas Nast. For Nast, Forrest spoke to various points. He used the general as shorthand for the brutality of the former Confederacy, the racism of the white South, and, first and foremost, the casual cruelty of the Democratic Party. The battle served as convenient shorthand not only for Forrest but for white southern aggression and dishonor. Tellingly, these stories became part of the Forrest myth as pro-Forrest writers employed them to underscore his brashness.

In the immediate postwar period, Forrest attempted to reclaim his prewar wealth built on slavery in the inhospitable (to him) soil of emancipation and free labor. Most of these ventures kept him in the public eye throughout the mid-1860s as he attempted various railroad and insurance schemes. Forrest's military fame afforded him diverse opportunities in a transforming South. Politics, too, circulated around him as the former alderman mingled with politicians and former Confederate officers. Forrest's political views tended toward the pragmatic. Several interwoven affairs defined much of his political viewpoint, including local and state elections and the dense knot of issues related to freedmen and voting rights. On a more personal level, however, Forrest devoted much of his energy to obtaining a presidential pardon. Forrest navigated the intersection of local, state, and national politics in the years after the war, though Fort Pillow continued to shape these interactions. The fight for a presidential pardon and his trip to New York in 1868 underscore how the Fort Pillow massacre shaped his public image. The twentieth century hinged on the general's other associations and actions. Still, for the next four decades, Fort Pillow served as the shorthand for Forrest, the unrepentant white South, and racist violence coursing through much of the nation.

Between 1865 and 1868, Forrest repeatedly appealed for a pardon from President Andrew Johnson for his service during the war. The history of pardoning former Confederates tracks with the larger history of Reconstruction. Abraham Lincoln devised a pardon policy in 1863, but Republicans in Congress deemed it too lenient. This dynamic defined the question of pardons through the end of the war. In May 1865, just weeks into Andrew Johnson's presidency, the administration announced a new policy incorporating a wide range of exemptions. These new provisions—including Confederates who served above a certain rank and prewar monetary and property holdings—effectively barred Forrest from a pardon. Despite these new requirements, which placated congressional Republicans, Johnson began pardoning large numbers of Confederates that summer. Forrest first applied for a pardon in July 1865. Arguing that he "owed his first allegiance to his state," Forrest wrote that he entered the war as a private and had "acquiesced in the fate of war" before returning to his Mississippi home. Forrest's case for amnesty centered on his contention that he fought for his home state, implying he had little regard for the politics of secession and that he ended the war "fairly whipped" and ready to enter postwar America as a patriotic citizen. The administration denied his appeal.[17]

Forrest was always a pragmatist, and his attempts at amnesty led him into several political friendships. In 1866, Forrest allied with Frank Blair, a Union major general who left the Republican Party after the war. Blair wrote a personal appeal on behalf of Forrest and noted that "his courage, in more than a hundred battlefields," outweighed any condemnation stemming from Fort Pillow. Unmentioned in his 1865 appeal, Fort Pillow emerged as the centerpiece of Forrest's pardon search from 1866 into 1868.[18] Several months later, in November 1866, Forrest wrote another petition, this time arguing in far more personal tones about his situation. "I am also aware," Forrest wrote, "that I am at this moment regarded in large communities, at the North, with abhorrence, as a detestable monster, ruthless and swift to take life, and guilty of unpardonable crimes in connection with the capture of Fort Pillow on April 12th[,] 1864." "Perhaps at a time of political excitement so fierce and high as at present," Forrest noted, "this [misjudgment] of my conduct and character should not surprise me. Nevertheless[,] it pains, and mortifies me greatly." Forrest's acknowledgment of his position in society shows a degree of self-knowledge. However, self-interest plays into his plea as travel restrictions, more than any other limits, hurt his business ventures (including possible activities with the Ku Klux Klan). Regardless, Forrest had to confront his image as the Butcher of Fort Pillow before he could move forward in other areas of his life. Forrest (or likely Gallaway) wrote of the "heavy wounding weight of undeserved obloqy [*sic*]" pressing down on the general. "In conclusion," Forrest wrote, "I take occasion to say that I shall continue to do all that I can to assuage ill feeling, and promote a spirit of moderation, and accommodation. Moreover, I will say further, that should your excellency deem it as likely to subserve the purposes of pacification, I would even waive all immunity from investigation into my conduct at Fort Pillow, that might attach to my parole."[19] This 1866 push resulted in an extension of Forrest's parole, which allowed greater travel freedoms, but his application for a pardon again failed.

Whether or not Fort Pillow functioned as the political stumbling block for his pardon, Forrest worked to mitigate the damage—to a degree. Forrest never apologized or even admitted to any wrongdoing at Fort Pillow. Instead, he focused on undermining the veracity and integrity of the many sworn statements and testimonies from the congressional report that repeatedly appeared in northern newspaper coverage of the general. Fort Pillow and Forrest's public infamy and intermittent interest in politics coalesced in the summer of 1868 as he pressed upon his network of influential friends to obtain a pardon. Forrest threaded the needle between seeking a pardon and advocating for white southern political victories for the Democratic Party. A lack of a pardon limited his political aspirations—if he had any—and opportunities, but he used soft power to influence local and state politics. His friendship with Gallaway helped, too, as the *Memphis Avalanche* continued to publish pro-Forrest articles as well as featuring an editorial slant in line with Forrest's overall agenda. Forrest left few specific indications of his ideological viewpoints, though he generally and unsurprisingly supported the platform of statewide Democratic leadership, on the one hand, and detested what he saw as the radical agenda of Republicans such as Governor William Brownlow, on the other.

In early June 1868, Forrest attended the state Democratic convention in Nashville. The leadership of the state Democratic Party sought to select delegates for the national convention to be held in New York City later that summer and sort out diverse political matters, including a statement opposing "the negro supremacy of the Congressional plan of reconstruction."[20] On June 9, Forrest's name surfaced during deliberations over possible delegates at large. His nomination caused not a little consternation and perhaps confusion. Division characterized West Tennessee Democrats over considering Forrest as a delegate, and the two major Memphis newspapers sparred over the decision. Much of the tension, at least on the surface, concerned procedural issues as party members had already submitted a slate of delegates, but Forrest's notoriety played a role. The chairman of the convention argued to associates that Forrest's "nomination as a delegate for the State at large would produce incalculable injury to the Democracy in the approaching struggle." For his part, Forrest gave a speech punctuated with cheers and laughter from the crowd where he argued "he was willing to withdraw his name" and that he "had not come there for self-aggrandizement."[21] The convention soon named Forrest to the delegation, though he admitted to the *Memphis Avalanche* that "Conservative Tennesseans acted very strangely when they wished to proscribe him." The Republican-backed *Knoxville Whig* used the general to contest the pro-Confederacy aspects of the convention and referred to him simply as "N.B. Forrest, the Fort Pillow Butcher."[22]

Once in New York City, Forrest pushed for Andrew Johnson's nomination at the national convention after his first choice, George Pendleton, stalled out in votes. Johnson's bid began to falter, and the convention turned to Horatio Seymour as a candidate with Frank Blair, Forrest's friend, as running mate. Quiet throughout most of the proceedings, Forrest rose to cast Tennessee's vote for Blair. Later, Forrest contended that he had worked hard to get delegates to support Johnson and shifted only after the vote deficit proved insurmountable.[23] Yet, regardless of his personal political views, Forrest's overt and loud support of Johnson paid off in ways unrelated to the national scene. On July 17, 1868, after three years, Andrew Johnson pardoned Forrest.[24] Perhaps Johnson wanted to ingratiate himself with southern Democrats during the nomination process. Perhaps Forrest's explicit service to Johnson's cause procured a last-minute change of heart. At any rate, personal, regional, and national politics played a role in the decision. They underscored Forrest's interpersonal strengths even as the media outside the white conservative South struggled to comprehend the general's inclusion. The *New York Tribune*, perhaps exhausted by the entire story, simply mocked Forrest as the "hero of the Massacre at Fort Pillow."[25]

Instead of dissipating, the attention on the Fort Pillow massacre only intensified as Forrest played a more public role throughout 1868. Four years did little to assuage northern (and southern Republican) assessments of Forrest—and the massacre showed more relevance in the run-up to the 1868 presidential election than at any point since 1864. Between Forrest's presence in New York City, his pardon, and the publication of the only biography written with his support, Forrest held the national spotlight longer than at any other point in his life. This exposure received enhancement through a series of cartoons published in a national magazine. More than a speech or an article or an editorial, the brashest condemnation of Forrest and Fort Pillow came from the pen of Thomas Nast, a staff artist for *Harper's Weekly.* Between July and October of 1868, Nast published seven cartoons featuring Forrest and Fort Pillow in some capacity. His first Forrest cartoon appeared coincidentally the week the general received his pardon and centered on the different components of the Democratic Party. Throughout the summer leading up to the election of 1868, Nast lampooned the Democratic Party as a coalition of Irish immigrants, New York bankers, and white southern former Confederates united by racism. Nast places Forrest on the far right of the drawing wearing a small pin marked "FP," his shorthand for Fort Pillow.[26] Near Forrest stands Frank Blair, another target of Nast's as the vice-presidential candidate's outspoken racism framed the cartoonist's view of the Democratic Party.

The best-known of Nast's 1868 cartoons ran in *Harper's Weekly* on September 5. Entitled "This Is a White Man's Government," this image stands as the quintessence of Nast's art related to Reconstruction generally and the election of 1868 in particular. The drawing centers on the Democratic Party, represented as a triune of a crudely caricatured white Irishman holding a club marked "a vote"; August Belmont, a Jewish banker from New York City, gripping money for voter bribes aloft; and in the center, Nathan Bedford Forrest—the three men pressing their boots onto the back of a Black man reaching out for the ballot box. Forrest, occupying the focal point of the heavily detailed tableau, wears a "CSA" belt buckle and clutches a dagger labeled "THE LOST CAUSE" over his head; on his lapel sits a badge featuring a skull and the words "Fort Pillow." Nast knew Forrest's notoriety would carry enough meaning without much more than a representative portrayal of his face and a few signifiers. Forrest was far from the most visible Confederate officer during or after the war, but the collision of his inclusion at the Democratic National Convention and the constant low hum of the clamor created by the massacre at Fort Pillow made the general one of the most recognizable southerners in the nation. Nast deepened the racial connotation of the cartoon by adding a whip protruding from the general's back pocket. Between the massacre at Fort Pillow and the slave trade, Nast intensified his representation of the Democratic Party as unrepentant, violent, and racist.

After "This Is a White Man's Government," Forrest and Fort Pillow appeared in several other cartoons before disappearing after the election. For

Thomas Nast, “This Is a White Man’s Government,”
Harper’s Weekly, September 5, 1868.

Nast, Forrest and Fort Pillow represented the violent shadow self of the Democratic Party, and the cartoonist used these images to puncture what he saw as the superficial nature of the platform. In addition, Forrest served as a key example of the racial hypocrisy of the party. In one cartoon, Forrest sits at a table beneath a banner reading: “Gen. Forrest late CSA heroe [*sic*] of Fort Pillow, and your best friend.” In a later image, Nast quotes the Confederate commendation of Forrest’s “late brilliant and successful campaign” at Fort Pillow. Nast also simplified the image to its essence with a four-panel image mirroring a wanted poster entitled “The Leaders of the Democratic Party.” The general stands in the upper right corner, clutching a flag marked "No Quarter" and the caption: "The Butcher Forrest." Irony and actuality blurred into a collage of brutality, complicity, racism, and revulsion, as Nast's 1868 series of cartoons both satirized the contemporary political scene of postwar America and, at the same time, served as a template for images of the general in the twentieth century. These later images, though, would come from supporters of the general. Thus, Nast unwittingly created an image that found its use in oppositional ways. Nast's portrayal of Forrest setting fire to a globe while firing a pistol in the air, published in October 1868, could easily find a home in pro-Forrest tableaus today. Removing Forrest from Nast's context, with the satire and irony leached from the ink, the exaggerated anger and raised dagger of the Lost Cause with a holstered pistol and bullwhip became simply the lens through which his advocates saw the general. Within a century, the cartoonish metamorphosized into the literal and a new form of viciousness eclipsed Fort Pillow.

Besides Nast and newspaper copy, the summer of 1868 also passed down two Forrest stories flecked with enough myth to call into question any historical veracity and underscore why Forrest held the public imagination in such a peculiar way after the war.

Somewhere between Nashville and New York City, a train congested with former Confederates made a water stop at a depot. Word of the passengers on the train had spread out along the route, and crowds had started to collect at various points along the way. Three years after the Civil War, tensions intensified as northerners and southerners circulated once more into public spaces. Nathan Bedford Forrest had boarded the train in Tennessee to travel to New York to serve as a delegate for the Democratic National Convention. Four years had failed to dull northern public opinion of Forrest, known colloquially as the "Butcher of Fort Pillow," and the general's service as a delegate at large for the Democratic National Convention only inflamed long-simmering animosities. Fort Pillow acted as a mist around the general—preceding, following, and enveloping Forrest's actions for the rest of his life. Fort Pillow allowed northerners to caricature Forrest as the embodiment of white southern cruelty and depravity. As a result, he stood as the most obvious villain in any retelling of the Reconstruction story—a role the general cultivated with purpose and a gleam in his eye. Basil W. Duke, a Confederate officer from Kentucky, shared Forrest's coach. Duke had befriended the train conductor, who had fought for the Union but "was a very fine, manly young fellow." As the train pulled to a stop, the conductor informed Duke about brewing trouble at the depot as "the town bully, a very truculent fellow," made his intentions clear to storm the train and confront Forrest. Duke writes this chronicle as if he, too, wanted to see what the general might do.[27]

"Where's that damned butcher, Forrest? I want him."

The boldness of this unnamed man in the unnamed town electrified the passengers on the train. Forrest, however, barely responded to the news or the implied threat of violence. He had encountered this reaction repeatedly since he had reentered civilian life. To that point, Duke's narrative devotes as much space to the former Union conductor as to the confrontation with Forrest. The conductor, Duke emphasizes, stood to protect Forrest and the other passengers as nervous excitement careened through the train. Duke takes pains to bring the conductor into the Forrest fold. Once the man enters the train car, the attention shifts to Forrest, with Duke in awe of the change that took over the general. "I never in my life," Duke writes, "witnessed such an instantaneous and marvelous transformation in any one's appearance as then occurred with Forrest." The general sprang from his seat and "strode rapidly down the aisle toward the approaching champion." From reserved and retiring to quick-tempered and unpredictable, Forrest stormed toward the man with "perfect, invincible determination." "I am Forrest," the general declared, "what do you want?" With a glance, the northerner shrank away and jostled his way off the train with Forrest in brief pursuit before bursting into laughter. Forrest, Duke notes, made "new friends and admirers" as he made his way back to the train.[28]

Twenty years after Duke compiled his memoirs, Andrew Lytle published his biography of Forrest. Lytle wedged into his book several stories that read more like exaggerated folktales—and some of these accounts may have been oral tradition in the Forrest family. Lytle includes Duke's train-car clash and adds to the convention narrative with a confrontation at Forrest's Manhattan hotel room. The general and his son Willie shared a room, and during the convention, a knock on the door disrupted Forrest's slumber. Still in bed, Forrest asked Willie to attend to the unexpected visitor. Willie opened the door to a stern, angry woman looking to confront Forrest. The woman pushes past Willie and barges into the room. "Are you the Rebel General Forrest," she demanded. "[I]s it true," she continued, "that you murdered those dear colored people at Fort Pillow?" Lytle's account turns to the curious as Forrest lies half-dressed in his bed. As with Duke's narrative, the significant element relates to Forrest's quick transformation from passive to electrified in moments. "Yes, madam," Forrest replied, "I killed the men and women for my soldiers' dinner and ate the babies myself for breakfast." The woman screamed, turned, and ran out into the street.

Regardless of their place on the spectrum of invention, these two stories tell us a lot about postwar Forrest, the complicated landscape of Reconstruction, the mythic contours of reconciliation, and how white southerners could contort the general to advance any agenda. Duke devotes specific attention to the general's physical attributes: his form "erect and dilated," his face of "heated bronze," his eyes "flaming, blazing." Forrest manifested "perfect, invincible determination." Lytle, too, focused on the corporal with Forrest rising from his bed, still in his sleeping attire, to his "full height, his hair on end." In a preface to the hotel story, Lytle writes of Forrest's introduction to the public spaces of New York, where he drew considerable attention. To clear a path, Forrest "swept his mighty shoulders around," which resulted in a traffic jam. These stories also characterize the nameless northerners as frenzied ciphers that crash into a calm and resolute Forrest. Forrest's initial composure leads to action, but only in response to the unwarranted interruptions. The explosive Forrest is also the point. His physical and rhetorical response produces the crowd-pleasing climax. Duke's and Lytle's audiences expected this version of Forrest. Still, it matters, too, that the general is outside of the South (on a northbound train, in a Manhattan hotel room); the general commands even in unfamiliar surroundings and situations. He is at once recognized, applauded, loathed, cheered, and detested, and Forrest's postwar life played out in public, with volatile confrontations becoming the norm.[29]

All of this was true to the spirit of the general, if not true to the facts. These tales allow Forrest's military strengths to play out in the civilian arena. Outnumbered and in enemy territory, Duke's Forrest calmly waits for the opponent to show his hand before leaping onto the offensive. The bully's "purpose evaporated" and fled, but Forrest kept up the pursuit, "following him into the midst of the crowd outside." Duke writes the scene as comedy, with Forrest erupting into laughter and "the entire crowd joined in his merriment and seemed to be in complete sympathy with him." For Duke, Forrest represented the spirit of conciliation—only on his terms—as the general had attained celebrity status. Lytle echoes these sentiments in his description of Forrest on Fifth Avenue, where his frustration with onlookers led to a growing throng of curiosity seekers. Where Duke allegorized Forrest's military tactics, Lytle pairs Forrest off against a "spinster," which helps to highlight his southern manhood. Lytle inverts the roles, with Forrest underdressed lying in bed and the firm-jawed "spinster" playing the aggressor as she pushes aside Willie Forrest, then in his early twenties. These two stories encapsulate much of what the postwar Forrest image contained. Central to an understanding of Forrest's appeal in the years after the Civil War is his infamy, his celebrity, and his use of these two elements to craft a persona at once fearsome and self-aware.

Fort Pillow circumscribed Forrest's postwar public image. Yet, as the public all but focused on the massacre, Forrest's actions in 1867 and 1868 centered on a series of associations that would define the general's image from the twentieth century onward. At some point, in the first eighteen months after the Civil War, Forrest joined the Ku Klux Klan, an enigmatic guerrilla organization twisted out of a white social group formed in Pulaski, Tennessee, in 1866. Forrest had no connection to the origins of the group, though he knew several of the group's early leaders. By 1867—stories differ as to when exactly—Forrest worked with the group in various capacities before very quickly being named "Grand Wizard," a title based on "wizard of the saddle," his nickname during the war. Forrest's connection to and leadership of the Klan spanned the late 1860s and occupied his time during the run-up to the 1868 election. For his part, Nast mentioned the Klan in various cartoons but never explicitly connected Forrest to the group. As the twentieth century progressed, however, talk of the Butcher of Fort Pillow yielded to a focus on Forrest as the "Grand Wizard." Still, the organization's purposefully secret origins and a general absence of records and self-serving (false) recollections make it nearly impossible to reconstruct Klan leadership's specifics. For his part, Forrest flirted enough with the truth to give credence to his role in determining the direction of Klan activities during this period.

Throughout the twentieth century, Forrest's supporters continued to roil the historical waters by developing competing narratives that argued some blending of (a) proud defiance ("of course, Forrest led the Klan"), (b) vague equivocation ("Forrest led the Klan only until it became violent"), and (c) blurry concession ("Forrest may have played some role in the Klan, but his military record is more important"). Detractors of the general complicate the story further by unambiguously arguing a range of discursive points framed by the ahistorical (Forrest started the Klan) to the decontextualized (Forrest's actions writ small mirrored the Klan's actions writ large). Somewhere within this whirlwind of truths, half-truths, and inventions lies a relatively simple story: a group forged in post-Emancipation rage devoted to white supremacy and racial violence appealed to Forrest, who served as the natural figurehead to grow the organization through a multifaceted network of social, business, and political connections. Forrest understood the postwar white South—its fears, challenges, and myths—and had the fame and the leadership skills that made him attractive to the early organizers of the Klan. The Klan had no reason to cajole or instruct Forrest; the entire situation worked symbiotically and offered both parties incentives.

The history of the Ku Klux Klan encompasses several entangled pieces and lacks a straight line connecting the earliest meetings and the white terrorist organization into which it would evolve. White rage festered across the post-Emancipation landscape of Tennessee, and a combination of real and perceived threats to the southern white (Democratic) social order motivated elites across the state to assert social and political power. The earliest incarnation of the Ku Klux Klan began within this context as a club of six white men in Pulaski, Tennessee. Unfortunately, a lack of detailed sources along with blatant and purposeful dishonesty shroud much of the origins of the Reconstruction-era Klan, and much of what exists tends toward the contradictory. Lacking a centralized organization and emulating a military hierarchy from their often-shared Confederate past, the Ku Klux Klan was a blanket identifier for numerous disaffected groups of mainly white southerners with fluid allegiances, shifting ideologies, and ever-changing goals. In terms of early leadership, however, everyone knew everyone, and these relationships shaped the early Klan's outreach and development. What started in Pulaski in December 1865 spread quickly through these interpersonal connections. Fraternal, secretive, rageful, militant, violent, and amoebic, the Reconstruction Klan evolved rapidly and chaotically in its first year. Muddled in its structure, the Klan cohered to the southern wing of the Democratic Party and operated socially and politically to advance white supremacy along local, regional, and national lines. Self-identifying as the bulwark against the immeasurable changes confronting white southerners after the Civil War, the Ku Klux Klan fused complementary pieces into a workable organization devoted to racial antagonism. But they lacked a leader.

Forrest's connections to the Klan stemmed from a series of friends and acquaintances already connected to the organization. During the war, Forrest's artillery captain, John Morton, wrote extensively about his former boss's introduction to the Klan. Morton's book, *The Artillery of Nathan Bedford Forrest's Cavalry,* published in 1909, outlines Forrest's involvement with enough hedge words and passive voice to elide responsibility. "It is believed," Morton wrote, "that the 'Grand Wizard' was no less a personage than Nathan Bedford Forrest." "As the possessor of dauntless and sustained courage, resourcefulness, and a grim disregard of all consequences," Morton argued, "no more ideal leader of such a movement ever appeared upon the American stage."[30] Morton's testimony and tone serve as essential sources as the artillery commander more than likely brought Forrest into the Klan. Two decades Forrest's junior, Morton adored the general and worked hard to stay in a favorable relationship with him. In 1866, Morton, still only in his early twenties, allegedly invited Forrest to the Maxwell House Hotel in Nashville to induct him into the Klan. Morton hints at this relationship while simultaneously downplaying the fundamental objective of the organization. The Ku Klux Klan, to Morton, "was at first merely an association of college boys for the playing of those mysterious pranks in which the ebullient heart of youth takes keen delight."[31] Ignoring its racial violence, lynching, and terrorism, Morton purposefully diminished the organization's intent while also bolstering Forrest's role in the Klan.

Morton's tale may well be true or true-ish, but a conflicting narrative places George Gordon (who later would serve an essential role in the memorialization of Forrest) at the center of the initiation. This story centers on Forrest's excitement at the prospect of Gordon's proposal, with the general responding: "That's a good thing; that's a damned good thing. We can use that to keep the niggers in their place."[32] Some retroactive jockeying took place between Gordon and Morton as people wrote themselves into Forrest's Klan history, but Forrest represented an obvious choice for the organization given his infamy, his contacts, and his reputation. Regardless of who did the initiating, the Klan welcomed Forrest readily into the organization and soon carved out a leadership position named after his Civil War nickname of "wizard of the saddle." Forrest thus served as the first "Grand Wizard" of the Ku Klux

Klan. However, when Forrest took over the Klan leadership, the organization's alleged prankish origins had long mutated into anti-Black violence and anti-Republican political activism. Masked, cagey, secretive, and purportedly anonymous, the Ku Klux Klan spread throughout the South rapidly as the goals and methods of the organization enticed white southerners across the class spectrum. Although Forrest's leadership links the group to an ever-widening circle of influential former Confederates, the Klan proliferated because it connected to various organizations already crisscrossing the white South. Democratic associations, rifle clubs, and local and regional groups dedicated to blocking the rights of freedmen and women already populated the post–Civil War southern landscape, and the Klan—with its famous adherents—plugged directly into this fertile mix of racism and fury.

Much of the modern interpretations of Forrest's tenure with the Klan by his supporters hinge on his assumed actions to restrain the organization. As the summer of 1868 progressed, violence became more and more pronounced against Black southerners and white Republicans. These actions led to an emerging anti-Klan movement. Tennessee governor Brownlow signed into law a series of acts meant to disrupt and dispel the Klan and like-minded organizations. Brownlow also sought to use the state militia, including Black volunteers, to oust the Klan from specific counties. Forrest saw these movements, especially the use of Black militiamen, as a personal offense, and in August, gave a blistering speech arguing that Brownlow endeavored to label all Democrats and Confederates as Klansmen to instigate a Civil War in Tennessee. "But if they send the black men to hunt those Confederate soldiers whom they call Kuklux," Forrest argued, "then I say to you, 'Go out and shoot the Radicals.' If they do want to inaugurate civil war, the sooner it comes the better that we may know what to do." Defensive and angry, Forrest's intentional misreading of Brownlow further escalated the talk of civil unrest. Forrest almost immediately backtracked from these remarks and claimed a reporter misrepresented them. In an interview a few days after his original speech, Forrest pushed back against a reporter who questioned the viability and even existence of the Klan. Forrest responded that the organization extended "all over the South" and that "in all the Southern states about five hundred thousand men" served as members. "I could raise 40,000 men in five days," Forrest threatened, if Brownlow sent Black militiamen after the organization. The *New York Times* published this interview, which pressed Forrest to reply that he "did not mean to convey the idea that I would raise any troops." These exchanges characterized Forrest's relationship with the press after the Civil War. First, say something exaggerated and inflammatory that played well with his supporters—in this case, fellow Klansmen. Then deny you ever said the printed statements to maintain a semblance of professional decorum—all while blurring threats with crowd-pleasing humor. Forrest played it both ways: upholding a fearsome persona for newspapers and the opposition and casting enough confusion to muddle criminality or culpability.[33]

Mirroring the organization's shadowy origins, the end of Forrest's leadership of the Klan rebuffs a firm conclusion or date. In late 1869 or 1870—dates differ—Forrest issued a proclamation for all Klan chapters to cease all terrorism and destroy all regalia.[34] Since the 1860s, Forrest's decision has created a swirl of explanations. With a positive spin, John Morton argued that Forrest disbanded the organization once it had earned political and social victories. "When the white race had redeemed six Southern states from Negro rule in 1870," Morton maintained, "the grand Wizard knew that his mission was accomplished and issued at once his order to disband."[35] Modern interpretations cohere to a combination of Forrest disapproving of the violent turn of the organization, presumably during and after the election of 1868, and the general's annoyance at not having more control over the group. Neither of these positions makes much sense as Forrest rarely shied away from violence—particularly delegated violence—and he generally distanced himself from directly implicated Klan violence. The control issue breaks down because the Klan had always been undermanaged, decentralized, and locally anarchistic. Still, Forrest may have tired of reporters calling on him to answer for all Klan actions everywhere. His political acumen, or at least political contacts, may also have alerted him to increased anti-Klan pressure from Washington, DC. Ultimately, Forrest probably saw a lessening return on his overall investment in rebuilding his prewar wealth. Klan notoriety, after all, paid few bills.

On a national level, the Ku Klux Klan's impact on civil rights and the larger Republican platform during Reconstruction pushed Congress to investigate the organization and enact legislation to protect Black Americans' legal and voting rights. The Fifteenth Amendment, ratified in February 1870, established constitutional protections regarding voting rights for men. In May, Congress passed the first of several Enforcement Acts that banned terroristic threats against citizens wanting to vote. Under this act, the president had the power to use the army and state militias to counteract groups such as the Klan. In April 1871, a new Enforcement Act (also referred to as the Ku Klux Klan Act) allowed the president to suspend *habeas corpus* to combat the Klan and comparable groups. These acts led to the arrest of hundreds of suspected Klansmen and significantly curtailed the machinations of the first iteration of the Ku Klux Klan. As part of the legislative process, Congress held a series of hearings related to accounts of Klan terrorism. Congress eventually summoned Forrest to appear before the committee to discuss his actions and connections with the Klan. Forrest's testimony veered from manipulative half-truths to outright falsehoods, with many of his statements a noncommittal haze of evasion and prevarication. Still, he explicitly laid out the white supremacist context of the Klan: "negroes . . . were becoming insolent," he says at one point, or "[white] ladies were ravished by some of these negroes."[36] Pushed to explain the political motivations of the Klan, Forrest responded: "There was a great deal of insecurity in the country, and I think this organization was got up to protect the weak, with no political intention at all."[37] Later, Forrest told a friend, "I have been lying like a gentleman."[38]

Despite Forrest's dismissiveness of the Klan and his leadership of the organization, he elucidated his position in the eyes of the white Reconstruction South. "I was getting at that time [1867] fifty to one hundred letters a day," Forrest argued, "and had a private secretary writing all the time." "I was receiving letters from all the Southern States," Forrest explained, "men complaining, being dissatisfied, persons whose friends had been killed, or their families insulted, and they were writing to me to know what they ought to do."[39] Although Forrest confronted a range of issues, financial and otherwise, on a personal level, his public persona as the hard-fighting cavalry officer offered white southerners a suitable symbol of resistance. Regardless of his leadership position in the Klan, Forrest cast a formidable shadow across the white South. White southerners no doubt respected his martial prowess as much as his tendency towards ferocity, and the Butcher of Fort Pillow resonated far beyond the bluffs north of Memphis. White southerners intuitively trusted Forrest to speak to their fears and interests, particularly in Tennessee and the Deep South. Perhaps they did not join the Klan, disagreed with specific parts of his past, or had concerns far afield from the general's focus, but they still saw Forrest as a dependable and trusted warrior on their behalf. Forrest reflexively understood the knotted roots of white fury more than most other southern leaders. He understood the racism that snaked across the fractured southern landscape. He understood the white rage that spiraled out of Confederate defeat. He understood the myths that turned these facts upside down. He understood the sword's symbolic power and the gun's harsh reality. Forrest served as a hero to a particular slice of the unrepentant and aggrieved white South. "I had," Forrest declared, "the confidence of the southern people."[40]

In May 1865, just days after surrendering his command, Forrest encountered a northern writer, Bryan McAlister, near Meridian, Mississippi. In a "small cabinroom," McAlister noticed a group of Confederate officers encircling Forrest "neatly dressed in citizen's clothes of some gray mixture, the only indication of military service being the usual number of small staff-buttons on his vest." Forrest cut a striking figure to McAlister, who noted that he "should have marked him as a prominent man had I seen him on Broadway; and when I was told that he was the 'Forrest of Fort Pillow,' I devoted my whole attention to him." McAlister transcribed most of his conversation regarding Fort Pillow and related matters. "Any one hearing him talk," McAlister argued, "would call him a braggadocio. As for myself, I would believe one half he said, and only dispute with him with my finger upon the trigger of my pistol." McAlister's remembrance shifted from the military (the general retold Fort Pillow and Streight's Raid from his perspective) to the personal—Forrest confessed that he looked forward to fishing and not seeing "any one for twelve months." Still, McAlister threaded through his piece Forrest's predisposition towards violence and brutality. The writer concludes with a brief story of Forrest killing two young men, incorrectly thinking they had deserted. "The fathers of these youths," McAlister notes, "are upon Forrest's track, sworn to kill him." "Poetic justice," McAlister writes, "requires that [Forrest] should meet a violent death." Forrest struck McAlister as a maelstrom of humor and ferocity, equally attracted to and repelled by the general. "What a charming hero he would make," McAlister argued, "for a sensational 'King of the Cannibal Islands!'"[41]

Even in the immediate dying ember twilight of the Civil War, McAlister, like Duke and Lytle after him, understood the mythic proportions of Forrest's public image. Forrest cut a compelling figure—at turns aggressive, astute, humorous, dishonest, and racist. McAlister grasped the volatility and horror embedded in Forrest's posturing, just as Duke witnessed blindered honor and strength, and Lytle saw a comical tableau steeped in regional retribution. These three (white) narrators grasped the sometimes-conflicting elements stitched together to shape the Forrest persona, even if McAlister, Duke, and Lytle diverged in plotting their significance. In the decades after the Civil War, as history slid into myth, the various components of Forrest's personality and character coalesced into an identifiable, if mutable, form. His military exploits settled into the hardening amber of static set-pieces. With few written records connected to his personal life, Forrest drifted quickly into the two-dimensional world of caricature and distortion. After he died in 1877, most northerners moved on, relegating him to the soon-to-be-forgotten drawer of Fort Pillow. White southerners, however, worked to keep his public memory active through commemoration and memorialization. By the early twentieth century, these celebrations severed Forrest from his historical moorings and allowed the general to serve limitless purposes for limitless audiences. The decontextualized echoes of the 1860s continued to reverberate in various ways and directions in the decades after his death. Those closest to Forrest—his fellow warriors, business partners, and political allies—had some say in his legacy. As this group died off, the Forrest image experienced a resurgence as younger people, mainly connected to Memphis, saw Forrest from a fresh perspective. No longer frozen in the past with the Civil War, the Forrest image entered the twentieth century amorphous, alluring, and fluid enough to signify practically anything. The Butcher now occupied the infinitely redefinable Present.

2

MEMPHIS, 1905

> So far as Memphis is concerned, the unveiling of the Forrest monument will be one of the noteworthy episodes in her history. We have no hesitation in saying that it will mark a new era not only in Memphis, but in the South.
>
> —Memphis newspaper editorial, 1905

> Public art claiming to represent our collective memory is just as often a work of historical erasure and political manipulation. It is just as often a violent inscription of myth over truth, a form of "over-writing"—one story overlaid and thus obscuring another—modeled in three dimensions.
>
> —ZADIE SMITH, 2020

Nathan Bedford Forrest, dead and buried in the sludge end of Reconstruction, pulled at Memphis in ways large and small in the late nineteenth century. His specter magnetized white Memphis, and as the daily interactions with a difficult neighbor began to fade in death, the *idea* of Forrest increased in worth. In 1877, an outsider journalist witnessed Forrest's funeral and noted that the general "was actually quite unpopular with a large portion of the community, who feared and disliked him about evenly." This white animosity drifted away over the years and allowed for the emergence of a multivalent symbol far removed from personal grievances. Throughout the twentieth century, Forrest developed into a useful icon for many white southerners and a growing number of white northerners as personal traits blurred into an amalgam of half-truths and fictions ready-made for new realities and meanings. Memphis sat at the center of this fabrication, and the city forged most of the crucial components of the Forrest myth into an image at once attached to a historic tableau and yet disconnected enough to serve endless purposes. Thirty years after his death, Forrest helped define the civic culture of Memphis, and the city reciprocated by giving new importance and significance to the general. Memphis in 1905 represents the fulcrum of Forrest's public memory as white southerners replaced the rapidly vanishing experiences of the Civil War with a narrative defined by the needs of the present.

In May 1905, the city of Memphis unveiled its long-awaited bronze statue honoring Forrest. The ceremony capped off three decades of Forrest's shadow-like presence in the city as Memphis melted into civic crisis after civic crisis. The bronze figure of Forrest on his horse emerged as a particularly potent symbol of white Memphis history, present and proposed future. "The future of Memphis is great," one newspaper editorial claimed after the statue's unveiling, "but that future has its foundation perhaps in a greater past."[1] As a kaleidoscopic avatar of Memphis, the 1905 statue of Forrest radiates variegated flashes of history and myth, folklore and dishonesty. Much had changed since Forrest's death, and the monument spoke to new concerns as white Memphians struggled to make sense of their city, their region, and their place within the national conversation. Reconciliation helped ease the old wounds of the Civil War, and white northerners condoned and bought into a hero separated from dogmatic regionalism. The Forrest monument reflected this extra-regional approach as both white northerners and southerners came to Memphis to proclaim the greatness of the Confederate cavalryman. By the early twentieth century, regionalism began to buckle and ceased to serve as the motivating energy within the Forrest image. He still represented certain traditions of white southern society, but by the 1900s, Forrest attracted new audiences and enthusiasts as race and racism trumped regional affiliations. Jim Crow animated the racism embedded in the Forrest image, and throughout the late 1890s into the 1900s, a new version of the general emerged.

The racism of the Forrest image coincided with white Memphians confronting a tumultuous and changing city. Between the Civil War and the 1905 Forrest statue, Memphis suffered through several crucial catastrophes, each profoundly affecting the city's Black community. The Memphis Massacre of 1866, the economic disorder of the 1870s, and the yellow fever epidemic of 1878 radically altered the ways in which the city worked. This decade of anxiety—mapped alongside the regional and national tensions of Reconstruction—reverberated across the political and social landscape of the city, simultane-

Forrest statue in Memphis, unveiled in 1905.
Prints and Photographs Division, Library of Congress.

Memphis statue with roller skaters, ca. 1906.
Prints and Photographs Division, Library of Congress.

ously uprooting established patterns of interconnectedness and reinforcing bedrock patterns of white southern culture. By 1905, Memphis represented a very different city than the one that had experienced the Civil War. At once more Black, more economically viable, and more socially agitated, Memphis held promise at the dawn of the twentieth century, even if the direction forward was unclear. White Memphians, though, felt the seismic shifts as the city drifted away from what they assumed was the rightful power structure defined by race and racism. Thus, as incidences of anti-Black violence came to define this period, the city looked backward to celebrate a white hero-general. No longer a symbol of unrealized military victory, Forrest in 1905 served as a blank canvas of white supremacy and the protection of white governance.

The entwined story of Forrest and Memphis helped push these competing narratives of racism and boosterism as the image of one tended to burnish the other. Unlike many other Civil War personalities, Forrest and his image were baked into a specific place, which allowed for a blurring between individual and city. This convergence meant that white Memphians tended to cast any attacks on Forrest as attacks on their hometown while simultaneously absolving the city of any accountability regarding the general, which crafted a slippery tableau of narrative-building and responsibility-shirking. In the century-plus years that the Forrest statue stood on Union Avenue, Memphis attempted to have it both ways even as the Black population grew. The city maintained and preserved the memory of Forrest through its most visible monument while, at the same time, quietly distancing itself from the general through renaming and shifting ownership of the land on which the monument stood as criticism heated up in the late twentieth century. The image of Forrest, as centered on the Memphis monument, suggested multiple meanings and variable implications. The hallmark of the Forrest legacy in the city related to the ways in which it shifted along with public opinion. The story of Memphis after the Civil War is a narrative driven by change, adjustment, reframing, and recontextualizing the meaning of the city. Memphis shared part of the New South trajectory with other southern cities, but a set of unique issues helped set it apart, too. Economic collapse(s), yellow fever epidemics, demographic upheavals, and waves of racial violence transformed the city—creating a space defined by agitation, unease, and white anxieties. Forrest offered confidence and future-centered optimism, and white Memphians rallied around the general as a talisman to ward off urban disaster.

The Civil War altered the development of the critical Mississippi River port as Union soldiers occupied the city from 1862 through the end of the war. Still, Civil War Memphis represented a fluid, volatile landscape of smuggling and sliding allegiances. The Union occupation's most noticeable impact on the city was the influx of enslaved Black individuals and families, who fled neighboring farms and plantations and entered theoretically protected Union-controlled Memphis. During the war, the Black population of Memphis quadrupled, a demographic shift that redefined Memphis society and politics during the late 1860s and 1870s. White refugees and returning soldiers entered a radically altered landscape without their previously held positions of power. The tensions embedded in the city's demographics—racial, regional, and ethnic—played out in various violent ways throughout Reconstruction. In the months after the war, Memphis regained its prewar power structure as the Union army left, and the Union-controlled Tennessee legislature allowed the city to reconvene a civil government. The upheaval of Memphis society churned for years as many white Memphians attempted to reassert their antebellum prominences, white northern transplants looked to improve upon their newly arrived status, and Black men and women worked to carve out new spaces in the emerging new, urban South. Whatever sense of optimism, potential, and promise circulating along the bluffs of the Mississippi River in the summer of 1865 soon drifted elsewhere. Within a year, Memphis lay in disarray once more.[2]

Profound demographic changes characterized Reconstruction-era Memphis, as well as the racist violence sparked by these shifts. Black people coming into Memphis after the Civil War led to increased racial tensions, culminating in the violence of 1866. This combination of resentment and violence coursed through the city in the years following the war. As the city's Black population grew, white Memphians resorted to brutal responses and a more quotidian dependence on white supremacy. The matrix of postwar Memphis society represented a complex series of fault lines divided by wealth, race, ethnicity, and regional background. During this period, several different groups collided in Memphis, including recently arrived white northerners, former Confederates (and returning members of the rebel army), Black men and women (many originally from the surrounding rural areas), and white Irish immigrants. This fourth group—white Irish, who generally rebuffed Confederate pleas for service—experienced an upsurge in political power as many former Confederates lost suffrage rights. Thus, as many white city elites lost political power, Black Memphians and white Irish Memphians gained influence. Emancipation and shifting suffrage laws transformed the city and created space for Black people looking to start new lives apart from slavery and upturning white political expectations. As a result, Memphis emerged from the Civil War as a contested space. Fort Pickering, too, served as a source of tension within white Memphis as the presence of uniformed Black soldiers served as a reminder of the real-world ramifications of the war. In the year following the Civil War, white fears and anxieties defined the city: political turmoil, social turmoil, and economic turmoil were all exacerbated by fears of real and imagined Black resistance.[3]

The Memphis Race Riot of 1866 resulted in the deaths of forty-six Black Memphians as well as a white police officer and a white fireman. The timing of the massacre played directly into the hands of Republicans, and the local, state, and national political scenes shuddered with the partisan fallout of the May bloodshed in the city. Ricocheting tensions crisscrossed postwar Memphis society, but the racial divide between white and Black Memphians, generally, and the Irish power structure and freedmen and women (both relatively new groups in the city), specifically, portended calamity. The flashpoint of these strains emerged in part from issues of public safety. White Irish Memphians controlled the politics of Memphis in the years after the Civil War as well as the fire department and police force of the city. This bloc of primarily public-facing power allowed for many antagonistic interactions between Black Memphians and white public officials. Harassment and brutality defined the relationship between white Irish policemen and Black Memphians and helped build a culture of violence and distrust. The presence of Black Union veterans in the city further drove white supremacist anger, fueled in part by loss and Black empowerment. Fort Pillow loomed over Memphis, too, and the massacre just two years prior helped frame much of the tensions. The 1866 Memphis riots stemmed from the issues surrounding Reconstruction as well as from Forrest's actions in the Civil War. On a more individual level, Black survivors of Fort Pillow found themselves mustered at Fort Pickering and thus involved in the riots of 1866, too. The 1866 actions stemmed as much from local webs of racism, violence, and memory as they did from the larger counterrevolution developing between Black and white southerners confronting postwar unknowns.[4]

Much of this narrative of the development of the Black community in postwar Memphis can be tracked along with Forrest's public actions in the years before his death. Forrest is missing from Memphis during the May turmoil, and we do not have specific evidence of Forrest's thoughts concerning the matter. However, two examples of Forrest's actions—one early in Reconstruction and one later—help illustrate the shifting nature of Memphis society after the war. In 1866, just weeks before the Memphis riots, Forrest murdered a Black worker on his Mississippi farm. This murder tends to hover just below the surface of the Forrest myth. Although a relatively large regional story in 1866 (the murder occurred in March and the trial was in October), few biographers noted the events until the 1990s. The proximity of the murder to the May riots helps illustrate the racial tensions and violence in the area. Nine years later, however, in 1875, Forrest offered a seemingly more conciliatory approach to Black Memphis. After years of actions related to the Ku Klux Klan and the racial politics of the white southern Democratic Party, Forrest began to speak in a very different language in the final years of his life. Through this lens, Forrest's 1875 speech to a local Black mutual aid society reflects a more pragmatic angle as he attempted to rebuild his life and finances in a city with a growing and empowered Black community.

In March 1866, Forrest confronted Thomas Edwards, a Black worker on his home property in Coahoma County, Mississippi. According to various accounts, Edwards had a considerable temper and had allegedly been involved in multiple altercations with other people on the farm. Edwards, some reports claimed, had physically attacked his wife, too, although she provided testimony counter to these suppositions. "He was generally considered to be a bad man," another worker on Forrest's land argued. Forrest, who had recently been in Memphis, returned to his farm to prepare for a fast-spreading cholera outbreak. He ordered the Black workers on his property to dig several drainage ditches and clear out an area of stagnant water. Edwards, in some form or another, refused, which led to a confrontation with Forrest. The exchange of words turned physical, and Forrest killed Edwards with an ax blow to the head. News of the killing spread quickly, and reports suggest Black workers in the area worked to keep Forrest detained near his home. The general eventually surrendered to authorities and stood trial several months later, in October. The jury found him not guilty.[5]

Much of what we know of this story comes to us through a Freedmen's

Bureau report and Coahoma County court documents, which serve as the basis of the story as constructed by historians since the 1990s. The story is straightforward: Thomas Edwards angered Forrest by ignoring a work order; Forrest kills Edwards with an axe; a jury finds Forrest not guilty. However, the way the story is retold and reframed underscores the power of the Forrest myth. Much of the narrative relates to Edwards's abuse of his wife, as if to support Forrest's actions related to the work order. "I will whip my wife when I damn please," Edwards reportedly told Forrest's foreman. Forrest, the former slave trader, takes Edwards's actions as a particular affront to the supposed rules of decorum on his property. In her testimony, Sarah Edwards denied that her husband "abused me in his life in any way." She would also argue that Edwards never pulled a knife on Forrest—clouding a critical element of Forrest's defense. But modern writers also embody Edwards with many of the same qualities seen as strengths of character in Forrest: he had a quick temper, he could be profane, he was aggressive, and he was physically strong and imposing. Here, the Forrest myth is flipped as the general is the peacekeeping rationalist—who still bludgeoned a man to death with an axe. We do not know much about Thomas Edwards—and much of the documentation we do have is contradictory—but we do know Forrest. This inversion of the central elements of his legacy to correlate with a "not guilty" judgment illustrates the complexity of both Forrest and the convoluted plotlines of white southern masculinity and honor.[6]

Nine years later, Forrest addressed a local Black benevolence and mutual aid society known as the Pole-Bearers. This speech, which coincided with a Fourth of July celebration in 1875, has been framed as Forrest's attempt at racial conciliation. The history of the Independent Order of Pole-Bearers in Memphis mirrors the creation and activity of numerous other Black-led mutual aid societies that emerged in the years immediately after the Civil War. This Memphis organization comprised a large number (newspaper references range between 250 and 500 members at various events in the 1870s) of Black veterans of the Union Army. The Memphis press first couched the Pole-Bearers in racist terms, especially by writers for the *Daily Appeal*. In 1870, for example, following a public showing of the group, the *Daily Appeal* noted that the organization numbered "250 strong (numerically—rather stronger by odorometer), bearing banners with the legend, 'Hope and Prosperity to All,' 'We trust in God and our other Friends,' etc." Four months later, the newspaper drove the racist invective further in a story on a Pole-Bearers picnic. "The mokes had a picnic yesterday," the reporter for the *Daily Appeal* wrote, and "[a]s usual the pole bearers (better pole-*cat*ers) were out in force, with Masonic aprons and other toggery." "The procession was headed by a band of nigger music," the writer concluded, "and had every mackerel in town at its heels." The *Memphis Public Ledger* offered less overtly bigoted language about the organization. In 1873, for example, the Pole-Bearer band performed outside of the newspaper's office, eliciting an article that acknowledged and thanked the musicians and concluded, "It is gratifying to record the fact that a better era is dawning and a better understanding exists in this glorious State of ours between the white and colored people."[7]

As offered by the *Daily Ledger,* the perspective shifted in 1874 after an alleged confrontation between the Pole-Bearers and various white merchants at a Decoration Day celebration. According to the *Daily Appeal,* the Pole-Bearers, "who were armed with muskets and bayonets and battle-axes," disrupted a group of merchants selling refreshments and other items outside of the National Cemetery. "But instead of paying the honor due to heroism and the bravery of the Union dead," the article proclaimed, the group "enacted the most BRUTAL AND DISGRACEFUL SCENES that drunken ignorance or political malice could invent." The newspaper writer blamed "bad whisky or the advice of wicked leaders" for the melee. However, given the newspaper's racist descriptions of earlier Pole-Bearers actions, it is difficult to know what actions occurred during that celebration. It is interesting, however, to note the rather gracious tone taken while discussing the Union dead. Still, the *Daily Ledger* followed up on these charges with a series of articles on the affair, focusing on how the group obtained the muskets and bayonets. "It has been well known," the *Daily Ledger* argued, "that the Pole Bearers Association was not only benevolent but military in its purposes, but where did those companies of pole bearers get those regulation muskets and bayonets? Forming as it were a secret but standing army in our midst." Two days later, the newspaper reminded their readers that the "Pole Bearers Association is composed principally of negroes who served in the Federal army. It is a military organization, about six hundred strong, and they are regarded as bullies and fighters by the other colored associations." "Indeed," the paper continued, "other colored organizations have but little use for the Pole Bearers, who are a terror to their own people." Ending on a threatening note, the newspaper writer warned that, "should the insolent Pole Bearers ever start a riot not one of them would be left to tell the tale on the bluffs. We give them this advice gratis."[8]

News coverage on the Decoration Day fight and the gun issue died down after a couple of weeks, though the Pole-Bearers would show up occasionally in both the *Daily Appeal* and the *Public Ledger.* A year later, however, a marked shift occurred in the public relationship between the newspapers and the organization on the occasion of the Pole-Bearers inviting a slate of white Memphians to address the group on its annual Fourth of July picnic. The invited group included Gideon Pillow, the former Confederate general who had built a law practice in Memphis after the war (and for whom Fort Pillow was named); Matthew Gallaway, who had worked as aide-de-camp for Forrest during the war and later owned the *Memphis Daily Appeal;* a real estate broker; a lawyer; and Nathan Bedford Forrest. Thus, just over a year after the contentious 1874 picnic, the group invited on the most celebrated patriotic holiday to speak the most infamous former Confederate general most known for the slaughter of Black soldiers at a fort named for another person invited to the platform. Forrest's inclusion captured most of the press attention to the event. "Of all the white leaders in the South, during or since the war," a writer for the *Nashville Union and American* proclaimed, "none has been represented as a more dangerous enemy to the colored race than the famous Confederate *sabreur.*" "'Remember Fort Pillow!' was long the favorite rallying cry of a political adventurer when a full negro vote was needed," they continued, "[y]et this same Gen. Forrest has not hesitated to promptly recognize the tender of restored good feeling." The *Memphis Daily Appeal* labeled the invitation "courteous" and published the invited group's response. "Feeling that the prosperity and happiness of both the white and colored races in the southern States, in a great degree, depends upon kindly relations and a good understanding and mutual friendly offices," the group wrote, "we will probably all accept your invitation to be present, and some of our number will address you upon matters affecting your interest and future welfare; but we will, as far as possible, avoid all discussions of existing political questions or issues."[9]

On a hot July day, Forrest addressed a predominately Black audience with a speech alluding to political differences and "many things" that had been said of him "which are wrong." Overall, the overt tenor of the speech ran towards the reconciliatory and sociable. "I came to meet you as friends," Forrest noted, "and welcome you to the white people." Forrest, forever self-aware, recognized that his appearance would raise an eyebrow or two in the white community—and he enjoyed playing the role of the provocateur throughout his postwar life. Forrest, for his part, seemed to relish the opportunity to speak to a crowd (his last major public speech before his death) as well as to court controversy simply by showing up. His remarks began with his acceptance of a bouquet from a young Black woman. The image of Forrest accepting flowers from a Black woman alone represented a shocking tableau for all involved. Forrest leaned into the moment. "Ladies and Gentlemen," he began, "I accept the flowers as a memento of reconciliation between the white and colored races of the southern states." "I accept it more particularly as it comes from a colored lady," Forrest continued, "for if there is [anyone] on God's earth who loves the ladies[,] I believe it is myself." "I came here," Forrest later noted, "with the jeers of some white people, who think that I am doing wrong." However, he believed he had the power and sway to improve race relations in the city. "I believe I can exert some influence," Forrest argued, "and do much to assist the people in strengthening fraternal relations, and shall do all in my power to elevate every man to depress none." A thread of reconciliation (racial, regional, national) ran through the brief remarks—as did a line of politics: "we have but one flag, one country," Forrest declared, "let us stand together. We may differ in color, but not in sentiment." He spoke as someone interested in civic rebuilding and social uplift and, publicly at least, interested in the electorate's power. "I have been in the heat of battle when colored men asked me to protect them," Forrest explained to the crowd in a rather stunning counterbalance to the Fort Pillow story, "I have placed myself between them and the bullets of my men, and told them they should be kept unharmed." "I," Forrest concluded, "assure you that I am with you in heart and in hand."[10]

More than his specific words—and we must rely only on the *Daily Appeal*'s transcript of the event—the context of the event and the relationship between Forrest and the audience imbued the afternoon with a much more considerable significance. According to the *Daily Appeal,* the crowd responded with "immense" and later "prolonged" applause, and the general mood of the remarks and commentary, at least in Memphis, was quite positive. "The affair," the *Public Ledger* noted a few days later, "did more to twine the two races together than any incident since the war." The *New York Times,* in their obituary of the general in 1877, noted that he gave a "friendly speech" when "he appeared before the colored people at their [Fourth of July] celebration." However, as Forrest expected, some white southerners expressed apprehension and anger at the general's presence at the celebration. An organization called the Cavalry Survivor's Association condemned Forrest's actions and "address delivered before a black and tan audience." One of the group members argued that Forrest had forever tarnished his heroic name by accepting the flowers. "To mar all the lustre attached to his name," the newspaper writes, "his brain is turned by the civilities of a mulatto wench who presented him with a bouquet of roses." "What can," they asked rhetorically, if exasperatedly, "his object be? Ah! General Forrest!" To these Georgian men, Forrest transgressed their racialized and gendered expectations of white southern masculinity, and his public embrace of a Black woman forced them to reevaluate his heroic status. Their version of Forrest disappointed them. Ultimately, the group unanimously passed a resolution stating their disapproval and "that we allow no man to advocate, or even hint to the world, before any public assemblage, that he dare associate our mother's, wives', daughter's, or sisters names in the same category that he classes the females of the negro race, without, *at least,* expressing our disapprobation."[11]

What Forrest actually meant (*what can his object be*), or even said for that matter, in 1875 represents less than the ways various writers have used it to forgive Forrest for the slave trade, Fort Pillow, and the Ku Klux Klan. Due to the paucity of public speeches from Forrest, not to mention the historic nature of this particular gathering, the focus on this speech makes sense. And yet, the address did not enter the Forrest myth until the late twentieth century. Most biographers of the general before the 1990s tended to focus almost exclusively on the war years and paid relatively scant attention to his pre- and postwar activities. One exception was James Harvey Mathes's biography, published in 1902, but his account incorporated several factual errors, including dating the speech to 1868. Robert Selph Henry, writing in the 1940s, places the events of 1875 (without mentioning the address) in the context of Forrest's late-life religious conversion. The speech remains challenging to fit into the Forrest story on one level since it is a rare moment where the race and racism of his persona collide in such a public way. On a deeper level, however, the speech puts Forrest at odds with some of the central tenets of his mythos; thus, it runs against the militaristic focus of most of his biographers. The story gained traction in the 2000s as various Confederate-themed groups began to circulate the speech on online forums. This resurgent interest in the address tended toward the hyperbolic as defenders of the general used his words (the address runs under 350 words as published by the *Daily Appeal*) as a way to absolve Forrest of his connections to slavery, Fort Pillow, and the Klan. These few words, then, allowed proponents of the general to reframe him as an advocate for civil rights through a late-in-life conversion. The centrality of Black women in both narratives also underscores the various ways in which race and gender frame Forrest's postwar life. The Thomas Edwards murder received scant coverage before the 1990s and has generally only been touched on in passing. The axe murder of a Black worker played less into the ideologies of various groups in the 2000s than a decontextualized and malleable oration. These two events—separated by nine years—illustrate the fluidity of Reconstruction Memphis and the multiple ways white Memphians negotiated a rapidly shifting culture.[12]

Forrest's actions after the Civil War coincided with a complete upheaval of the Memphis economy as the city limped along with a broken network of railroads, a small number of working banks, and wide-ranging deflation. The collapse of the cotton economy furthered the economic instability of the area, as did the Panic of 1873, which significantly increased Memphis's debt. For white Memphis, the loss of enslaved labor and its accumulated capital signified a further dampening of economic fortunes. By 1878, the city had suffered through enough interconnected monied crises that Memphis declared bankruptcy. In August, just seven months after declaring bankruptcy, the city was hit by the worst yellow fever epidemic in Memphis's history. Approximately twenty-five thousand Memphians fled the city in less than a week, including most white business leaders, government officials, and much of the police and fire departments. The disease had a massive impact on the city's racial makeup as Black Memphians comprised over 70 percent of the population who stayed in the city. The evacuation of much of white Memphis would profoundly affect the city for decades, both in real demographic change and in the perceptions of what Memphis looked like during the 1880s and 1890s. The city lost a large part of its white elite during the epidemic, which created a power vacuum within the city government and business districts. By the late nineteenth century, a stronger Black business coalition would emerge. Still, in the 1870s, the heavy reduction of the white governing population laid bare the city's shaky economic foundations. In January 1879, the city government—in an attempt to escape the meddling of external creditors—voted to transition control of Memphis to the state of Tennessee. The city implemented a commission style of government, and Memphis (stripped of its charter) became the "Taxing District of Shelby County." Not two years after his death, Forrest would have hardly recognized his city.[13]

As white Memphians fled and Black Memphians survived, the city drifted into new existences. As white Memphis slowly returned, a new order emerged. The racism, white antagonism, and racial violence of the late nineteenth century stem from this period of chaotic undoing. Instead of viewing the Forrest statue of 1905 as a localized remembrance of the Civil War, the fundraising and plans make more sense as a public memorial to the changing landscape of the near past and vacillating present. This combination of history and presentism provided the Forrest image with such power. The general gave historical meaning and present direction at a time when white Memphians struggled to remake the city in ways that made sense to their lived experiences and expectations. Black Memphians, outside of the city's power structure, built their own neighborhoods and businesses, and Memphis's capitulation to Union troops early in the war gave the city a different trajectory than other southern cities as northerners moved into the area. White northerners entered the business sector and, after the war, helped work toward Black voting rights and education. The history of Memphis from the Civil War into the early 1900s is defined by the connections and tensions between aggrieved white southerners, transplanted white northerners, and Black men and women making early steps toward self-determination. Sometimes these stresses led to outright conflict, as in 1866, but this era of anxieties often served as a backdrop to more subtle interactions and confrontations. An ever-present duality emerged as white and Black Memphians worked and struggled to build a city representative of their needs. Postwar Black Memphis emerged from this challenging matrix of enslaved spaces, freedom-driven entrepreneurship, racial violence, and the faint promise of a better Memphis in the future.[14]

In the late nineteenth century, the narrative of Black Memphis ran through Holly Springs, Mississippi—a farming community southeast of Memphis. Here, two individuals born into slavery but separated in age by two decades would come to define the parameters of Black Memphis. Robert Church, born in 1839, and Ida B. Wells, born in 1862, represent much of the map of Black Memphis as they lived through slavery, emancipation, postwar unrest, the yellow fever epidemics, and worked to build new (sometimes entwined) paths forward. Different in temperament, ideologies, and practically every other way, the intersection of Church and Wells underscores the interconnectedness, diversity, and shared roots of Black Memphis during this period. Through his quasi-legal entrepreneurship: racially proud at times, racially fluid at others, pandering to white customers and politicians while maintaining Black connections, Church and his career speak to the unpredictability of postwar Memphis, where the yellow fever demographic shifts were comprehensive. Through her activism and writing, Ida B. Wells spoke to more significant concerns of white supremacy and violence toward Black people. Together, Church and Wells laid the spatial and intellectual groundwork for a multifaceted and complex Black community within a turbulent, transforming city. The narrative of Black Memphis surviving (and sometimes thriving) in the late nineteenth century and the myriad ways these successes, near-successes, and even failures led to pushback as white Memphis attempted to reclaim control of the city decades after the Civil War provide the context for the memorialization of Forrest, which culminated in the 1905 statue. The escalating friction of social unmooring, rather than memories of the war, led white Memphis to seek a hero for turbulent and unsettled times.

Robert Church epitomized much of this transformation as he worked to build an operating and profitable Black Memphis. Born into slavery in Holly Springs, Church would emerge as one of the most important figures in Memphis history. The two prominent crucibles of postwar Memphis society—the 1866 riots and the yellow fever epidemic of the 1870s—established Church as a leader and entrepreneur. Shot in the neck during the 1866 riots as his saloon was ransacked, Church asserted himself at a center of a Black community in transition. After the riots, Black Memphians worked to secure a geographic space within the city to provide security and community. Church often stood at the heart of much of this rebuilding. In the 1870s, Church began to acquire real estate devalued significantly by the epidemic. He bought various other properties concentrated in downtown Memphis between Second and Gayoso, which helped solidify his position within city affairs. Church tended to work on one side or another of Memphis's relatively fluid legal boundaries as he expanded his hold on brothels and saloons. Coming from the turbulent world of cotton merchants and riverboat gamblers, Church understood the contours of speculation and built a dynasty in downtown Memphis. Church's legacy in Memphis is simultaneously convoluted and straightforward. He used his wealth to help create a space for Black Memphians while still ingratiating himself to white businessmen and seekers of various vices. These tensions and connections played out through local politics as well as real estate deals and everyday gives and takes—perhaps as social responsibility, perhaps as grift—as Memphis struggled to escape epidemics, financial ruin, and existential loss. Church's wealth and success represented a path forward for Black Memphians, and he symbolized Black uplift during a tumultuous time.[15]

As Church worked to build his real estate holdings in Memphis, Ida B. Wells focused on education. A schoolteacher in Holly Springs, Wells relocated to Memphis after her parents died of yellow fever. Wells soon became active in Black Memphis society as she honed her political perspective. In 1883, Wells successfully sued the Chesapeake & Ohio Railroad for forcefully removing her from a train. This lawsuit brought her to the attention of Black Memphis, and she soon began to write for a local Black newspaper. Much of her early forays into journalism focused on the Black elite who chose individual wealth over community uplift. Consequently, her criticism tended, veiled though it might have been, toward people like Robert Church. Still, Church took notice of her lawsuit and journalism and eventually even supported Wells through a loan outside public knowledge. Throughout her time in Memphis, Wells emerged as a formidable moral crusader interested in pushing wealthy Black Memphians to commit to advancing their communities. At this point, her writing and activism stemmed from the local complexities of a growing Black community within the unsettled environment of late-nineteenth-century Memphis. The nexus of entrepreneurship, poverty, strength, and limitations within Memphis's Black population was not necessarily unique in postwar southern cities. Still, Wells's writing and activism underscored the various fault lines that defined much of the internal dynamics of the city. However, more significant and critical issues began to take up her attention and would eventually force Wells out of Memphis and into Chicago and then the nation.[16]

In 1892, a Black grocery store served as the epicenter of a violent confrontation between white and Black Memphians. The resultant murders of three Black men came to personalize the latent racist tensions that seethed below the city's New South surface. The lynchings represented the bloodiest explosion of racism since 1866. The murders spun out from a clash between a white-owned grocery store and a newer, Black-owned store located in a mixed-race neighborhood of Memphis known as the Curve. William Barrett, the white proprietor, had become increasingly annoyed at the success of Thomas Moss and his Black grocery store, known as the People's Grocery. Race relations in the area were initially shaky, and Moss's success further irritated Barrett. These tensions worsened after a fight between two young children playing near the grocery store broke out. The white father began assaulting the Black child, and this fight then grew as Calvin McDowell and Will Stewart (both employees of Moss) came to the boy's defense. The next day, an armed Barrett entered the People's Grocery with a police officer to arrest Stewart, but a fight broke out and shots were fired. Over the next several days, white mobs formed to pursue the three main targets of their rage, though dozens of Black people in the area were the focus of various levels of abuse. Eventually, police arrested and jailed Moss, McDowell, and Stewart. Early on the predawn morning of March 9, a mob of as many as seventy-five masked white men rushed the Shelby County jail and absconded with the three men. The white abductors forced Moss, McDowell, and Stewart out to an empty field near the Wolf River, where they were brutally murdered. "If you are going to kill us," Moss purportedly said, "turn our faces to the west." "Scarcely had he uttered the words," the *New York Times* reported, "when the crack of a revolver was heard." In one historian's words, it was "the worst atrocity against blacks since the Memphis police riot of 1866."[17]

A group of Black pastors in Memphis prepared a statement bringing together different pieces of the story from a Black perspective. "The citizens about the Curve," they wrote, "in a mass meeting, have denounced Barrett, the white grocer, as the instigator of the whole affair, and made direct complaint to the criminal authorities, and yet he is at large—not a white man arrested." The pastors emphasized Thomas Moss's role in the community—he, they wrote, "especially was known as a quiet and well-behaved man"—but they also spoke to the concerns of the Black community at large. "So far as we can learn now," they argued, "the Colored people are terrorized." The fear and anger that swept through the city's Black neighborhoods led some citizens to pack up and leave. "With the utmost cause for feeling deeply wronged and falsely accused," the pastors wrote, "our people have maintained so far a quiet demeanor, giving away only to their fears in trying to get away from the city or planning to remove." For Wells, the lynching provided her with new resolve to counter the white supremacy of the city. "The good colored citizens of Memphis who have been interested in and worked for the prosperity and success of the city," Wells wrote, "who stood by the white people when the plague of '78 and '79 threatened to sweep the town from the face of the earth, demand that the murderers of Calvin McDowell, Will Stewart and Tom Moss be brought to justice." A friend of Moss's, Wells took this brutal killing personally. Her activism from this point forward took on lynching as her primary topic and the lens through which she saw white supremacy as well as white masculinity. "If Southern white men are not careful," Wells wrote, "they will over-reach themselves and public sentiment will have a reaction, or a conclusion will be reached which will be very damaging to the moral reputation of their women."[18]

Wells's activism and journalism gained her national and international support as well as the vocal admiration of Frederick Douglass. The period of white rage and disruption—epitomized by the careers of Church and Wells and lynching and Jim Crow—upset racial, economic, and public health norms. The attempts of white Memphis to reassert their power and dominance in the late nineteenth century produced the opportunity to memorialize Forrest while imbuing his image with newer, more civic-minded ideals. White Memphis adopted the imperfect hero as a symbol of what could be. Before, during, and after the war, Forrest's exploits became muddled into a useful set of tropes rooted in history yet flexible enough to serve multiple purposes. Both historical and ahistorical, Memphis and not Memphis, real and imagined, these blurry-edged stories provided enough context to connect them to the city and enough fluidity to fill many different roles. A statue commemorating Forrest stood, one Memphis editorial proclaimed, "not for the good it does for the departed hero, but for the good it does for us and the good it will do for those who are to come after us." Memphis would reverberate with these tensions throughout the twentieth century, but in 1905, white Memphians understood their past, present, and probable future through the life and legacy of Nathan Bedford Forrest.[19]

The organizing of a memorial to Forrest coincided with two significant streams in Memphis history: the reestablishment of the city as an independent entity (it reclaimed the name "Memphis" in 1891) and the intensification of white supremacy and racially motivated violence. Unlike memorials to other fallen Confederates, such as Robert E. Lee, the efforts to memorialize Forrest dealt very rarely with the emerging standard array of declarations and platitudes that came to define the Lost Cause. The memory of Forrest was explicitly centered on the white needs of Memphis at the turn of the century. Rather than a piece of a larger arrangement of Confederate heroes, Forrest stood alone, or at least off to one side. Forrest and Memphis became entwined in the 1890s and 1900s, and celebrating one meant celebrating the other—both images defined by—and forged in—white supremacy. Throughout the last decades of the nineteenth century, Memphis erected relatively few memorials or monuments to honor its Confederate past.

The move to memorialize Forrest originated a decade after the general's death. In 1887, two Confederate veterans and a businessman who had moved to Memphis in the 1880s attempted to raise money for a statue honoring the general. This early effort failed after receiving $55 in cash and less than $2,000 in signed subscriptions. Four years later, another group of businessmen endeavored to restart the process to honor Forrest with assistance from individuals connected to the construction of the Robert E. Lee statue in New Orleans. A Memphis attorney then chartered the Forrest Memorial Association (FMA) with a leadership group that included Samuel T. Carnes as president, George W. Gordon as first vice president, W. A. Collier as second vice president, James Beasley as treasurer, and George H. Cunningham as secretary. These men represented a convergence of business elites and Confederate veterans, a dichotomy that came to define not only the FMA but the honoring of Forrest as well.[20]

This combination of civil and military connectors underscores the various fundraising events of the 1890s as the FMA sponsored both theater benefits and competitive veterans' drills. The committee's leadership, too, represented a merging of past and present as George W. Gordon—born near Pulaski, Tennessee, in 1836—headed much of the fundraising, and Carnes—born in West Tennessee in 1850—directed the general mission of the FMA. Gordon, the Civil War veteran with military bona fides and Ku Klux Klan connections (and who possibly indicted Forrest into the organization), signified the white Memphis past shaped by military valor, real and imagined. A statue commemorating Forrest as the untrained military hero born into poverty who found wealth and power through slavery and the war connected directly to this group of veterans. Too young to fight in the war, Carnes represented, instead, the New Memphis as the businessman who introduced electric lights to the city, brought in the first Bell Telephone franchise, and owned the first automobile in town. He also represented the most significant individual donation to the statue. Forrest signified something different to this younger generation, more myth than history, and the general's connection to the city was more expansive than old war stories. Military heroism was important, but the money and drive came from a younger generation less tethered to the Civil War and connected to turn-of-the-century issues affecting Memphis. The present, in other words, defined the memorial efforts more dynamically than the fast-receding memories of the past, and the FMA eventually succeeded because of the multidimensional fusion image of Forrest.[21]

Various fundraisers and financing drives shaped the early years of the Forrest Memorial Association. A martial tinge colored these early efforts as they centered on Confederate drills. Still, the FMA also hosted events at local theaters and other public spaces to underscore the civic nature of the undertaking. A certain aimlessness defined the early years of the FMA as money started to come into the organization, but no sculptor had been appointed, and there did not seem to be much consensus as to what would come out of the enterprise. By 1900, however, the FMA had raised $14,000 in "cash and signed pledges," and the organization created a committee to request design ideas from various American sculptors. That same year, Mary Latham helped lead a Woman's Auxiliary Association that raised money for several years. Latham, the wife of a Memphis attorney and a member of both the United Daughters of the Confederacy and the Daughters of the American Revolution, brought together several other women to raise money outside of the FMA's immediate purview. By 1904, Latham and the Woman's Auxiliary Association had raised almost $3,000. "Without disparagement to the others," Samuel Carnes later said, "I think Mrs. Latham was the most active worker of them all, and the most effective." Women's groups would play a smaller role in developing the Forrest statue than with other Confederate monuments. Still, Latham and others worked within their circles to support the project as it came together.[22]

As the money rolled in for the monument, the FMA started work on the spatial plans for whatever form the memorial would take. The plans for the space emerged simultaneously as many American cities began experimenting with arranging urban life around small parks serving various urban functions. Memphis would establish several parks during the early twentieth century, including in 1899, "Bedford Forrest Park," which would stand on the grounds of the old city hospital. In 1900, Memphis created a park commission to oversee the establishment of small urban parks. Louis McFarland, the city's first parks commissioner, had deep connections with the Confederate organizations of Memphis (he had served in the war) as well as the FMA, to which he had donated money. McFarland and the parks commission appointed George Keesler—a German-born landscape architect out of Kansas City—to draw up plans for Forrest Park. Keesler's original plans provided for a "passive recreational space in the Picturesque style," but the space would undergo numerous changes before and after the statue was erected with assorted ponds, roller-skate paths, tennis courts, playgrounds, and gardens built, moved, and removed over the years. "It is the design of the commission," McFarland wrote, "to subordinate everything except its utility as a park in the treatment of these grounds to the fact that it is Forrest Park and to the accentuation of the monument itself." Race, too, played a role in these designs as the parks represented white public spaces. In June 1905, just a few weeks after the Forrest statue unveiling, a Memphis horse breeder objected to forbidding Black people in the park with specific attention given to his Black "servant." After "considerable discussion," the parks commission decided to "instruct the policemen at Forrest Park to preserve order, and to use discretion in ejecting objectionable characters . . . but not to prohibit the passing of negroes through the Park."[23]

Contracting for the design and construction of the monument began in late 1900. After almost a decade of intermittent work, the FMA formalized its plans regarding a statue honoring Forrest. The year 1901 represented a crucial turning point for the Forrest statue project as Memphis hosted the Eleventh Annual Meeting and Reunion of the United Confederate Veterans. The FMA used the Confederate Reunion to bolster fundraising efforts and lay the foundation for the proposed monument. The 1901 reunion prefigured the 1905 unveiling, bringing together civic and military elements to honor Forrest on a citywide scale. The reunion, which ran from May 28 through May 30, featured an array of events set to celebrate the living Confederate veterans as well as to spotlight Forrest and the FMA's fundraising for the statue. After surviving the fiscally disastrous decades following the Civil War, Memphis entered the twentieth century eager to boast its newly stabilized economy. The 1901 reunion allowed the city to assert New South growth to a wide range of visitors. A central part of Memphis's host status centered on the construction of the Confederate Hall—an 18,000-seat exposition space that cost $80,000 to build and would be torn down after the reunion. The program for the reunion prominently featured most of the board members of the FMA, and organizers adorned public spaces with Forrest's image. One speaker noted that the gathering signified "the proudest day the old veterans of Memphis have seen since the war ended." The mayor of Memphis proclaimed the occasion "fitting that [the veterans] should meet in Memphis, because here was the home of that great soldier and cavalryman whose daring deeds and daring in war have won the admiration of military critics in Europe and in America—Nathan Bedford Forrest."[24]

For the FMA, the reunion held a dual purpose: continued fundraising for the proposed statue and the laying of the cornerstone of the monument in Forrest Park. Most of the invited speakers commented on Forrest, and many of the orations mentioned the monument project. These references included the usual military hyperbole of establishing the historic nature of Forrest's various martial feats. "Here in this Memphis no Alexander the Great ever worshiped in life or laid in state when dead," a Civil War veteran and former senator from Georgia argued, "but here lived, here fought, here died and here rests the honored ashes of Nathan Bedford Forrest, the wiliest horseman of modern times and the equal in native, untutored genius of the greatest cavalryman of any age." The "untutored genius" line of tribute would appear again and again in the proceedings (and would recur again and again in the century-plus afterward) as speakers spoke to Forrest's innate talents on the battlefield. Another orator echoed these remarks, arguing, "that wonderful man, Nathan B. Forrest [was] easily the greatest cavalry general the world ever produced." "If he had enjoyed early military training with equal opportunities as others," Bennett Young concluded, Forrest "had talents which would have made him the greatest soldier amongst men." Many of these speeches sounded like standard Civil War encomia. Still, orations on Forrest tended to bring out a strong thread of defensiveness about his background as well as a tinge of the uniqueness of his abilities and circumstances. One veteran, for instance, argued in one speech, "If Forrest had been a Northern man he would have had many monuments, a whole square in Washington." Likewise, a Methodist preacher spoke on the "greatest chieftain of the Confederacy" but strove to refute Forrest's illiteracy—a theme that would be amplified in the 1930s and 1940s. Throughout the twentieth century, Forrest would inspire more and more exaggeration and hyperbole. Still, even in 1901, speakers talked about him in a way that they did few other Civil War figures. In his recounting of Forrest's military career—particularly his bluff of Union general Abel Streight in 1863—Young defined the general as "some insatiate monster." No one talked about Civil War personalities as they did Forrest, especially using "monster" not as pejorative but as a compliment. Foreshadowing his modern image, the 1901 reunion underscored the various ways in which Forrest upended memorial discourse and played a distinctive role in Lost Cause dialogue.[25]

In fundraising, the FMA relied on informal appeals such as passing baskets at the various events. Mary Latham, who one writer described as "a happy combination of amiability and unceasing courage in whatever she may undertake," headed up much of these efforts. "I can not make a speech," Latham said on one occasion, "but there is a name on my tongue that will thrill you through and through. That name is Forrest." "I will appreciate," she implored, "the poor man's quarter as much as the rich man's $100 and more." Latham collected over $100 at the Reunion, "mostly in small coins with many one cent pieces being found in the basket." In addition to Latham's pleas, the FMA sold various items decorated with Forrest's image. Souvenir spoons, cigars, badges, paperweights, letter openers, and ribbons were sold throughout the city and helped fill the FMA coffers. This early commercialization of the Forrest image foretells a growing use of the general's visage to market a specific virile interpretation of military manliness. Two images appear repeatedly in these souvenirs—which show up only fleetingly later: one, a studio portrait of the general with rather foppish hair and a full goatee, and the second, a later, white-haired Forrest from sometime in the late 1860s. The older Forrest photograph (sometimes presented as a photo illustration) brings a certain gravitas to the proceedings and connects him visually to Robert E. Lee. Selling Forrest, selling the FMA, selling Memphis, selling the New South, these images offer an early glimpse at using the general's image to represent someone like other more famous generals and simultaneously looking and acting like no other person from the Civil War at all.[26]

After a memorial service featuring George Stainback, who had eulogized the general at his funeral in 1877, the veterans and onlookers gathered to witness the laying of the monument's cornerstone and to hear more speeches about Forrest's life and military career. Once the addresses ended, members of a Masonic order daubed the cornerstone with oil and incorporated a copper box holding sheet music, Confederate badges, and a poem. The cornerstone laying represented the culminating moment for the FMA, but the event was a bit of a ruse as "the masonry blocks used for the event were apparently carted off at a later date." The building of the base occurred three years later, in 1904, and primarily out of public sight. However, the occasion of the cornerstone laying marked an essential moment in the FMA's history as the organization needed to present the monument project as something tangible and achievable. Forrest Park existed, but "little or no formal development" had happened at the space since the city had torn down the old hospital in the late 1890s, and the statue still appeared only in rough artistic sketches and models. Money poured into the FMA during this period, but the financial undertaking was immense. Despite the great success in fundraising and attention-raising for the Forrest monument project at the 1901 reunion, the FMA ran into several organizational issues in the months immediately following the gathering in Memphis. Four months after the reunion, the FMA realized it needed to reconstruct its charter since the progress had been slower than anticipated. In November 1901, the FMA reorganized under a new charter "in view of the further fact that the purposes for which this Association was incorporated have not been [fully] accomplished and cannot be carried out for several years to come." For ten years, the FMA had overseen an expansion of fundraising and publicity for the project, but by late 1901, the statue and park tentatively came into sharper focus. Still, the FMA had succeeded in bringing attention to Forrest and the monument task. "This reunion," one newspaper writer argued, "has done more than all the histories and reunions of the past thirty-five years to bring the deeds of the famous cavalry leader to the attention of the world."[27]

In August 1901, sculptor Charles Henry Niehaus visited Memphis and began collecting photographs and paintings of Forrest and his horse, King Philip. Niehaus constructed several quick studies and models, which he then shared with the committee. The FMA specifically requested a life-size head of the general as an indicator of artistic and historical direction and perhaps even a sign of good faith for the project. Satisfied, the FMA and Niehaus signed a contract dated August 12, 1901. Born in 1855 in Cincinnati, Ohio, and trained in Munich in the 1870s, Charles Henry Niehaus had extensive experience with public and commemorative art. Between the 1880s and 1901, Niehaus designed and built sculptures ranging from presidents (fellow Ohioans James Garfield and William McKinley) to Union heroes (Abraham Lincoln and David Farragut) and several other pieces with midwestern and German connections—and even Moses. In some ways, Niehaus represents a peculiar choice for such a prominent symbol of white southern pride, but the FMA had an eye on his heroic civic pieces.[28]

The tension between artistic desires and civic constraints defined much of this relationship as Niehaus consistently pushed the FMA to consider the public framing of his sculpture. Much of the correspondence between Niehaus and the FMA concerned the size of the monument, which the association's finances tended to dictate, and the placement of the final statue. Niehaus disapproved of the Forrest Park location as he considered its size wrong for the statue. "If it is to be placed in the park," Niehaus wrote the FMA in 1902 regarding Forrest Park, "the perspective will greatly diminish its apparent size, and to be imposing and of permanent value, it should be at least [one- and one-half life] size." In response, the FMA asked Memphis for $15,000 via a city tax to increase the statue to "colossal" rather than life-size. "It has been pointed out," one newspaper writer noted, "that statues in Northern cities of Grant and other Yankee heroes are mostly of colossal size." The city refused, and in 1903, Niehaus responded that he was "sorry to learn that you have not been successful in making provision for the larger size, after all your efforts and trouble." "However," he added, "we must do the best we can with the heroic size, and I hope you will consider the points I once made in regard to a one and a quarter size equestrian monument going in a site like Forrest Park, where the trees will dwarf it in comparison, and where it will generally be viewed from a distance, thus lessening its apparent size."[29]

On May 16, 1905, Memphis once again inundated Union Avenue to celebrate Forrest as Kathleen Bradley, Forrest's eight-year-old granddaughter, pulled the cord to unveil Niehaus's statue to the public. With a band playing "Dixie," Memphis revealed the long-awaited tribute to Forrest as public space, as memorial, as grave (Forrest and his wife were reinterred in front of the pedestal). The day's festivities centered on a familiar group of orators who gave speeches on the relevance and necessity of Forrest, the FMA, and the statue. The 1905 celebration shared themes and speakers with the 1901 reunion but with a distillation of the Forrest image at the center of the proceedings. The speeches given in honor of Forrest cohered to two basic themes: the general's military genius and his civic pride representing Memphis's past, present, and future. George W. Gordon, from the FMA, gave the longest speech of the afternoon, talking at length about Forrest's life and military career. Gordon ignored explicit comments on slavery—Forrest was simply a "dealer in live stock and real estate" who later "engaged in cotton planting on a large scale." Gordon also omitted the Klan. Forrest, in his final days according to Gordon, "engaged in railroad building and other industrial pursuits." Most of his lengthy speech focused instead on Forrest's military exploits. The general covered Fort Pillow fleetingly, stopping only to suggest the battle was a fair fight under no flag of truce nor surrender. In contrast, the battle at Brice's Crossroads took up over twenty paragraphs of text—Fort Pillow received two—as Gordon recounted in detail the various maneuverings of Forrest in 1864.

Cornelius A. Stanton, formerly of the Third Iowa Cavalry, followed and echoed Gordon's remarks. "Impartial history," Stanton argued, "has given Gen. Forrest high rank as one of the greatest cavalry leaders of modern times." As a Union veteran, Stanton brought a unique perspective among a dais crowded with southerners. As expected, Stanton continued to gild Forrest with military praise. Yet, much of his speech focused on the similarities between white southerners and northerners as they reflected on the meaning of the Civil War four decades earlier. "It will be the verdict of history for all time," Stanton argued, "that the soldiers of the South and the soldiers of the North both fought for what they believed was right . . . and they fought with the same Anglo-Saxon valor." More interestingly, Stanton took the time to honor the men who served with Forrest. "Forrest's men," he noted, "are prominent and influential in every community where they now reside." These men, long after fighting for Forrest, returned to their war-torn South and "repaired and rebuilt the wasted and ruined towns and farms and homes; they devoted themselves to the development of the wonderful resources of the South, and the enterprise, the business sagacity and financial ability of Southern men have made Southern fields and Southern industries contribute to the wealth of all the world." If Gordon spoke to the military meaning of Forrest, Stanton underscored the living network of white southern men working to remake and cohere with the values of the general.[30]

The motif of Forrest as civic hero demarcated much of the 1905 celebration, bringing into sharper focus the Memphis elements seen in 1901. Senator Thomas B. Turley and Memphis mayor John J. Williams made the most of the coalescing of Forrest and the city in their speeches. Turley took an existentialist tone with the city and noted that, if Memphis were to collapse into nothingness, "still she would be remembered as the home of Forrest." Echoing Stanton's comments, Turley proclaimed, "the principles of the cause for which Forrest fought are not dead, and they will live as long as there is a drop of Anglo-Saxon blood on the face of the earth." Mayor Williams took a more traditional stance, noting that the people of Memphis "will see to it that this statue will be cared for and prized . . . as it will to the coming ages, of a chivalric race, of a glorious past and of a glorious Forrest." David C. Kelley's benediction struck a similar note. "We here dedicate it," Kelley announced, "to the promotion of patriotism, chivalry, and devotion to country as God gave him to see these duties." Despite the militaristic praise, the desire for a civic-minded warrior held strong. For example, the week of the unveiling, an editorial in the *Memphis Press-Scimitar* contended that Forrest "loved humanity; he took no delight in the suffering and sorrow of others." "The cause is lost," they declared, "but Forrest shed no blood in vain." At the end of the festivities, the *Memphis Commercial Appeal* echoed these sentiments. It argued simply that "the unveiling of the Forrest monument yesterday was one of the proudest triumphs of Peace."[31]

The need for a real, *present* Forrest can be seen in the emphasis on the physicality of the statue and of the man. George Gordon's speech is the best example of this focus, as he continually referenced Forrest's size and stature. Early in his remarks, Gordon noted that Forrest's "native endowments, both mental and physical, were extraordinary." "Physically," Gordon said later, in a section devoted to the general's physical attributes, "our hero possessed all the attributes of an athlete and a champion," and he had "an active step and bearing erect." "His eyes were a dark gray," Gordon noted, "and singularly vivid, searching and piercing." Gordon contended that "his appearance was striking and engaging" and that he struck witnesses as "a knightly and gladiatorial figure." Stanton later noted that he had "never witnessed a nobler example of self-respecting manliness" than Forrest. This focus on Forrest's corporeal features would play a large part in the general's magnetism in specific quarters in the twenty-first century. Still, in 1905, it also mirrored the interest in the specificity of Niehaus's statue. The sculptor had contact with Forrest's tailor, who had maintained records of the general's measurements for his uniform to allow for a good representation of Forrest's dimensions and proportionality. Unlike most other Civil War monuments, which focused much more on an idealized imagining of the celebrated person, the Forrest statue in Memphis held onto the physical elements of the general as it also served as his grave site. Not only did Niehaus work to get the details of his size, frame, and visage down to a specific point, but the statue stood over the actual bones of Forrest and his wife. This combination of the corporeal and the imaginary shaped how Forrest was seen outside Memphis throughout the twentieth century. Forrest was real, 1905 Memphis proclaimed, but he was also otherworldly—a man of his time and simultaneously of no time, a blurring of past, present, and future into a usable symbol of white masculinity unbound by chronology or context. A Forrest for Memphis, perhaps, but also a Forrest for the white South and beyond.[32]

The completed statue stood twelve feet tall on a seven-foot marble pedestal—with a final cost of $32,359.53 (roughly $950,000 in 2020 USD). The sculpture weighed almost ten thousand pounds. On the western face of the pedestal was inscribed: "Erected by his countrymen in honor of the military genius of Lieutenant-General Nathan Bedford Forrest, Confederate States Army, 1861–1865." The eastern face featured a stanza of Virginia Frazer Boyle's poem, focused on the line "those hoof beats die not upon fame's crimsoned sod." Niehaus's sculpture represented an image of Forrest in transition. As a civic symbol, the statue reflected the needs of Memphis in 1905—the calm repose of a city leader. Niehaus conveyed none of the ferocious elements—the "insatiable monster"—of Forrest's life and legend, opting instead to focus on the composed side of the general. With four hooves planted on the ground, King Philip stands still and looks off to the right while Forrest's face turns to the left. In many ways, Niehaus crafted the apotheosis of Forrest as a symbol of reconciliation and civic pride. At the same time, more and more testimonials to the general incorporated references to the Ku Klux Klan, and a more complicated picture of Forrest began to emerge. The statue straddled the traditional—with the visual restraint connecting it to the nineteenth century—and the modern—it served as a blank slate to project increasingly conflicting views. Ultimately, it provides much more of a story about 1905 white Memphis and their needs, desires, uncertainties, and fears (and their embedded sense of history) than it gives in terms of Forrest, the man. Niehaus's Forrest would stand in as the most prominent monument to the general for most of the twentieth century, the stasis of the statue belying the roiling complexity of Forrest's modern image. After the unveiling, and once the statue's shadow finally fell across the park, Niehaus made one final comment on the project: "I never had a more grateful subject than Forrest." By the 1930s, a much more raucous image of the general emerged—one much more likely to inflame, incite, and inspire. Never again would Forrest be viewed through the lens of stillness and immobility. The different pieces that had been merged in 1905 to craft a civic hero for white Memphis seemed hopelessly old-fashioned in a few decades as white southerners wanted a more virile idol, and Black Americans sought to challenge and undermine everything Forrest—and 1905 Memphis—represented.[33]

One month before the 1905 unveiling, the *Memphis News-Scimitar* ran a cartoon that explicitly linked Forrest to racism and the Ku Klux Klan. The cartoon "Forrest Again in White Shroud" featured an image of the Forrest statue hidden beneath a protective cloth surrounded by a group of marauding phantasmic Klansmen on horseback. "Forrest has come to his own again," the

"Forrest Again in White Shroud," *Memphis Press-Scimitar,* April 30, 1905.

accompanying article declared, and the trope of Forrest as leader of the Klan was resurrected. Filled with flowery hyperbole, the article sought to reassert Forrest as the white leader of the South as he once again commanded the Ku Klux Klan "for the protection of the honor and independence of Southern social conditions." "It may be only a mirage of a war-loving brain that peoples the park again with men in spectral garb," the writer admitted. Still, he saw in Forrest the image of a "leader whose iron hand held the reins of safety over the South when Northern dominion apotheosized the negro and set misrule and devastation to humiliate a proud race." The cartoon made the implicit explicit, and Forrest once again served as the archetype for white southern racial aggression and antagonism.[34] These moments, where the racism fundamental to the Forrest image leaches into public discourse, emphasize the myriad ways the supporters of the general skidded around the warped historical record. Sometimes explicit, sometimes veiled, the Forrest image could reflect and refract everything and nothing, depending on the context and the audience.

The 1905 unveiling occurred during the peak of the first wave of Confederate monument-making and the ideology-building of the Lost Cause. After 1905, Forrest would emerge as a much more radicalized and useful figure for the white South. Throughout the twentieth century, white southern writers enabled a Forrest image with a national audience. Memphis faded into the background as the more prominent themes of masculinity and race came to define much of the dialogue surrounding Forrest. Untethered from Memphis, Forrest became a much more useful symbol of white southern masculinity and the backdated promise of undefeat. The sanctification of Forrest in 1905 would be short-lived as white supporters of the general wanted something more earthbound and virile than what Neihaus's historicized general could provide. Still, the 1905 monument and the surrounding celebration underscore the desires of white Memphians to establish Forrest as their central civic signifier. He served as shorthand for the mythologized tales of their past, for their chaotic present, and for their hopeful, if unclear, future. But in the building of this monument, white Memphis erased a giant swath of the past as public art trumped a complicated past. A testament to white civic pride, the Forrest statue signified an erasure of Black Memphis as a public, segregated space that defined the history of a divided city. As history collided with myth, Forrest Park served as a tangible symbol of the intersecting ways civic pride, white supremacy, and racial violence have defined so much of the history of Memphis.

3

FORREST AS HISTORY, FORREST AS FICTION

> Through the long winter nights, before the leaping fires, the men who rode with Forrest told over what Old Bedford did on the Streight Raid, what he said at Murfreesboro, how he looked at Brice's Cross-Roads. And as they talked, their children and, years later, their grandchildren heard only of victory, never of defeat.
>
> —ANDREW LYTLE, 1984

> The exploits of Nathan Bedford Forrest are balm for the soul during these days of defeat and retreat before the Red menace. For here is a man, tho dead, whose memory lives on to inspire us to Victory!
>
> Letter to the *Memphis Press-Scimitar,* 1962

Decades after the Memphis statue and celebration, Forrest had drifted into the ether of the unremembered. In life, Forrest cut a captivating figure for southerners and northerners alike. Newspaper stories trailed his exploits—intrepid and rousing to white southerners, threatening and sinister to everyone else. His actions found a national audience. After his death, and certainly after 1905, Forrest faded from the national consciousness. Less immediately important to white Memphians and no longer a cipher for former Union soldiers to demonstrate their spirit of reconciliation, Forrest's power in the early twentieth century dissipated. July 13, Forrest's birthday, provides a benchmark to measure the energy of the general's public memorials in Memphis and Nashville. The state legislature elevated the date to a state holiday in 1921, and celebrations centered on the Memphis statue. Some years, as in 1906, the United Daughters of the Confederacy celebrated Forrest with flowers,

Postcard of Memphis statue, ca. 1930s.
National Druggist Sundry Co., Memphis.

speeches, and a splash of fanfare. More often, especially after World War II, not much took place at all. By the 1930s, the birthday disappeared from the public eye as the only local newspaper coverage of Forrest related to the patina of the Niehaus statue as the bronze morphed into a greenish tinge. Tennessee removed Forrest's birthday from the slate of state holidays in the late 1960s, in the aftermath of Martin Luther King Jr.'s murder, and transferred it to the more ambiguous category of "special day of observation." Forrest fell through the cracks as civic concerns gave way to a dialogue about the racism embedded in the general's image in the 1990s. The gravitational oblivion of time helped deconstruct the Forrest myth: the factual elements of his life shattered into a whirlwind of half-truths and exaggerations. At the same time,

Memphis statue in 2010.
Photo by Thomas R. Machnitzki, licensed through Creative Commons.

the racism that braced much of the context of his memorials sluggishly came into focus. As fact and fiction blurred, the racism at the mucky crux of the celebrations hardened into a fixed monument to the past.

The dismay of some white Tennesseans broke through the concrete of forgetfulness. In 1974, a Memphian rediscovered a rusted sign marking the Bedford Forrest "Memorial Highway." More rutted gravel than paved road, the site embarrassed devotees of the general. One newspaper article asserted that the sign "really is disrespectful to the memory of our great General Forrest. And a gravel road isn't a fitting tribute either."[1] Andrew Lytle, writing in the 1930s, helped create a practical and present-facing Forrest. For Lytle, Forrest signified the yeoman history of the white South, and his life and career embodied the promise of a New South built on traditional values. Colorful, virile, necessary, Forrest spoke to white southerners disappointed at the direction taken by—and, in their view, forced on—the South in the decades after the Civil War. Lytle's book, *Bedford Forrest and His Critter Company,* inspired writer Shelby Foote to take an interest in the general. By the end of the century, however, everything had changed. Despite his apparent regional symbolism, Forrest resonated less and less outside of the Memphis orbit—and even there, a tiredness began to show. The story of Nathan Bedford Forrest at the end of the twentieth century is a whorl of knowing and unknowing, celebration and condemnation. To plot a line through the peaks and valleys of Forrest's presence, then absence, then presence between 1905 and 1995 requires a study of the biographies published on the general. From staid studies of military tactics to eccentric retellings of folktales to more nuanced renderings grounded in historical context, the modern image of Forrest ricocheted between history and fiction and back again. Forrest played well within this blurring of what happened, what could have happened, and, by extension, what should have happened.

Silence defines large parts of the Forrest story, and the lack of sources helps energize any number of fictions about the general. Equipped with only rudimentary writing skills, Forrest left very few written records. Military records, almost entirely written by adjutants and aides, dot the historical record, but they provide only glimpses of the career aspects of Forrest's life. Forrest talked openly about corresponding with various well-wishers, politicians, and opponents in the years following the war. Still, secretaries wrote out most of these letters—many lost or in private hands today. Without legitimate memoirs or caches of correspondence, much of what Forrest thought comes to us through newspaper accounts, professional military records, or not at all. Still, much of the power of the Forrest image precisely comes from these silences and gaps. Incomplete records allow lines between even the faintest array of dots to materialize. By the late nineteenth century, as writers began excavating aspects of Forrest's nonmilitary life, a hazy outline of a biography emerged. Much of this writing veered toward the mythic as source material outside of the tall tales of Memphis remained untapped. The vacillation between fact and fiction—not to mention the narrowly defined gray area of unprovable, if marginally believable, fabrications—defines much of the Forrest story. As the Civil War receded into the amnesiac past, a reframing of Forrest took place throughout the twentieth century as writers began to portray a military hero burnished of the racism and racial violence that defined much of his life. Bookended by a statue in Memphis in 1905 and appearances on American televisions and in bookstores in the early 1990s, the twentieth-century Forrest image snaked around crumbling pillars of memory and commemoration, amnesia, and racism. At the end of the century, Forrest was everywhere.

Between 1868 and 1931, four biographies of the general were published.[2] First, Thomas Jordan and J. P. Pryor published *The Campaigns of Lieut.-Gen. N. B. Forrest, and of Forrest's Cavalry* in 1868. Written with the cooperation of Forrest, the book served as the only sanctioned biography of the general.[3] For thirty years, Jordan and Pryor's work stood as the only significant take on Forrest's military career. Then, in the late 1890s and early 1900s, three new books helped expand the historical record. In 1899, John Wyeth, a surgeon with personal connections to Forrest, published the first full-scale biography of Forrest, with particular attention given to his prewar life. Then, in 1902, J. Harvey Mathes published *General Forrest,* another biography that worked to clarify factual information and once more to extend Forrest's prewar and postwar existence. Together, these authors quietly brought Forrest into the twentieth century, but the fourth biography, published thirty years afterward, would bend the arc toward the future. Finally, in 1931, Lytle cast these earlier contributions into an animated and usable facsimile of white southern skepticism. At once fabulist and political, Lytle's Forrest loomed large over the twentieth century, smudging fact with fiction and creating new connectors between the past and the present.

Originally from northern Virginia, Thomas Jordan graduated from West Point and fought with the U.S. Army in the far west and against the Seminoles in the Southeast. Jordan resigned in May 1861 and worked as a chief-of-staff under P. G. T. Beauregard and then later Braxton Bragg. After the Civil War, he moved to Memphis, serving as the editor for the *Memphis Appeal.* Little is known about Jordan's coauthor, J. P. Pryor, who may not have even seen the book through to print. Historian Albert Castel notes that only Jordan signed the preface and alludes to Pryor's alcoholism and possible prepublication death. Correspondence exists from February 1867 between Pryor and contributors to the Forrest book, but the historical record beyond those fragments is sparse.[4] Jordan and Pryor worked to compile as factual an account of Forrest's military exploits as possible by gathering testimony from as many of Forrest's colleagues and Forrest himself. This insistence on incorporating Forrest's viewpoint led one historian to refer to Jordan and Pryor's study as Forrest's "quasi-memoir," arguing that the "book is free of some of the tall tales found in later biographies."[5] In October 1867, as Jordan and Pryor completed their manuscript, Forrest provided a brief note explaining his connection to the project and his insistence on its veracity. "In the work," Forrest notes, "will be found an authentic account of the campaigns and operations in which I took part during the war for the independence of the Confederate States." "I placed," Forrest contends, "all the facts and papers in my possession or available to me, in the hands of accomplished writers, who have done their part with close and conscientious research, and have endeavored to make up a chronicle neither over-wrought nor over-colored as I can testify."[6] Memoir or not, Forrest wanted to distance himself from the accusation of inflated anecdotes.

Although the vast majority of Jordan and Pryor's study concerned the military career of Forrest—the first chapter begins with Forrest's enlistment, and the final chapter ends with his farewell address—the manuscript includes an introductory sketch that briefly summarizes Forrest's lineage and early life. From this first foray into delineating the life of the general, the frontier myth proved a formidable aspect of contextualizing Forrest and his lineage. "Thus it will be seen," Jordan and Pryor argue, "Nathan Bedford Forrest is of pure, though mixed, British stock and springs directly from those hardy, stout-handed pioneer families who, ever far out on the border, wrested the wilderness from the savage by their ready rifles."[7] Forrest's frontier bona fides helped define his character to the authors, served as a signifier of whiteness, and introduced the cultural and geographic map of his life career. As for slavery, Jordan and Pryor note that he "established himself in Memphis as a broker in real estate and a dealer in slaves."[8] However, a footnote to this paragraph opens a key line of defensiveness in the general's historiography by claiming that, contrary to white southern cultural norms, Forrest was quite popular despite his slavery business. "[T]here were many dealers," Jordan and Pryor contend, "who overcame the prejudice by their individual worth and standing . . . and prominent in this class stand Bedford Forrest." Forrest, they maintain, "carried on his business with admitted probity and humanity." They assert that he never separated enslaved families, and he worked to purchase family groups as a unit. "Habitually kind as a master," they conclude, "we are satisfied his slaves were strongly attached to him."[9] Later authors would expand on this mythology. Still, as early as 1868, the foundation was set to allow platitudes and self-justifying white defensiveness. Edging toward the curiosity side of the axis since later studies and biographies have supplanted it, the Jordan and Pryor entry postulates a Forrest trapped in the resin of old-fashioned military history—a die-cast model figure useful for fantasy quests but lacking historical context.

Much of the basis of the twentieth-century myth of Forrest found its origins thirty years later when John Allen Wyeth published *The Life of Nathan Bedford Forrest* in 1899. It also propelled forward many stories that Forrest devotees would soon canonize. Wyeth wrote within the living memory framework of the Civil War, which allowed for an engagement with the past that evoked a particular presence. Born in northern Alabama in 1845, Wyeth fought for the Confederacy before attending medical school after the war and moving to New York City as a surgeon and a pioneer in medical graduate education.[10] At some point after the war, Wyeth became acquainted with and worked for Thomas Jordan. This relationship stimulated the surgeon's interest in Forrest.[11] Unlike Jordan's book, Wyeth's biography endeavored to tell the larger story of Forrest's life. Though borrowing obvious organizational aspects, the later writer had access to the *Official Records of the Union and Confederate Armies* (published in the 1880s), allowing a more complete look at the Civil War. Wyeth introduced a slew of soon-to-be canonic stories to the Forrest myth. Tales of a young Forrest confronting rattlesnakes and panthers played into the narrative of the general as a fearless frontier archetype. With so many gaps in the Forrest backstory, Wyeth and other early biographers built bridges of imagined stories to situate and contextualize a wobbly childhood. "Of the boyhood life of General Forrest," Wyeth admits openly, "I have been able to obtain but little of interest which is reliable."[12] This combination of fact and fiction would be a hallmark of Forrest studies well into the twentieth century. Forrest as symbol mattered more than Forrest as historically grounded person.

As for slavery, Wyeth expanded on Jordan and Pryor's defensive take by bringing in commentary from George Adair, a Nashville newspaper editor and probable slave trader who served as an aide to Forrest during the war. "Forrest," Adair attested, "was kind, humane, and extremely considerate of his slaves."[13] This trope of his alleged compassionate treatment of enslaved Black people caroms through the Forrest myth. More than defensive posturing against northern attacks on his character, these counterfactual rationalizations served as a convenient workaround to any acknowledgment, not to mention confrontation, of the realities of Forrest's prewar life. Adair goes much further than alleging a specific benevolence. Forrest, Adair argues, "was overwhelmed with applications from a great many of this [enslaved] class, who begged him to purchase him." Much of Adair's testimony concerns Forrest's appearance, which he claims to be "foppish," and that Forrest demanded cleanliness from "these creatures" as he demanded of himself. "The slaves who were thus transformed," Adair concluded, "were proud of belonging to him."[14] With his apparent connections to the slave trade, Adair certainly pushed for normalizing the myth of a benign system. This lurid defense of a profoundly terrifying aspect of a horrifying system of oppression would be less explicitly echoed by later writers. Still, the core elements of this fiction of slave trading altruism would adhere firmly to discussions of Forrest's prewar life. Wyeth's willful misrepresentation of slavery and his clichéd takes on childhood tales illustrate the challenge of documenting the historic Forrest.

In 1902, soon after Wyeth's biography, J. Harvey Mathes published *General Forrest*. Underrepresented within the Forrest historiography (and routinely out of print in the twentieth century), Mathes's study represents a link between the nineteenth-century publications and the more modern versions of Forrest in the first half of the twentieth century. Mathes fought in the Civil War and served as a correspondent for the *Memphis Daily Appeal*—one of the many journalists in Forrest's circle. Mathes follows Wyeth in the opening section on Forrest's prewar life, though he is more straightforward about slavery. Mathes omits overt mentions of the Adair material but does assert that "the negroes were proud to belong to [Forrest], for he required them to be neat and tidy in appearance, and of course they were well fed and housed."[15] Mathes shows few qualms with the institution of slavery but adds that men like Forrest faced "some prejudice" for trading enslaved people, "although it was as legitimate as horse trading or any other business."[16] The casual racism of Mathes's book did little to distance it from earlier studies. Mathes, however, did introduce stories into the Forrest narrative that would have growing importance across the coming decades. His book incorporates the 1857 John Able story, where Forrest rescued Able from an extralegal hanging. Forrest, according to Mathes, "had vindicated a principle in a time of wild excitement, and set the people to thinking as seldom have."[17] Later, in the postwar section, Mathes brings in the first appearance of Thomas Edwards, though not by name. Mathes argues that the Black plantation workers "expressed their approval of the killing," as Edwards "was a turbulent, dangerous character whom most of them feared."[18] Mathes also comments extensively on the Pole-Bearers speech, only mentioned as "a grand barbecue." Mathes satirizes the gathering—he describes the master of ceremonies as having "a face as black as the back of the moon"—with flippant references to a lynching. "It was an ideal barbecue day," Mathes writes, "but the distinguished Caucasian visitors were ill at ease, for they were aware that their roasting was near at hand."[19]

Mathes died the year his biography was published, and the book fell under the shadow of Wyeth's earlier book and the biographies to come. Borrowing the prejudice if not the defensiveness of Wyeth, Mathes's contribution to the Forrest bookshelf allowed the general to creep into the twentieth century with a few more facts and a lot more racism. The book ends with a mention of the progress toward the Memphis statue, and Mildred Spottswood Cash Mathes—the author's widow—worked to raise money for the monument. Several years after the unveiling of the statue, a bust of Mathes went up in the newly consecrated Confederate Park. In late 2017, as attention swirled around the Forrest statue and other Confederate markers in Memphis, Mathes tumbled into the maelstrom. Following the removal of the Forrest statue, the bust of Mathes quietly came down, too. The Mathes family expressed their anger as they had tried to remove the bust on their terms. "The bust of Capt. Mathes is being stored in a safe and secure place," the director of the nonprofit that purchased and removed the monuments said. "If the Mathes family wants it," he noted, "they should probably have preferential status in that process." With all the attention paid to Forrest and Jefferson Davis, the bust slipped through the cracks of public memorialization and condemnation. "No one," the newspaper noted, "paid much attention to Capt. Mathes."[20]

Fort Pillow provides a convenient lens through which to view these early perspectives. Not all the books covered the slave trade other than in defensive glances, nor do they all cover the Ku Klux Klan. But Jordan and Pryor, Wyeth, and Mathes devote space to examining and explaining the 1864 battle, and the ways these writers confront and contort Forrest's actions underscore this early iteration of this historiography. Each of the early biographers of Forrest offers various levels of defense to counter the media reports and congressional testimony on Fort Pillow. These writers share an eagerness to reframe Fort Pillow around questions of actions taken under a flag of truce and the conduct of Black members of the garrison. Jordan and Pryor's coverage of Fort Pillow set the standard for much of what would follow by Forrest-friendly writers: deny the worst elements of brutality, omit specifics, and blame Black troops for anything else that may have happened. A prominent aspect of Jordan and Pryor's defense of Forrest relates to the actions of Black soldiers, whose activities the authors describe as "stupid."[21] Wyeth and Mathes take this further and claim the Black garrison was at turns drunk and "defiant." Mathes stressed the supposed aggravations in the area by Union soldiers as a reason for the battle in the first place. He also claims the fort's leadership was "weak" and "vain." A "fondness for intoxicating drinks," argues Wyeth, "especially so with the Negroes just free from slavery," led to greater violence. This charge of drunkenness, and the implication that it led to a more ferocious Confederate response, emerged as a centerpiece of much of the white southern defense of Forrest. No excessive violence occurred, they argued, but if it did (which, they claim, it did not), then it was the fault of a drunken garrison who responded with insolence in the face of unconditional surrender. "The garrison," Wyeth contends, "had resolved to die—*not to surrender.*"[22]

After the battle, as survivor accounts of post-surrender violence and brutality emerged, these pro-Forrest accounts tended to blame the Black soldiers and emphasize supposed acts of Confederate kindness. Jordan and Pryor focus primarily on a narrative centered on Forrest's men working to end fighting and tending to Union wounded with a keen emphasis on the role of prisoner taking—in direct opposition to the media claims. Wyeth goes further and blames most of the post-battle violence on the garrison. "Terror-stricken Negroes," Wyeth writes, "either insanely intoxicated or convinced from the slaughter that had transpired that no quarter would be shown them, and determined to sell their lives as dearly as possible, still offered resistance and continued to fire at the Confederates." Mathes repeats the drunkenness allegations but adds a new justification for the confusion: Confederates worked hard to bury the dead, and these funeral pyres led to unfair accusations of Black soldiers being burned to death. Confederate considerateness thus led to, in Mathes's description, charges of brutality. In all, the writers refuse to refute the allegations as much as they attempt to provide explanations and rationalizations for Forrest's actions. Some of this narrative would get hard-baked into the Forrest myth, though later writers would tend to deemphasize the overt racism of the first fifty years of Forrest historiography. From the 1860s to the first decade of the 1900s, these writers helped shape Forrest's biography. The resultant image fused an underdog military story with a muddle of fiction and hyperbole tacked together with implicit and explicit white supremacy—a biography easily connected to the Memphis statue in connotation and significance. The substantive changes would come in the 1930s.

In 1931, Andrew Lytle brought the various pieces of the Forrest myth into one robust package with his biography. Lytle sought to craft a usable Forrest who spoke as much to white southern concerns of the 1930s as to the past. To Lytle, Forrest represented the "plain people" of the South.[23] Blending bloody militarism and racialized social history profoundly shaped the public memory of Forrest over the next fifty years. As much as earlier biographers wanted to cast Forrest as a hero, Lytle desired something more specific: to craft a functional representation of white southern masculinity. The image of a quick-thinking and bloodied warrior replaced Forrest's earlier, more composed perception during the late nineteenth century. Lytle effectively rescued Forrest from irrelevance by refashioning him as a signifier of contemporary southern issues, proving that Forrest could easily represent the modern South. Race factored into his characterization, and as the grand wizard of the Klan, the general represented to Lytle "the last ruler of the South," who helped shatter Reconstruction. "At the most tragic moment of Southern history," Lytle writes, "when all seemed lost beyond redemption, he appeared, unexpectedly, mysteriously, almost supernaturally and snatched the enjoyment of victory from the enemy's hands, from those Black Republicans who had set out to destroy the South and the Old Political Union."[24]

"This is a young man's book," Lytle wrote five decades after its publication. He places it at once in the youthful past and underscores the political energy coursing through the book.[25] Published in 1931 when Lytle was in his late twenties, *Bedford Forrest and His Critter Company* represents an anomaly within the Forrest historiography: simultaneously influential and dismissed. Lytle began work on the biography in the late 1920s, shortly after graduating from Vanderbilt University. Vanderbilt provided Lytle with a cohort of friends, students and professors, who shared enthusiasm in wrenching significance out of the southern past. Known as the Southern Agrarians or Fugitives, this educated coterie of white men pushed against the attacks on and stereotypes of southern culture and worked to craft an intellectual and artistic defense of the South—or at least their particular and selective version of it. Besides Lytle, the group included Allen Tate (poet and Lytle's closest friend of the group),

Donald Davidson (poet and the professor central to the group), Robert Penn Warren (poet/novelist and the most acclaimed writer of the group—who won the Pulitzer Prize for both fiction and poetry), John Crowe Ransom (poet and instigator for much of the group's efforts), and Stark Young (playwright, novelist, and critic). In 1930, this group published a collective manifesto as a series of twelve essays titled *I'll Take My Stand* (a phrase disliked by some members of the group). As they fixated on the tumult of the southern present, Allen Tate, Robert Penn Warren, and Andrew Lytle obsessed over their version of the southern past. Between 1928 and 1931, these three writers published their first nonfiction monographs—all biographies of historical figures that fundamentally influenced the South. In 1928, Tate published *Stonewall Jackson.* Warren followed the next year with his *John Brown: The Making of a Martyr.* Lytle's Forrest biography followed in 1931. Still in their twenties (Tate and Lytle were twenty-nine when their books came out; Warren was just twenty-four), these men looked to history to make sense of contemporary society. Lytle's Forrest, then, fits directly into this frame of reference.[26]

Lytle's contribution to *I'll Take My Stand,* "The Hind Tit," outlined his dismay at the evolution of American society, especially as to its relative perversion of his white southern ideal. At the center of his essay stood the small regional farmer—the southern yeoman, who Lytle argued was the central figure of the southern past. Lytle argued that most of the South's problems stemmed from a blind adherence to modernization and modernity (broadly defined) and the forsaking of the yeoman class. Much of "The Hind Tit" relates to industrialization and banking and how northerners pushed "progress" to keep the South subservient. Connecting the debates between Jefferson and Hamilton to Civil War battlefields, Lytle argues that the northern-centered economic power structure set out to corrupt the lives and livelihoods of the backbone of the white South: the yeoman farmer. In addition, Lytle wrote a two-page discussion of the war between the "rigid Theocracy" of the North and the "Feudal Aristocracy" of the South. "My general purpose," Lytle begins, "will be to show that the experiment that every man is entitled to life, liberty, and the pursuit of happiness, the natural rights of man, that is the rights inherited from the creator, was born of tainted parentage." "In the South," he argues, "slavery denied this right by the men who possessed it; in New England, Industry and a spirit of Commercialism put up material gain as the end of man instead."[27] These themes had little to do with the general himself other than through Lytle seeing the promise of this white yeoman ideal in Forrest. Instead, Lytle was focused on the long history of sectional division and southern distinctiveness. Lytle conceived of and wrote *Bedford Forrest and His Critter Company* within this context—a romanticized past coupled with a presentism shaped by industrial fears.[28] Lytle's finished book proposal mentions Forrest zero times.

Buried in his papers archived at Vanderbilt sits a fragment of an essay Lytle wrote, perhaps just as an exercise for himself. "First," Lytle writes, "the fabric of the Agrarian Culture of the Southwest was not a Ctton [*sic*] Aristocracy at one extreme and pore [*sic*] white at the other with the slaves in between. It was largely a country of the Yeomanry, the Plain People, owning modest-sized farms and occasionally a few slaves." Forrest's lineage connected directly to what Lytle saw as the real center of the white South. "That from these plain people the Cotton Aristocracy was recruited, and [in] the four generations of Forrest[s] is seen the gradual development from the pioneer stage to the more or less hardened culture of which Nathan Bedfor [*sic*] Forrest is the example. That this family may be taken as a type of the strong men who made themselves the rulers of what was becoming a Feudal Aristocracy, whose economics was based on the land, no[t] on slavery."[29] This war, too, played into Lytle's mythmaking narrative, with much of the brunt of the story being carried by Braxton Bragg. Forrest's superior represents the command system's inability to recognize Forrest's genius to his admirers, standing as the unimaginative foil to the crafty Forrest. Partially true, this stand-off energizes much of the debate regarding Forrest's role in the Confederacy. If only Bragg had understood Forrest, if only Davis had not listened to Bragg, if only Forrest had had more soldiers, and on and on. "The Western campaigns were the decisive campaigns of the war," Lytle argued, "and that Forrest was the particular genius produced by the west during the war. He was the only man in the west who consistently brought victory."[30] As much as he scattered discussion of Hamiltonians and Jeffersonians in his prewar chapters, Lytle would reliably bring in Bragg and other command figures to serve as hindrances and hurdles to Forrest's success. Much of Lytle's military narrative coheres to earlier iterations—his importance comes from his politicized and energized Forrest—but he still insisted on grinding as many axes as he could regarding Forrest's status.

Lytle's Forrest is important for several reasons. First, he helped modernize Forrest. Despite his misgivings of the modern overshadowing the traditional, Lytle wrenched Forrest out of the nineteenth century and crafted him as a useful heroic template for the contemporary white south of the 1930s. Secondly, he narrowed the gap between fact and fiction within the Forrest narrative by incorporating many of the tall tales central to his myth into a readable account for a mass audience. Third, Lytle pushes the aggression and bloodshed to the forefront. The violence is the point. Finally, Lytle offers an unapologetic Forrest tethered to the fundamental aspects of the primal white South. Lytle discusses slavery and the Ku Klux Klan openly. For Lytle, the slave trade, not slavery itself, represented an obstacle for Forrest. "It was honorable in the Southern feudalism to own slaves," Lytle argues, "but very dishonorable to traffic in them." "The close personal association between slave and master," Lytle writes, "particularly between slave and mistress, caused the planters tacitly to ignore the economics of his condition out of respect for him as a person." "The slave understood his relationship," Lytle argues, "that he owned the master as much as the master owned him." "Because the slave dealers looked on the negro only in terms of trade," Lytle concluded, "Southerners considered them debased." But Lytle also bought into the myth of Forrest as a benevolent dealer of enslaved men and women. He never separated families, treated everyone well, and "always did his best to find and buy the husband and wife."[31] Taking it further, Lytle argued that Forrest "treated his slaves so well that he was burdened with appeals from them to be bought."[32] On one level, slavery existed as a theoretical talking point. But on a deeper level, Lytle, a planter himself, had to have understood the labor needs connected to the structure of slavery within the southern system—not to mention the racial suppositions embedded therein.

Lytle's understanding of slavery stemmed partly from his upbringing and family, but it also borrowed strongly from historians such as Ulrich B. Phillips. Phillips—especially in his *American Negro Slavery* (1918) and *Life and Labor in the Old South,* published two years before *Critter Company*—conceived of Black American slavery as a predominately beneficial and even "benevolent" institution for all involved.[33] Racist language defined his descriptions of Black people defined as childlike and submissive. Despite the legitimate historical work present in his work, Phillips's prejudices time-stamped his books as hopelessly of the past. Still, Lytle's work borrows liberally the tone and perspective of Phillips. Lytle, no serious scholar of slavery, used sympathetic views of enslavement to exonerate Forrest. With his understanding of slavery as a prologue, the Ku Klux Klan represented the apex of Lytle's iteration of Forrest's position in southern history. Instead of running from the Klan associations or burying them under clouds of obfuscation, Lytle saw this chapter of Forrest's life as what elevated him to a true regional hero. In a brief flurry of paragraphs, Lytle at once belittles the origins of the group (he refers to the founders as "a group of boys") while elevating their aims (the "South was disarmed and helpless"). The Klan's actions related mainly to youthful pranking of Black southerners as well as wholly undoing Reconstruction. It was everywhere and nowhere, but Lytle saw Forrest as a leader. "The triumph of the Ku Klux Klan," Lytle writes, "was the triumph of the political genius of the South, a genius that had failed, because of its limitations, to save the Union but which, at last, managed to save itself by following the most typical, the greatest, leader its feudalism had fashioned."[34]

Lytle's allowance for slavery and his admiration for the Reconstruction-era Ku Klux Klan adhered to his polemical focus on the modern dismissal of an imagined feudal South of white yeoman farmers. However, a more insidious element was at work, especially as one looks at the context of Lytle's use of dialect and his correspondence with other members of the Fugitives. In an unpublished manuscript, Lytle uses southern language as a signifier to distinguish yeoman farmers and their supposed cultural elites. Forrest plays into this metric through his unschooled patois. "And that at last," Lytle writes, "notwithstanding his use of a more ancient form of speach [*sic*], he is the highest type of Southern leader the Old South produced." "That his kind and not the cotton snobs," Lytle contends, "must be called the Southern leaders."[35] Dialect thus plays a couple of argumentative roles within the book—and at some point, Lytle went back to the manuscript and added various "dialect" edits. In an early chapter, for example, handwritten corrections emended "children" to "chillan" and removed the "h" from panther. However, the book ends with Lytle using dialect more concretely connected to a (doubtless invented) Black woman. The final paragraph of his book, in fact, relates the memories of "an old negress, Georgiana," and her belief that Forrest's bronze horse in Memphis "show is gittin' poe." "I regon," Lytle has the woman conclude, "de Gin'ral must ride him of a night."[36]

This use of dialect mirrors what is found in various letters between Lytle, Alan Tate, and Donald Davidson. Tate, among others, uses "br'er" as a repeated form of address to Lytle, and in one letter, dated July 4, 1931 ("damn far from 1776"), Tate uses dialect throughout. Tate closes with "[w]e shore is honin' to see ye, Br'er Lytle, and we shore expects ye to come fore long." Davidson was more egregious. He and his wife sent Lytle a homemade Christmas card with a photo taped to a folded piece of paper of a Black child standing in a field, smiling and holding a cotton sack. The inscription read: "Us and de Davidsons sho' do wish you all a Merry Christmas." It was signed "E Pluribus." The casual nature of these exchanges spoke to how the writers interacted with one another. On the one hand, a self-conscious ruralification of their language and addresses—learned modern southern men trying on the pretend language of the poor; on the other, a racism that spanned the extemporaneous (Tate) to the flagrant (Davidson). Placed in the context of Lytle's discussion of slavery and the Ku Klux Klan—not to mention the larger war aims of the Confederacy—this language conveys something far more entrenched than some playacting in the past tense.

Lytle's book reflected a newfound audience for Forrest. Each of the earlier biographies tended to be aimed at white southerners with an eye toward a white northern readership. A line of defensiveness coursed through these books as the authors attempted to give their hero a wider audience. Lytle's aim, however, was different. Lytle maintained a sensitivity to the Confederacy and white southern culture but expressed less touchiness about Forrest's image than earlier writers. Seven decades removed from the beginning of the Civil War and only a toddler when the Memphis statue went up, Lytle wrote from a different perspective than Wyeth or the others. Paradoxically more alive, Lytle's Forrest came not from personal memories but instead from political ideology. Forrest mattered to Lytle in ways that eluded people who had actually known him. In his review of the book for the *New York Herald Tribune,* Civil War historian Avery Craven noted that, although "Mr. Lytle's work contains little of fact that is new," the author has "an intimate knowledge of the stage over which this leader fought and an understating of dramatic values in writing that gives this book real distinction."[37] Craven thought the book worked best as a heroic tale rather than as a work of history. "For those whose taste is for rugged heroes," Craven wrote, "for tales that reveal the lengths to which human endurance can go, this book is to be highly recommended."[38] Picking up on the animated nature of this new Forrest, "[t]he author appreciates," Craven writes, "the value of humor in his story of blood and storm."[39]

As World War II approached, this violent image of Forrest intersected with a growing American tolerance for bloodshed. To that end, the general's sword attracted keen attention when Mary Forrest Bradley, Forrest's granddaughter, allowed a reporter to photograph the weapon for the first time. The *Memphis Press-Scimitar* noted that "the bloodstains thereon are plainly visible."[40] Forrest took on greater appeal as the defensiveness of the late nineteenth century gave way to a more defiant and aggressive image in the mid-twentieth century. As the United States entered World War II, Forrest as military hero began to trump Forrest as Confederate general. By the 1940s, Forrest's image served a much more generic military purpose. Lytle's southern-man archetype gave way to the decontextualized fierce warrior. Robert Selph Henry, a Tennessee lawyer who had graduated from Vanderbilt in the 1910s, published a new biography of the general in 1944. Arriving with a cover drawing of a rangy and determined Forrest—part gunslinger, part Don Quixote—*First with the Most: Forrest* reflected a decidedly more sober approach to Forrest. Primarily a military history, Henry's book replaced much of the polemical elements of earlier biographies and wrote from a more matter-of-fact perspective. "[A]ny excessive loss of life" at Fort Pillow, for example, came down to "the character of the command and the plan of defense which permitted no definite, clean cut and readily understood surrender or end to fighting." Henry worked to create a narrative that played well across regions and regionalisms. Politics, Henry avers, played more of a role in the claims of massacre and therefore any sober assessment had to look at actions on both sides. Even with the Klan, Henry tried to broker the different vectors of white southern loss and all-out blame. "The original Klan," Henry writes, "was a desperate device of a people defeated and all but despairing." Henry softened some of the racism embedded in earlier Forrest biographies. His disinterest in the role of enslaved people within the Forrest story and concern for an unemotional retelling of military exploits led to a book long in action and perhaps short on significance. In 1992, at the height of Forrestphilia, Konecky and Konecky Press reprinted Henry's book, and the biography found a new audience as stacks and stacks of these books buckled into remaindered heaps in the front of every Barnes & Noble.

However, buried in plain sight in his title sits one of the lasting impressions of Henry's work. Henry took pains to end one of the more troubling, in his mind, aspects of Forrest's memory: the general's literacy. Since the 1860s, Forrest has been quoted as reducing his tactical aims of getting to the battlefield first and with the most men. The quote, taken as a given that Forrest even said something to that effect, soon found fame as Forrest getting there "fust with the most" and eventually "fustest with the mostest." Sometimes, commentators used the dialect-driven version to underscore Forrest's uneducated manner. By the twentieth century, many of Forrest's advocates had taken up "fustest" as a form of endearment to distinguish the general from any military snobbery. Family, however, still bristled. In a newspaper article published in 1940, Mary Forrest Bradley discussed her grandfather's literacy at length. "He had," she maintained, "a real gift for using words correctly." Nevertheless, Forrest had "atrocious spelling" since he "spelled by sound."[41] Henry would have none of it. He saw "fustest" as a bastardization and ultimately an embarrassment to Forrest's career and life.

In 1918, an exchange in two New York newspapers erupted over the use of Forrest's maneuvers as an example of proper military tactics. The British commentator emphasized Forrest's adage of getting to the battle "first with the most men." Forrest had used the phrase to explain his raid into Murfreesboro, Tennessee, during the Civil War, but the maxim was not widely repeated until after the general's death. Instead, the phrase often became "git thar fustest with the mostest." By the twentieth century, the idiom played an integral part in the Forrest myth. The commentator's use of the correct syntax sparked a debate between the *New York Times* and the *New York Tribune.* In response to the story in the *Times,* the *Tribune* published an editorial asserting that the cleaned-up phrase did "injustice to Forrest." The general, the *Tribune* reported, was "a stranger to book learning," spoke in a "cracker Southern dialect," and most certainly said "fustest with the mostest."[42] The next day, the *New York Times* defended the British correspondent's syntax as well as Forrest's schooling by arguing that no "uneducated man would think of such an intricate and complicated phrase." The *Times* also refuted the *Tribune*'s contention that it was "cracker" dialect; "it is not dialect but 'baby talk.'" The *Times* did agree with the *Tribune*'s military assessment of the general and compared him to Napoleon. "Forrest," the newspaper concluded, "was a genius whom the Confederacy discovered too late." Fifty years after the Civil War and forty years after the *New York Times*'s scathing obituary of the general, two northern newspapers competed to praise a former Confederate and slaveholder to correct any supposed "injustice" to his name.[43]

Despite Henry's pleas, "fustest" had a life of its own—sometimes overtly connected to Forrest, but often in the 1940s, not at all. As the Confederacy became decoupled from Forrest, "fustest" came to represent wide-ranging

American military might. For example, in 1944, it appeared in a full-color ad for Allis-Chalmers, a manufacturing company out of Milwaukee, promoting their M-4 military tractor. "Carrying on in the legendary tradition of Lt. Gen. Nathan Bedford Forrest," the ad copy reads, "Allied military commanders today are 'gittin' thar fustest' with their big guns to smash enemy resistance." No longer Confederate, no longer even southern, Forrest represented only American military power. A few years later, in 1951, a recruitment ad for the U.S. Army Airborne notes that "the Airborne gets there 'fustest with the mostest' . . . on the wings of huge transports carrying the finest fighting men in the U.S. Army."

A curious subsect of this renewed fascination with Forrest as a military commander relates to the uptick in references to the general as a precursor to German tank warfare. Throughout World War II, newspapers referenced Forrest as a German tank commander and the inventor of the German Blitz. In 1940, a newspaper article even made explicit the connection between Forrest and the war in Europe. Adolf Hitler, the article declared, exhibited the same military genius as Forrest. Nevertheless, the comparison remained positive, and the writer noted that "Adolph [*sic*] Hitler, more than anyone else has ever done, is applying Forrest's methods." "What Forrest did on horses," the article explained, "the Germans are doing in planes and tanks."[44] In 1941, accompanying a photograph of the snow-covered Memphis statue, the *Press-Scimitar* considered "what a leader of a hard-hitting panzer division Gen. Forrest would be today." Another piece referred to Forrest's tactics retroactively as "blitzkrieg warfare."[45] And in 1943, the paper related that Forrest "is credited with being the originator of blitz tactics made famous in this war."[46]

A long-lingering myth related to Erwin Rommel, the German tank commander, who admired Forrest to such a degree that he visited different Forrest-centered battlefields to understand the cavalry commander's tactics and perspectives. In the mid-1980s, Lawrence Wells wrote *Rommel and the Rebel,* an alternative history of Rommel's engagement with Forrest's career. Published before overt connections between Confederates and Nazis would have raised enough eyebrows to question the association (an early cover of the book featured a Confederate flag with a swastika in the center), this book took a playful spin—at one point, a drunken Faulkner takes Rommel on a tour of Shiloh—on what is a rather odd aspect of the Forrest myth. The story bounced around various newspaper columns and Internet chat rooms for decades. In 1996, however, a Tennessean reached out to Rommel's son and asked directly (though he wished not to "bring up sad memories"). Manfred Rommel replied simply that, despite rumors, his father never visited the United States.[47] Commenters rarely delved into the meta elements of this pairing as they seemed content only with their hero's fame as a tactician. The blurring of fact and fiction with the Rommel story plays directly into the contours of the Forrest myth: unverified or unverifiable stories pressed into a narrative that makes enough sense at a hazy distance fall apart with any critical research, yet the myth persists. Not true, not possibly true, but this story touches on so many overt and implicit parts of the Forrest story that it never entirely faded away.[48]

No mechanized or militarized product could avoid being connected to Forrest, no matter how far the analogy stretched or even snapped. Regardless of veracity, the unpretentious manner of Forrest's quip captured the imagination of journalists and advertising copywriters. Folksy and historical, or at least "historical," the phrase allowed writers to be engaging and to affect some sense of military or tactical understanding. After World War II, writers continued to connect Forrest's phrase to the Atomic Era, decontextualizing an already watery expression. In 1946, the *Chicago Daily News,* for example, featured a story on atomic bomb defense. "The successful commander," one admiral argued, will no longer 'git thar fustest with the mostest.' He will 'git thar with the leastest latest.'"[49] In 1949, the student newspaper for Eastern Illinois State College ran a piece on the state of the world in the first four years after the dropping of atomic bombs on Hiroshima and Nagasaki. They argued that "if the East and the West should ever clash in warfare both sides will realize that to survive at all they must strike hard and fast with their greatest weapons, the atomic weapons." This third world war, they concluded, "will be fought and won with the philosophy and tactics of a Civil [W]ar Confederate, General Forrest, who said, 'Battles are won by those who get there fustest with the mostest.'"[50]

In the 1940s, a Chesterfield cigarettes ad featured a serviceman ringing a doorbell for a date. A cigarette drifted from his lips as he held a carton of Chesterfields and flowers behind his back. "Getting there *First* with the *Most,*" read the copy. Forrest shows up only at a glance, but the heady combination of cigarettes, militarism, and romance defined the World War II era and beyond. Throughout the twentieth century, Memphis newspapers ran stories on the veracity of the phrase, using it in dozens of articles on military and military-adjacent issues, and whenever Forrest would hit the news. The regional papers, however, also inadvertently emphasized the absurdity embedded in the fustest focus. In 1946, the *Commercial Appeal* ran an ad for WeOna, a local grocery. "Fustest with the Mostest," proclaimed the ad, which pushed cans of deviled ham and fresh beef brains as cartoons of two white businessmen come running, one with tie flapping, the other in a three-piece suit and fedora. "We don't know," the copy reads, "if the good General ever really said those words, but they make it a mighty powerful formula for doing things right." In a box to the left, the store promised a visit from "Aunt Jemima in person." A tight snap-

Chesterfield Cigarettes print ad, 1944.

shot of postwar consumerism, gender roles, and racism, the ad makes clear to the hometown readers that Forrest may never have even said the words.

The highwater mark of "fustest" culture hit in 1948 as ad after ad used the phrase to connect to the postwar culture of ambiguous militarism, indefinite patriotism, and unabashed consumerism. Transportation and shipping companies still valued the expression, and Beechcraft aircraft used a painting of the general with the tag "Forrest Got Around." Half of the full-page, full-color ad, which ran in *Newsweek* and *Time* in March 1948, featured an oil painting of the general, sword in hand, leading a cavalry charge complete with a Confederate flag. After including the Rommel myth, the ad copy noted that the "secret of Forrest's success" was speed and mobility. "General Forrest," Beechcraft argued, "simply got to more places faster than his competitors." Likewise, an advertisement in *Yachting* magazine (in August 1948) sold a Higgins Deluxe nineteen-foot Sport Speeder boat via Forrest's words. "It was battles, not boats," the copy argued, "General Forrest had in mind when he said it, but his description of a winning combination certainly applies to this Higgins fast-and-roomy 19-footer."[51] A Spartanburg, South Carolina, radio station used "fustest with the mostest," as did a piece in *Traffic World*.[52] In February, an article in *Chess Review* reasoned that, "as a rule, the side that 'gits thar fustest with the mostest' is victorious."[53] That same month, the *Chicago Tribune* used the phrase in a short piece about a Russian publication that claimed a Martian spacecraft had crashed into Siberia. The Chicago writer implied that a hole in Arizona dating back to 760 AD proved alien spaceships had blasted into American soil long before. "Rocket ships, meteors, or atoms," the article claimed, "we get there firstest with the mostest."[54] Finally, *Milk Plant Monthly* used Forrest in an article on milkmen and bottle caps. "Get thar fustest with the leastest," the piece broadcasted. "General Forrest didn't say that. But we do. We think the dairyman shouldn't be loaded down with a whole year's supply of bottle caps."[55]

In October 1951, the *Chicago Tribune* ran a Hedda Hopper Hollywood news column on a motion picture featuring Gary Cooper as Forrest. "Can you think of anything more pat," Hopper exclaimed, "than Gary Cooper playing the role of Gen. Nathan Bedford Forrest, that favorite Confederate character who made the immortal crack—'Get there fustest with the mostest men?' Warner Brothers had purchased a story entitled "The Grey Ghost" that served as the basis of the film. The source material, written by Alan Dowdy, remains a mystery, especially since the Grey Ghost sobriquet was most associated with Confederate cavalry commander John Mosby. Gary Cooper, fresh off several terrible and terribly reviewed films in a row, including *Distant Drums* in 1951, which had the actor storming a fort in the Spanish-controlled Everglades and fighting Seminoles. These films may have led to Warner Brothers' decision to can the Forrest film. Instead, Cooper would go on to film *High Noon,* one of his most respected movies, the following year.

Hopper's column piqued the interest of Monroe Cockrell, a Forrest obsessive in Chicago who worked as a research assistant for Robert Selph Henry. Cockrell read a wide array of regional and national newspapers and magazines and built an extensive clippings file on all things Forrest. The Chicagoan fired off a letter to producer David Weisbart at Warner Brothers to inquire about the film's particulars. "I know that films are produced to attract customers," Cockrell wrote, "and historical accuracy is of minor importance in gaining public acceptance." Excited for the spectacle, Cockrell nonetheless worried that Hollywood would damage Forrest's reputation with ahistorical additions, omissions, or out-and-out errors. Pointing out a list of falsehoods and misrepresentations, Cockrell listed a host of inauthentic artistic renderings, including mistakes in the types of pistols he held, how he held them, and the size of his sword. "The preponderant evidence," Cockrell writes, "shows that Forrest was naturally left-handed but ambidextrous by training and that he wore his sword on his left side and drew it with his right hand switching it back and forth as occasion required." His sword, too, had to be exact. "[Y]ou'll never realize," Cockrell notes, "the length, weight and thickness of that sword until you try to lift it. To the average man, it would be like lugging around about half a section of a railroad rail."[56] Cockrell pleaded with Weisbart to take this issue seriously, to take Forrest seriously as a commander. Weisbart responded quickly and noted, "due to circumstances which I won't go into at this time, the project has been indefinitely postponed."[57] But, Weisbart assured Cockrell, "if and when this is ever filmed, we will be as factual as is humanly possible." Three years later, Weisbart produced his best-known film: *Rebel without a Cause.*

The back-and-forth over a movie never made sums up Forrest at midcentury: famous enough to be the center of a proposed motion picture, big enough to have Gary Cooper sign on to play the role, celebrated enough to hit a Hollywood gossip column, yet the film sat unmade. Forrest wandered through American culture known and unknown in equal measure. Divorced from slavery, Fort Pillow, and the Ku Klux Klan, Forrest was simply "that favorite Confederate character." The fight, or at least tension, over what constituted fact or fiction with Forrest remained superficial as the battle roared around hand placements and grammar. As Cockrell sweated over Forrest's factual place within a fictional environment, the larger contours of what made Forrest notorious in the first place disappeared under the weight of minor celebrity status. During this period, Forrest represented an unproblematic feature player from a faded past, someone who could be played as a military hero, western protagonist, or southern character, or, as it were, some muddled combination of all three. The fact that so much of this discussion occurred between a researcher in Illinois, a Tennessee biographer, and a California filmmaker also underscores these issues. Oh, and that Hedda Hopper column? The *Chicago Tribune* ran it directly below the review of *The Desert Fox*—20th Century Fox's biopic of Erwin Rommel, featuring James Mason.

The Forrest myth sometimes coheres closely with other Lost Cause narratives, especially monument building in the early twentieth century. But at different times, the public memory of Forrest zagged when the celebration of other Confederate figures zigged. As other Civil War personalities found newfound fame and attention in the 1960s, Forrest peaked in the late 1950s. The 1958 birthday celebration for Forrest marked a high point in civic tributes as crowds gathered for speeches and Forrest-centered festivities. The local press noted the historic size of the revelry that year. Twenty-five years earlier, the *Memphis Press-Scimitar* pointed out, the United Daughters of the Confederacy had openly complained about the lack of interest in the general and his birthday. In 1958, however, "it was about the best observation of the General's birthday since his death." Mary Forrest Bradley stood at the center of much of the merriment. "I'm the happiest I have ever been in my life," she claimed, "[i]t was a wonderful tribute to grandfather." The turnout and media attention in 1958 emerged from a couple of different directions. Bradley certainly played a role as she assumed a more prominent position within the Memphis Civil War memorial scene. It also coincided with the spread of the civil rights movement and the growing resurgence in the Civil War as the Civil War Centennial loomed. The combination of fighting for Black rights and the resurrection of Confederate iconography played out throughout the white South. "[I]t was possibly," the newspaper quoted Bradley, "the Supreme Court School decision of 1954 which revived interest in the Confederacy so strongly." Confederate flags, for example, flew at the 1905 statue unveiling but were not a large part of the Forrest monument tableau throughout the first half of the twentieth century. However, the Confederate flag came back strongly in the 1950s and would be a mainstay of the park for the next decade. In 1958, a descendent of Forrest sliced into a giant cake with a Confederate flag baked inside as part of the festivities.[58]

After 1958, birthday commemorations shrank considerably—sometimes only a small crowd and a wreath, sometimes not much of anything. In 1965, the city held no observance at the statue of any kind. Several months later, Mary Forrest Bradley, her grandfather's most prominent defender, died. The following year, perhaps in tribute to his granddaughter, the Memphis phone company chose a photograph of the Forrest statue for the cover of the phone book. The Forrest image fragmented into the spectral at the height of the civil rights movement and the Civil War Centennial. Without many public ceremonies in the 1960s, tracking the public connection to Forrest in Memphis is hard. The silences and gaps offer a counternarrative, especially given the shift in tone in the late 1960s and early 1970s. For a decade after the 1958 birthday celebration, Confederate flags crowned the park while crowds abated. Black Memphis plays a role here, too. Though overt park protests were rare, nonexistent, or written out of the public record, a growing Black electorate coupled with a robust Black legal fight helped craft a mounting Black Memphis political voice. Desegregation redefined Memphis busses, movie theaters, restaurants, and, much more slowly, public schools.

The assassination of Martin Luther King Jr. in April 1968 bisects the Forrest myth, cleaving it between a white-owned narrative of heroism and civic pride and a decentered story gradually reframed through Black activism. Written out of the public record, the Black response to Forrest and the Forrest statue only began to gain shape in the late 1960s and 1970s. King's murder accelerated much of this development. A few weeks after King's death, Nat B. Williams, an influential Black columnist and Memphis radio host, published an article in the *Tri-State Defender* that argued for accurately teaching Black history in area schools. Williams explicitly called out the use of Forrest in Memphis classrooms that glorified both the general and the slave trade. Shifts on this level would be slow, but a more vocal Black Memphis led to immediate changes in other ways. In 1969, Tennessee quietly designated Forrest's birthday a "day of special observance," effectively removing it from an official holiday to a fuzzier category. Less ambiguously, Black Americans succeeded in removing the Confederate flag that flew over Forrest Park.[59]

The removal of the Confederate flag from Forrest Park offered a clear signal that changes were afoot. Forrest's invisibility throughout the 1960s gave way to a growing roar of conflicting viewpoints. A Black counterpoint to the white normative view of Forrest emerged in the 1970s and helped shift the poles of the public discourse of the general. Tracking anti-Forrest discourse throughout the twentieth century remains challenging, especially as city newspapers omitted Black voices. In 1877, Lafcadio Hearn intimated that many Memphians—Black citizens included—spoke negatively of the general. Across the next century, however, few public protests either happened or were recorded, with most Black voices slanted only through the newspaper bias. This dynamic shifted dramatically in the 1970s—due to the energizing of the civil rights movement and political activation following King's assassination in Memphis. Memphis demographics played a role, too, as Memphis's general population began to decline throughout the 1970s. In conjunction with this decline, Black Memphians began to grow their percentage of the city's population. By the late 1970s and early 1980s, the Black population of Memphis had swelled. A more significant percentage of the city did not directly relate to electoral victories, not at first, but it did begin to shift the culture of the city. Black Memphis demographics confronted traditional Memphis power structures. Black Memphis cultural power challenged traditional Memphis cultural configurations. Black Memphis shifted the narrative of the city and of Forrest, redefining Forrest in the last decades of the twentieth century.

This growing counterbalance swelled with the proposed addition of a bust of Forrest to the Tennessee state capitol. The idea behind adding a bust of Forrest to the state capitol came from Douglas Henry, a state senator out of Nashville and a member of a regional chapter of the Sons of Confederate Veterans. He was also the nephew of Robert Selph Henry. Henry authored a state Senate Joint Resolution in 1973 to manufacture a bust to celebrate "Tennessee's greatest military hero in that conflict on the Confederate side." The 1970s bust story reflected, writ small, the Memphis statue seven decades earlier (private fundraising and so forth), but with a very different post-King dimension. Unlike the early 1900s, when white supremacy closed most avenues of public disapproval, Black opposition to the bust swirled directly as the sculpture appeared. Between increased general Black political activism and a fatigue of public silencing, resistance to the statue represented the first concerted anti-Forrest protest. Moreover, this unrest dovetailed with anger at the state government. In 1979, when Tennessee eventually placed the bust in the capitol, protests merged with a growing dissatisfaction with the governor. The *Nashville Tennessean* alluded to much of this unrest in an article covering the theft of a twenty-dollar portrait of Forrest from a city library. "For some time," the reporter noted, "black groups here have been objecting to the fact that a bronze bust of Forrest has been installed at the State Capitol."[60] A spokesperson for the NAACP noted that "anything that symbolizes the Confederacy is an obvious insult to blacks."

In addition to the NAACP, a local group calling itself Black Tennesseans for Action objected primarily to Forrest's connection to the slave trade, the Fort Pillow massacre, and the Ku Klux Klan.[61] In contrast, William C. Davis, the editor of *Civil War Times Illustrated,* claimed that "Forrest is not being memorialized for these things." "Forrest's racial attitudes," Davis argued, "would be abhorrent to all but a few Americans. We can only say that he was a product of his time and place and that, except in the most flagrant cases, it is unfair to judge people of the past by the standards of the present." Furthermore, Davis contended that claiming the bust of Forrest represented racism would be to argue that "a statue of [Ulysses S.] Grant endorses alcoholism or that a monument to [Benjamin] Franklin is a celebration of adultery."[62] As Nashville heated up, the West Tennessee chapter of the Congress of Racial Equality (CORE) distributed a petition to remove the Memphis statue. The statue, CORE argued, served as "a symbol of race hatred, bigotry, prejudice and racism that Memphis can ill afford to give recognition, maintain with tax money and sustain as a display of social acceptance."[63] The CORE protest and petition also undermine the argument, especially prevalent in the 2010s and early 2020s, that no one opposed the Forrest statue. Throughout the late 1970s and into the mid-1980s, more and more attacks on Forrest Park grew out of an increasing frustration within the Black community with the continued civic sponsorship of public memorials to Forrest.

The engagement of the Black community to object to the Nashville bust led to a growing protest movement throughout the 1980s. In 1985, the *Tri-State Defender* ran an article reprimanding white Memphians for their continued strangulation of "positive attempts at success." "Until the truth about the evil side of Memphis history is brought to light, confronted and corrected," the article argued, "all the image remodeling in the world will not help us to be the people [and] the city we strive to be." "Can we continue," the writer asked, "to ignore the truth and blindly hope that others outside of our area will never become aware that we honor murderers in Memphis?" The article asserted that the annual Forrest celebration restricted Memphis's growth, and Memphians of both races "must also be strong enough to strive for the truth and let truth become our goal and integrity our symbol."[64]

Throughout the early to mid-1980s, the Forrest statue in Memphis attracted increased attention, graffiti, and louder calls for removal. The mounting disagreements culminated in 1988 when the University of Tennessee Medical Center took over the maintenance of Forrest Park. The medical center abutted the park, and the school wanted to outfit the small area with fitness equipment and jogging trails. Memphis permitted the university to refurbish Forrest Park, which led to public protests. The NAACP feared that the park's renovation would increase the prominence of the Forrest statue. Maxine Smith, executive secretary of the Memphis chapter of the NAACP, asserted that "[t]he presence of this park is a daily slap in the face to blacks throughout the city, and we intend to see that it's removed." Smith and the NAACP demanded the removal of the statue, the reburial of Forrest and his wife in Elmwood Cemetery, and the park's renaming. "Let the historians and all those who are so fond of the general," Smith charged, "take him and do what they want with him."[65] For their part, the SCV responded that they would "in no way compromise or retrench on this issue."[66] Kevin Bradley (Forrest's great-great-grandson): "I'm outraged. If they remove the statue of Forrest, they will have to remove statues all over the U.S." "We will fight to the bitter end."[67]

Into the fray stormed writer and local Memphis celebrity Shelby Foote, who replied, "While I can understand why blacks might see the statue as a symbol of racism, I think they've overlooked the facts about Bedford Forrest." "He was certainly not," Foote contended, "the villain they perceive him to be." "You have to take the past as it is," Foote explained, "Bedford Forrest and Abraham Lincoln were, in my opinion, the two absolute geniuses to emerge during the Civil War. To try and remove a monument to either one of these men is just crazy." Foote also argued that "[t]he idea of moving his bones is outrageous, and shows that they don't know what he was all about. It's as if all you knew about Napoleon was that he was 5-feet-4." "The day that black people admire Forrest as much as I do," Foote concluded, "is the day when they will be free and equal, for they will have gotten prejudice out of their minds as we whites are trying to get it out of ours."[68] Shelby Foote's public connection to Forrest dates to the 1960s. In 1969, the year following King's murder, Foote spoke on the character of Forrest at a ceremony in front of the Forrest statue. Foote argued that, as a slave trader, Forrest "served as an example of much that was wrong about the South." "But," Foote insisted, "he also treated [his slaves] with compassion." Aware and unaware simultaneously, Foote noted the absence of Black Memphians at the celebration. Foote stated, "I am sorry there are no Negro citizens here today because Forrest is a man they could admire." "This is a truly great man," Foote concluded, "deserving of the love and respect of the whole country."[69]

Black Memphians responded to Foote's insensitive comments quickly and directly. In an article entitled, "Foote, You Put It in Your Mouth," a writer for the *Tri-State Defender* called Foote's appeal for Black Americans to admire Forrest "outrageous, insulting, bigoted and racist!" "Black people are already free and equal," the writer asserted, and "they did not get that way . . . by admiring Nathan Bedford Forrest." "Forrest is your hero," the writer alerted Foote, and "why you are so enamored with him, only you can answer for sure, but it is not hard to guess. You are a relative, if not by blood at least in spirit and outlook." Then, inverting Foote's own words, the writer concluded, "The day you become as sensitive to the feelings of Black people as you are to those of Whites who admire Nathan Bedford Forrest you will be free, for you will have gotten the racist prejudice out of your mind that you want to force your hero on the descendants of his victims."[70]

The following week, the *Tri-State Defender* printed two articles on the controversy that shared the headline, "City must not dignify Forrest. . . . he's no more than a murderer." One article presented unsubstantiated stories of Fort Pillow and even insinuated that Forrest beat his wife and Black "mistress." The writer concluded with a plea for Memphis to "make no attempt to memorialize and dignify Forrest. His military genius does not excuse his inhumanity." "If he cannot be replaced by a more appropriate symbol that would bring the city together," the writer amended, "at least all of us should be aware that his memory is extremely painful for many Memphians." The related article continued the attack on Forrest's character and compared him to Adolf Hitler, Charles Manson, and Jack the Ripper. "Our assertion," the writer declared, "is that General Forrest should never have been honored in that park nor any other public park; he was no more than a whore-mongering mass murderer."[71] In an editorial for the conservative and pro-southern magazine *Southern Partisan,* Matthew Sandel argued that the fight over Forrest Park was "a petulant nastiness" and "a sure sign that the civil rights movement is over." The NAACP—defined by Sandel as the "National Association for the Advancement of Comfortable People"—had "no more real worlds to conquer," he explained, "only the inner world of a growing black paranoia." The editorial included a personal attack on Benjamin Hooks, national director of the NAACP, and ended with a wish for the resurrection of the mighty Forrest. "If [Hooks and his associates] push [Forrest] too far, he may just come roaring out of the grave one day, eyes flashing, teeth-clenched—and then you will see some well-fed, middle aged black men run like they haven't run in years, on their way to catch the train to Yonkers, to confront the challenge they have so cravenly avoided for so long." The description of Forrest resembled Lytle's and Foote's.[72]

It is impossible to overstate the power Shelby Foote has had on the modern interpretation and meaning of Nathan Bedford Forrest. In Memphis, Foote served as the unofficial spokesperson for Forrest and the Forrest family throughout the 1970s and 1980s—and he was undoubtedly the most prominent name connected to the general as controversy heated up over the memory of Forrest. Foote sparred with Black Memphians throughout the 1980s, although he did count on several prominent Black activists as friends. He genuinely seemed driven to connect to Black audiences, if only to get people to sign on to his version of the general. Although easily typecast through a cursory reading of his comments, Foote defied easy categorization. Foote took the myths and half-fictions of a century of Forrest storytellers and melded them into a usable archetype that muddled historicism with enough wiggle room to engage a broad audience. Throughout the 1970s and especially the 1980s, Foote helped craft a flexible, malleable Forrest—not too mythic, not too untainted—an abstract personality that worked like a prism for various groups.

Foote met race head-on. Unlike earlier writers, Foote spoke directly about Forrest's involvement in the trade of enslaved individuals but noted that he attempted to keep families together. Some form of this statement had circulated since the nineteenth century, but Foote rarely equivocated regarding Forrest's role in the slave trade on a general level. The Klan provides another example where Foote threaded the needle just enough to distance himself from the overt racism of earlier writers by not exactly exonerating Forrest or Forrest's actions but instead focusing on the differences between the Ku Klux Klan of Reconstruction and the Klan that coursed through the twentieth-century South. Foote argued that Forrest led the Ku Klux Klan, but "it was not a hate group when Forrest knew it." "He was not," Foote assured, "a Klu Kluxer in the way we know them today."[73] Partly borne out of distancing Forrest from the contemporary version of the Klan and partly out of personal experience, Foote spoke out against the Klan of the twentieth century. In a lengthy piece in the *Memphis Commercial Appeal* in 1966, Foote spoke out on white supremacy, the extremism of the Klan, and racial discrimination. "I got the sort of feeling," Foote noted, "that I ought to carry a pistol." That extremism "helped me a lot to understand the extremists in the period I am writing about."[74]

Foote's parsing of Forrest's life and career built a symbol that uneasily straddled the past and the present. Forrest could be seen as an inspirational hero rooted in the Civil War but with lessons for the modern day, from one perspective. Then, often simultaneously, a more complicated man emerged, selectively woven into a narrative that explicitly pushes against any sense of relevance. Foote's insight allowed more people to buy into the Forrest myth by welcoming them with daring stories that thorned into their memory while providing modern audiences with multiple outs regarding slavery and the Klan. Foote told Memphis newspapers throughout his career that Forrest was just a man of his time, except for the many ways he should stand as an exemplar of the white South across any timeline.

Foote never wrote a biography of the general, which allowed him to avoid confronting the totality of Forrest's life. For Foote, Forrest served as a convenient symbol to challenge northern (and many southern) perspectives on the Civil War. At the same time, Foote could disregard slavery, the slave trade, and the Ku Klux Klan. Burnished to a selective luster, Forrest indicated paths not taken to Foote as a representative of the forgotten importance of the Southwest. Forrest was a military hero, first and foremost, to Foote, but he consistently spoke to the necessity of understanding the general in more significant terms. Knowledgeable and charismatic, Foote spoke most often on one of the more fictionalized episodes in Forrest's life: his actions at Fallen Timbers. In interview after interview, Foote returned to the story and wrote at length about it in his novel, *Shiloh.* Fallen Timbers relates to a skirmish after the larger battle of Shiloh, where Forrest ran into some of William T. Sherman's infantry. The basic story of Fallen Timbers remains a central text of the Forrest myth, and its barest outlines appear in Jordan and Pryor. Most early sources, certainly through Wyeth, included Forrest outrunning his men and coming into hand-to-hand combat with Union soldiers. Mathes's book, however, added a new detail. "In this desperate strait," Mathes writes, Forrest "reached down, caught up a rather small Federal soldier, swung him around and held him to the rear of his saddle as a shield until he was well out of danger."[75] This account was so unrealistic that even Lytle omitted it. Still, it showed up in Henry's biography, which is most likely where Foote first heard it. Shotgun blasts, miraculous feats of strength, human shields—Fallen Timbers had it all, even if the exploits wandered into the improbable. But Foote loved the tale.[76]

Foote's historical philosophy skirted academic training and evolved from a jumble of literary and academic sources. The names he reliably mentioned in interviews spanned time and genre. "I am," Foote once proclaimed, "what is called a narrative historian."[77] But his sense of narrative composition came from deep readings of Marcel Proust and Homer's *Iliad.* Foote's trilogy on the Civil War came from these foundational texts. He once mentioned that he had constructed the trilogy as a novelist as "climaxes were distributed."[78] Lytle's Forrest had an enormous impact on Foote, and Foote often spoke about the same social and class structure issues over which Lytle obsessed. Foote more discretely conveyed Lytle's yeoman in his writing, but similar values streamed underneath his prose. Foote's view of history overlapped with Lytle's—"I'm a hangover from the agrarian movement," Foote once said—but he developed a more nuanced view of history than the earlier writer.[79] He also spoke highly of Lytle's friend and fellow Agrarian, Robert Penn Warren, but Foote shied away from Warren's more mystic sense of history colliding with memory. William Faulkner played with history, too, but Foote reacted in dismay to his disinterest in detail. Although not a trained historian, Foote held strong views on what constituted history. To Foote, history was fact—eye color, walking stride, the timbre of voice. Only through this knowledge could any real historical sense be made. After he started publishing the trilogy, interviewers habitually asked him to elaborate on what made good history writing. Unsurprisingly, Foote struck with the traditional. In one interview, Foote claimed Francis Parkman, born two years after Forrest, as a historian to emulate. To Foote, history represented a specific form of narrative. In a dismissal of the Civil War as soap opera, Foote noted that "I have no objection to a whorehouse if they hang a red light on it. But if it poses as a decent house in a decent neighborhood, it's a disruption." "No good," he argued, "can come from historical distortion."[80] The Civil War incorporated large tectonic plates, but to Foote, it all came down to the particulars.

Three portraits hung over his desk at different times: Robert Johnson, Elvis Presley, and Nathan Bedford Forrest. These men function as a collage of Foote's unconventional perspective on the meaning of the modern South. Foote allowed the South to contain multitudes, but within a specific framework, with Blackness set apart into a separate category. In 1966, Foote argued that "Negroes are the true creators of the only true American music. They have taught us a lot." He also allowed that "[t]hey gave us most of our humor." Foote argued that the South encompassed Black music and Black laughter. Still, those elements had to coexist (however equally or unequally, proportionally or disproportionally) with everything Foote saw in Forrest. Foote compartmentalized. Robert Johnson: genius. Elvis Presley, at least early on: genius.[81] Bedford Forrest: genius. Each could easily coexist as arbiters of southernness for Foote. His complexity, often denied by his harsher critics, allowed for a complicated Forrest, but ultimately, Forrest stood as a white hero and a traditionalist guide to comprehending a rapidly changing region and world. The gap between the blues, the origins of the blues, the *need* for the blues, the totality of Robert Johnson's short life within the blues, Elvis as a blues shouter, and the spectral significance of Forrest, as slave trader, as Fort Pillow commander, as leader of the Klan yawned and stretched almost to the infinite. Yet the modern South could contain all these and much more.

Foote never seemed conflicted in his views on the South. His map was undoubtedly more inclusive than, say, Andrew Lytle's. But the fact/fiction dynamic within his take on Forrest compelled a much more modern take on the general and helped establish the template for the culture wars of the 1990s and 2000s. Foote expanded the shadow Forrest cast by allowing a celebration of Forrest that rejected a denial of slavery. Slavery and the Klan (and, to a lesser extent, Fort Pillow) could be part of the conversation even as Foote cast aside the more significant implications of what slavery or Blackness meant. Foote saw slavery as bad, mainly, but not to the degree that necessitated any real emphasis. The Klan, too, was bad, mainly, but only within its current configuration. This slippery sense of race and history formed a Forrest that incorporated enough factual material to be believable by an audience less willing to buy into the overt racist fantasies of earlier writers. Foote's Forrest, in other words, sustained central fictions that allowed the acceptance of a long list of terrible actions. In Foote's hands, Forrest straddled fact and fiction in ways that made drawing a line between the real and the imagined impossible.

Throughout his life, Foote often spoke about his continued support of the Confederacy. He saw the Civil War mainly as a primeval clash of abstruse regional values instead of a modern conflict over the nature of labor, race, and power. Slavery and race only existed in the abstract to Foote. Although he spoke highly of specific Black individuals and supported the civil rights movement in the most general ways, he could never make sense of the connection between Black enslavement in the past and Black life in his white southern present. To Foote, slavery was simply economics. "Slavery was perfect for cotton farming," Foote said in 1970. "It was a marvelous thing to have a couple of hundred slaves running the plantation," Foote argued, "and you could make a lot of money doing it, a lot of money was made doing it."[82] But throughout the 1970s and 1980s, Foote opined on various aspects of Black life. "I think this black separatist movement is a bunch of junk," he told an interviewer, "I don't think it amounts to anything. Not anything." "The only thing it does is to restore some pride to the Negro," Foote maintained, "'Black is beautiful' is the good part of the movement."[83] He went further. "If I were a negro," Foote argued, "I might be a violent Negro."[84] Foote claimed to know more about the Black South than James Baldwin: "I told some interviewer I knew a hell of a lot more about negroes than Baldwin even began to know."[85] "I think," Foote insisted in 1971, "that I am closer to Nat Turner than James Baldwin is."[86] In the 1980s, he spoke even more negatively about racial progress and Black American life. In 1987, Foote argued that "you can't hold people down for two hundred years, and then all of a sudden let them up and not expect them to celebrate being let up." But, he added, "they celebrated it in some pretty strange ways. Memphis is the rape capital of the United States today."[87] Foote's Forrest materializes out of this context.

It begins with Foote's voice: all blended pipe tobacco and Johnnie Walker Black, honey dripping onto broken granite. Not necessarily the content of the words but the voice itself—its timbre, its whispered power—could sell you anything. And through the filmmaking of Ken Burns, it does. Burns, a documentary filmmaker, began work on a large-scale project on the Civil War. If 1905 Memphis represents the first important scene within the modern Forrest story—where the dead general first found rebirth—then the early 1990s signified the realization of a near-century of animating factors. In 1990, PBS aired Ken Burns's nine-part, eleven-and-a-half-hour documentary on the Civil War. Shelby Foote, the writer that Burns situated throughout the film, was central to the appeal of the documentary. Foote had written extensively on Forrest throughout the post–World War II era, and the writer positioned the general into many of his filmed interviews. "He understood, as few historians do," Burns said later of the novelist, "that the word 'history' contains the word 'story.'"[88] The slurry of fact and fiction—which Foote played a crucial role in muddying—crafted a nebulous base for understanding the historical Forrest. By the early 1990s, his celebrity was at an all-time high. The Burns documentary had shifted the magnetic poles within the Forrest myth. The general materialized as one of the Civil War's most known and notorious generals. His clashes, aphorisms, and mythology drifted through magazine articles and television news broadcasts. Stories of Forrest's exploits operated as a new shorthand for Civil War dabblers, who could add Forrest to their Robert E. Lee and Stonewall Jackson narratives.

After a conversation with Robert Penn Warren, Burns turned to Foote as an interview subject. Burns conducted a series of interviews with Foote in the mid-to-late 1980s—around the time the author made his rape comments. These interviews formed the narrative backbone of Burns's documentary. Burns places Foote at the center of his project, and though the filmmaker incorporated professional historians, including Barbara J. Fields, Foote takes up the oxygen. Forrest runs through the Burns documentary, providing color and elation, primarily through Shelby Foote. Fallen Timbers shows up ("one gray uniform in a sea of blue"), as does Brice's Crossroads ("Forrest outdid even himself"). The seventh episode, though, places him in the center. From Forrest's recruitment exhortation: "Come on boys, if you want a heap of fun and to kill some Yankees," to Foote telling story after story, Burns presents 1864 as the year that "would cement his reputation as the most terrifying cavalry commander of the war." A greatest hits of Forrest (and of Foote), this section of Burns's documentary provided Forrest with his largest national audience. A viewer might not know much about Forrest as slave trader or leader of the Ku Klux Klan, but they would hear Foote equate the general to a great artist. "Forrest was a natural genius," Foote intoned, "[s]omeone said that he was born to be a soldier the way John Keats was born to be a poet." Burns brings in Fort Pillow and does not shy from the brutality of the event, though Forrest is decentered, and much of the context falls on the collapse of prisoner exchanges. However, much more emphasis falls on Foote's folksy anecdotes of saber swinging and his calling Forrest's granddaughter to tell her that he thought of Forrest as one of the war's two "authentic geniuses," the other being Abraham Lincoln. "Well, you know," she replied, "in our family, we never thought much of Mr. Lincoln." Later, Foote noted that "he had thirty horses shot from under him in the course of the war, and he killed thirty-one men in hand-to-hand combat, and he said, 'I was a horse ahead at the end.'" By the soft chuckle, the knowing wink, Foote saw Forrest as someone to be venerated despite the fractures and complications embedded in his life and career.

The connection between Foote and Mary Forrest Bradley offers a fascinating glimpse at Foote's working view of historical perspective. "Bedford Forrest's granddaughter lived here in Memphis," Foote recalls to Burns. "She recently died, and I got to know her. And she even let me swing the general's saber around my head once, which was a great treat." Foote swinging Forrest's sword gives Foote the closest proximity to Forrest of modern writers. And yet Foote offers a curious telescoping of time. Mary Forrest Bradley died in 1965 at ninety-six; she was eight when Forrest died. So Foote would have probably been in his late forties when he knew Bradley—and he would have been in his early seventies when interviewed by Burns. Still, the past and present collapsed into a storytelling "recently died." But, for the PBS viewer, none of that mattered. Like "Ashokan Farewell," the unofficial theme song of the documentary, which dated back only to the early 1980s yet conjured a past at once foreign and faintly recognizable, Foote's anecdote diminished time, his own delight filling in for the audience as he could claim access to an essential talisman of the Forrest myth.

In the aftermath of Burns's documentary, and after a century of myths and folktales folded into histories, near-histories, near-fictions, and fictions, two new biographies arrived in the early 1990s. In 1992, military historian Brian Steel Wills published *A Battle from the Start,* which cleaned up Forrest's martial career through the lens of a professional historian. Several months later, Jack Hurst, a journalist out of Tennessee, published *Nathan Bedford Forrest: A Biography.* Much like Wills, Hurst removed the more untrustworthy elements of the Forrest narrative. The strength of Wills remains the military material, even if Fallen Timbers continues the trope of a human shield, even as he sees

Forrest as a "tainted hero." In contrast, Hurst was among the first writers to question the Fallen Timbers story openly. However, he concludes that a human shield "is the only plausible explanation" for Forrest's survival. Wills often gives Forrest the benefit of the doubt, especially in the central controversies.[89] For example, with Fort Pillow, Wills argues that there "were many causes for the 'massacre,'" allowing him to negotiate the different reasons. Many reasons played into the bloodshed, including lousy decision-making on the Union side and racial animosity on the Confederate side. At the same time, "massacre" gets placed in quotes, allowing for a certain distance of what happened during and after the battle. If Wills wrote the first military study of Forrest adhering to professional historical standards, Hurst's triumph was expanding Forrest's prewar and postwar life. By sourcing more of Forrest's origins, Hurst enlarged the early map of the general. He still lets him off in various ways—especially with slavery—but Hurst, more than any earlier writer, crafted a compelling case for the complexity of the forces that made Forrest. Expanding the postwar side, Hurst provided more detail and context of the final years of Forrest's life.

These biographies had the backing of large publishers (Wills, published by HarperCollins, and Hurst by Knopf). They had a bookshelf presence far exceeding earlier biographies, many of which had been out of print for years. Wills and Hurst received high-profile reviews in both the popular and academic press, which were generally positive. Reviewers overwhelmingly commended both books for adhering to modern scholarly standards to craft a Forrest drawn in less cartoonish hues. In contrast, the criticisms tended toward a lack of interest by either writer to come down too hard on the most troubling aspects of the Forrest story. Wills, one reviewer wrote, failed "adequately to explain the motivations" of Forrest.[90] Hurst, a reviewer argued, maintained a "hands-off attitude" which "results in an absence of strong conclusions about Forrest's conduct when the evidence is conflicting."[91] These books, however, met an audience primed by Foote and Burns for Forrest lore. Writing for the *New York Times,* Caleb Carr wrote a positive review of Wills's book, though it tended to dismiss Forrest's overall significance. Carr argued that the progressive impact of the civil rights movement ultimately made "it difficult indeed to accept the traditional view of men like . . . Forrest in our own time."[92] The newspaper published an angry letter to the editor a few weeks later, which argued that Carr's review "is an egregious example of politically correct claptrap."[93] Together, these biographies might not have moved the needle on viewers enamored of Foote's mash note to Forrest, and both authors maintained a pro-Forrest approach to various degrees—these are not reimaginings of his larger significance and meaning—but they do bring Forrest closer to the world of fact and out of the bog of fiction.

Burns made Foote a household name as well as a millionaire. Foote's trilogy sold hundreds of thousands of copies after the series aired. For the rest of his life, Foote would hold forth on the meaning of Forrest. Many of the same stories would be told and retold, but a growing sense of defensiveness crept into Foote's interviews. In 1997, Foote spoke again on the Klan, reiterating that Forrest ended the organization once it got "ugly" and "rough."[94] He took pains, however, to distance Forrest from the Klan of the twentieth century. "The Klan you're talking about," Foote maintained, "rose again in this century and was particularly powerful during the 1920s." "Forrest would have had no sympathy with that later Klan," Foote argued, and the "last thing in the world was he anti-Catholic or anti-Semitic, which is what that Klan was mainly in the twenties."[95] In the late 1990s and 2000s, Foote struck a more defeated tone as he feared Black people were not living up to his ideals of racial harmony and integration. At one point, Foote declared that the "behavior of blacks are fulfilling every dire prophesy the Ku Klux Klan made."[96] Discussions of the Confederacy went further as he got older, too. "I would fight for the Confederacy today if the circumstances were similar," Foote told the *Paris Review.* "There's a great deal of misunderstanding," Foote argued, "about the Confederacy, the Confederate flag, slavery, the whole thing." "The Confederates," Foote said directly, "fought for some substantially good things."[97] In 2001, Foote argued that "if"—that "if" doing a lot of work here—"I was against slavery, I'd still be with the South. I'm a man, my society needs me, here I am."[98] The following year, Foote contended, "I'm for the Confederate flag always and forever."[99]

A century of biographical writing fleshed out specific details, and a century of memorial building provided material space, yet a PBS documentary energized the Forrest legacy beyond even these markers. By the 1990s, Forrest, especially through Foote, had more recognition on a broader scale than at any other time since the Civil War. Nevertheless, the fluctuation of fact and fiction continued to animate discussions of the general. As historians provided a more substantially sourced base for Forrest's life, his exploits still careered through a mapless landscape rutted by exaggeration and fabrication. In June 2005, one hundred years after Memphis unveiled its statue of Forrest,

Shelby Foote died in Memphis. "Shelby had a way of talking about the war that blew everyone else out of the water," Ken Burns said. "I'm really going to miss him," Burns noted, "miss the sound of his voice."[100] Foote was crucial to Forrest's prominence in the 1990s and beyond. Without Foote, Forrest would have wandered through the modern era without a meaningful public memory outside Memphis. Forrest's newfound recognition in the 1990s led to new audiences, new statues, and a new iteration of white masculinity defined more explicitly through the lens of race and violence than it had in generations. The years after Foote's death ultimately proved chaotic as historical ambiguities gave way to culture-war absolutes. Forrest represented a particular strand of white southern attributes, real and imagined. In death as in life, the general's shadow skulked around the edges of Shelby Foote's legacy as the writer was interred in Elmwood Cemetery, a slight few footsteps away from the century-long emptied burial plot of Nathan Bedford Forrest.

4

THE MOST MAN IN THE WORLD

> Forrest is one of the most attractive men who ever walked through the pages of history.
>
> —SHELBY FOOTE, 1999

> Well, I hate Nathan Bedford Forrest
> He's the featured artist in the devil's chorus
> And damn, they're looking ugly to me
> Damn, they're looking ugly to me.
>
> —KURT WAGNER, 2006

It begins with the eyes. Gray, gray-blue, blue. Intense, even in repose. On the battlefield: blazing and violent. Nathan Bedford Forrest's eyes demand attention with equal parts terror and allure. His image sears.

A central piece of the Forrest myth relates to the most obvious yet weirdly hidden aspect of his image: his body. In life, in death, and in remembrance, Forrest's body held power. Forrest's promise and threat lie coiled within his build, size, wounds, physicality, strength, and bones. His admirers delighted in detailing his bodily attributes—especially his height—and his memorial landscape reflected this interest. The people who placed the Memphis statue in 1905 remarked constantly on the sculptor's use of real-life measurements, even of his horse. Later, in the 1990s, a statue in Nashville would take this preoccupation to cartoonish heights as Forrest's likeness grew to three stories tall. This emphasis on his anatomy inversely mirrored the focus on the bodies of the Black men, women, and children forced into his Memphis slave pens. In many ways, the body—his body, the control of other bodies, the battlefield destruction of bodies, the use of physical force, and the brutalization of the Black body—defines Forrest and his image. The convergence, therefore, of his treatment of Black bodies, based primarily on their physical attributes, and his admirers' cataloging of his physical qualities represents the fundamental nature of Forrest's power across time. Inherent within this corporeal preoccupation lies an underexplored piece of Forrest's appeal: the sexualized nature of many of these interconnections. The gendered components of the Forrest image help explain the complex contours of his public memory. In addition, the sexual energy permeating these factors, as seen in advertisements, cartoons, novels, and memorial rhetoric, underscores his magnetism. Using gender and sexuality as a lens, in other words, illuminates why Forrest continues to appeal beyond the battlefield.

Few photographs of Forrest survive—several military portraits, a handful of cartes de visite (small, inexpensively reproduced calling cards), perhaps one from before the war, and one or two late in life. A study of four images, in particular, provides a look at the elemental power embedded in the Forrest myth. Perhaps the earliest photograph of Forrest places him in a dress suit with a vest and necktie. He looked more gambler than businessman, though he was a bit of both, and his eyes gaze just past the viewer. With heavy, sleepy eyelids, bristly goatee, and a pomaded coif of dark hair (he generally wore his hair on the cusp of long on the sides with a greased wave at the top), Forrest communicates a professional, detached attitude. Often cited as a prewar photo—a notation in the Memphis library probably erroneously dates it to 1858—this session most likely occurred right before the beginning of the war when Forrest was about forty years old. Sitting (un)comfortably in this Nashville studio before the toll of war warped his body, Forrest looks out to the viewer without a real command of his power. Like many of the posed photographs of military men in the nineteenth century, this photograph remains just out of reach emotionally. The passivity startles us not only because of what we, the viewers, know was to come but also because of what has happened. Whether Forrest sat for this photograph in 1858 or 1861, as an alderman or as a newly enlisted private in the army, he already had made a fortune dealing in enslaved Black men, women, and children. This juxtaposition frames all photographs of Forrest, though the military iconography of the best-known images obliterates this past.

A couple of years later, probably in 1862, Forrest sat for a session that produced one of several cartes de visite he would make during this war. This im-

Portrait of Forrest, ca. 1862.
Prints and Photographs Division, Library of Congress.

Forrest in 1864.
Carte de visite by Bingham & Brother's Gallery, Memphis.

age features Forrest as a colonel—his face hollowed out and sunken. His eyelids, so heavy in the earlier photograph, are smudged dark shadows, his gaunt cheeks accentuating his goatee, which creates a dark whorl at the center of the image. The war had already taken its toll. Probably taken after Shiloh and Fallen Timbers, most definitely after his early success at Fort Donelson, this carte de visite shows a Forrest in transition. Facing the camera square on with a proverbial thousand-yard stare without much of an established pose, Forrest's posture drifts slightly to his left as his eyes meet the viewer directly. One version of this photo has been touched up—the brow line lightened, the uniform manipulated to show a later promotion. The original image, though, stuns with its near vulnerability. The format of the carte de visite assists by providing a wealth of space as Forrest floats disembodied at mid-chest in aging, tattered beige. This image stands alone within the Forrest iconographic record as less modeled—the eyes giving away a bit too much war-weariness. The fact that someone retouched the photo, with a specific emphasis on the

Forrest in 1865.
Prints and Photographs Division, Library of Congress.

eyes, shows that others at the time found issue with the original presentation. With these photos, the viewer has no power over Forrest—no looking away, no diversion as the gaze connects too openly. He has the upper hand. The editor crafts a more utilitarian Forrest by removing the shadows and providing just a hint of fuller cheek. Yet, these edits offer more power to the original photo. Stark and natural, this miniature calling-card portrait pulses with a searching contemplation far removed from other photos. There was no self-doubt, necessarily, but a moment of presence within what seemed at the time a never-ending conflict.

Two years later, Forrest sat for a third—and by far his best-known and reproduced—photograph. Sitting at an angle to his left, the portrait captures him at the height of his military powers. The cheekbones here are less scalloped, though the angle helps; the hair brushed back with the back and sides long; the goatee features a wisp of gray (Forrest would be white-headed within a few years of the war); Forrest stares out into photographic space with glowering assurance. An abrasion shadows his forehead, serving as a reminder of the battles surrounding this one moment of calm. Taken most likely in 1864, this photo would be within months, if not weeks or days, from Fort Pillow, perhaps, or Brice's Crossroads. The staggering weariness from the carte de visite transmutes into knowing confidence. We know he is a year away from defeat, but his eyes allow none of this possibility of loss. Reproduced on book covers and across the internet, this image defines the general. When people conjure up an image of Forrest, in other words, this is the face, and these are the eyes. Piercing, direct, and intense, Forrest's gaze dares the viewer to doubt his determination. An inertia filters through these photos, however, and a subjectivity. The photo captures the one-dimensional warrior devoid of ideology, stripped of context—one more military portrait to hang on the wall. It is this face that Tom Hanks attempts to approximate in *Forrest Gump* as the film explains in a ruthlessly quick flashback the namesake of the titular character. And it is this exact photograph that shows up in a more recent Tom Hanks movie, *Elvis,* as a signifier of Senator James Eastland's racism. This photograph's omnipresence allows it to serve multiple purposes at just a glance.

In 1865, Forrest sat for a final wartime photograph. Posed to his right, in opposition to the 1864 photo, Forrest has a bit more fire in his expression—anger, maybe, or a rageful frustration. His hair has pronounced lightness in this image—grayer, thicker, and wavier. His goatee spreads across his collar. His face seems slightly fuller here, too. Still, the eyes draw the viewer into the photo as they eradicate any plane dividing the audience and subject. After four years of war, with almost consistently hard fighting, Forrest appears less exhausted, especially in contrast to earlier photos. If anything, the photo transmits an even stronger aura of resilience to whatever end. Later photographs, only ten years in the future, show a prematurely aged, white-haired Forrest with a close-cropped goatee. But here, in the twilight of the Civil War, those photos could have been taken many decades later. The difference is stark. More than any other photograph, this 1865 image broadcasts his authority. In other photos, some feature of Forrest's face either drifts from focus or overtakes the composition. Here, however, a balance is struck with the central whirl of graying hair set off by the dark expanse of his goatee. Whatever vanity Forrest held onto—and he clearly maintained a specific look throughout his adulthood—this image brings everything into a particular focus. The creased brow brings the attention back to the eyes. No longer a newcomer to the photography studio, Forrest knew where to look and how to use his body to broadcast his status and authority.

Forrest's Civil War contemporaries consistently noted the general's attractiveness. Forrest, one wrote, "was a man of fine appearance, having piercing eyes, carefully trimmed mustache and chin-whiskers, dark as night, with finely cut features and iron-gray hair. His form was lithe, plainly indicating great physical power and activity."[1] Forrest's "muscular, well-proportioned figure, over six feet in height," a fellow soldier noted, "was indicative of extraordinary physical strength."[2] Another one took this further and underscored what he saw as feminine attributes. Forrest, they wrote, "was more than six feet high, well proportioned, with hands tapering like those of a woman, small feet and very high instep, exceedingly graceful in his movements, a swarthy complexion, and a look of the eye that indicated absolute fear of nothing."[3] This focus on his hands, feet, and physical motion, combined with his swarthiness and gaze, provides an intimate glimpse at the magnetism in the Forrest image. Battle scenes brought out more emphasis on Forrest's physicality. One witness noted that Forrest's "complexion, which was naturally sallow, changed completely in color" in battle. "The capillaries became so engorged with blood that the skin of the face and neck took on almost a scarlet hue," he continued. "The blood vessels of the eye took on the same congestion, giving him an expression of savageness that could not be misunderstood."[4] Another recalled Forrest on the battlefield, "[h]is face the color of heated bronze, and his eyes flaming, blazing."[5]

Biographers routinely introduced Forrest via adjective-rich prose. "In person," his first biographers wrote, "he is six feet one inch and a half in height, with broad shoulders, a full chest, and symmetrical, muscular limbs." "Erect in his carriage," they continue, "his average weight is one hundred and eighty-five pounds."[6] At the turn of the century, James Harvey Mathes noted, "Having led an active and strictly temperate life, he was in full enjoyment of perfect health and physical vigor." Mathes described Forrest as "straight as an Indian, of perfect symmetrical frame, confident of his strength and resources."[7] In the 1940s, Robert Selph Henry noted, "There was six feet two of him, lithe and powerful build, with steady eyes of deep gray-blue set wide in a lean, high-cheeked, swarthy face crowned with thick, wavy, iron-gray hair and set off with a short black chin beard."[8] A half-century later, Jack Hurst argued that

Forrest was "[a]lmost gigantic by the standards of his time, he was six feet one and one-half inches tall and weighed 180 pounds, and in disputes with fellow officers the threat of physical violence was always at least implicit."[9] This fascination wandered into the Memphis press, and the *Commercial Appeal* reiterated these comments throughout the 1940s and 1950s. In a discussion of his birthday celebration in 1940, for example, the newspaper noted that Forrest was "[p]hysically a massive man."[10] Later, in 1954, the paper reassured readers that Forrest stood "tall, robust, but not fat."[11] The numbers shifted. He stood over six feet, maybe six feet, one inch, just shy of six two, and weighed 180 pounds, maybe 185 (but not fat). Still, the fixation on his physical stature and look remained a constant biographical refrain.

A focus on Forrest's physical attributes makes sense given the interest in crafting a larger-than-life hero. His height and strength played directly into his battlefield actions. Also, in defeat, pro-Confederate accounts wanted to counter any hint of emasculation with a commitment to overtly white masculine virtues. Still, threads of racial and gendered ambiguities wormed through these descriptions and encomiums. Witnesses regularly undercut Forrest's white masculinity with commentary on his swarthiness, darkness in battle, and looking like an "Indian." So, the descriptions of his hands and feet are also uniquely feminine. This discourse fueled by competing depictions of manliness and femininity creates a curious vortex of colliding gendered images. His first biographers argued explicitly that his "dark hair, mustache, and beard worn upon the chin, a set of regular white teeth, and clearly cut, sun-embrowned features make him a much handsomer man than any of his pictures."[12] A contemporary of Forrest noted with excitement that "Forrest was a handsome man with a face, figure, movement, and bearing that no one, once seeing, was apt to forget." "You felt," he continued, "that he was a combination of enormous activity, endurance, and strength. That's what he was! Grace too!"[13] Authors of a study on Forrest published in the 2000s remarked on Forrest's bending towards foppishness. Forrest, they argued, "was noted for his meticulous appearance and attire, in spite of his reputation as anything but a gentleman."[14] Later, the general's beard captured the attention of Civil War bloggers in the early 2010s as a post on the attractiveness of beards segued into a discussion of Forrest's facial hair. "Ah, Forrest's stylish, Mississippi gambler's chin beard," one user named "Diane" exclaimed. "Neatly trimmed," they continued, "tidy, tasteful, and covers a too pointy chin and a too sensitive (at least in Forrest's opinion) mouth."[15]

Connected to the recurrent interest in his height and strength, writer after writer referenced the general's eyes: their inconstant color, ruminating intensity, and hinted violence. An eyewitness brought attention to this facet of Forrest back in the 1860s. "But it struck me," he recalled, "that his most wonderful feature was his piercing blue eyes which flashed and changed so rapidly with every emotion that it was difficult to distinguish its true color." "He was," he continued, "a man to catch the look and hold the attention of the most casual observer."[16] Biographers picked up on these comments. In 1868, Jordan and Pryor referenced his "[d]ark gray eyes, singularly bright and searching."[17] Later, in the 1890s, John Wyeth noted, "his eyes twinkled as he spoke, giving an attractive expression to his face."[18] "Forrest's bright gray eyes blazed," Mathes wrote in the early 1900s, continuing the trend.[19] Forrest captivated, compelled, and threatened in equal measure, or as one contemporary noted simply: "I devoted my whole attention to him."[20] One hundred and fifty years later, in a post on Civil War hairstyles, one blogger admits: "Goodness, Mr. Forrest, if I'm not careful I'll get a crush on a dead man." "But honey," she concludes, "when it's all said and done, I don't go for a racist."[21]

Forrest clearly stirred something up. His stature, his movements, his hair, his eyes, his entire *body* elicited an electrical response. Some part of this excitement, however unconsciously, could stem from Forrest's look of modernity. Forrest's entire affected mien, with his deliberately fashioned beard and coiffed hair, stands out from many of his contemporaries with its smearing of the practical and the considered. A glance at the few extant photographs of his brothers underscores Forrest's distinctiveness. His younger brother, William Hezekiah Forrest, could be from another earlier century or some far-off timeline—even his name evokes an ancient existence. The only man Bedford apparently feared, William ("Bill" does not quite cut it here), helps frame his older brother's singularity. In his photographs, Bedford Forrest projects an impulse that cuts through past the nineteenth century. Looking at William is like looking at the yawning chasm of history. The younger man (*ten years* Bedford's junior) could not conceivably exist outside of the deep, disremembered past. Yet, with his gaze and bearing, Bedford translates to the present or at least the present adjacent. This invented time-adaptability allows Forrest to exist outside of his historical moment. For his advocates, Forrest's photographic countenance enables him to transcend history. Not quite modern but far from an inert relic, Forrest's face blurred the past with the present in ways that gave him influence beyond Lost Cause rhetoric.

In its most provocative state, this bodily Forrest sits at the center of the confrontational, sometimes unhinged, novel *Devil's Dream* by Madison Smartt Bell. Based on history as much as rumor and innuendo, Bell's novel uses fiction to explore the less heralded aspects of Forrest's life. Forrest, in Bell's hands, is aggressive and sexual. The novel strikes more at the historic Forrest than many of the biographies committed more to battleground scenes of victory and loss. Forrest's relationships with women (free and enslaved, consensual and coerced, Black and white) define how his barbed image maintained such energy. If overt symbols of masculinity, heroism, and militarism represented the surface of Forrest, then these more obscured relationships with women help explain the dynamism of his public memory. These vectors of sex, sexuality, and sexual assault shape the waves of attraction and revulsion that crash against the Forrest image. Bell's placement of Henri, a Haitian Creole related it seems to Toussaint Louverture, in the center provides a racial foil to Forrest. Henri courses through the book as half real, half ghost (he narrates his own death, for instance), which allows a cosmic element to seep through the text. This time-slanted, racially fluid novel underscores the centrality of Blackness to Forrest. Forrest seems preternaturally to understand Henri and his race-straddled position within society, and this tension plays out in different ways throughout the novel. The phantasmic Henri situates Forrest both in terms of the Civil War via his omniscient eye and by emphasizing the significance and strangeness of race in the South. With some degree of irony, then, Bell complicates Forrest's image by inserting him directly into his historical context of enslaver. By taking slavery on straight-faced, Bell underscores the brutalities of the system while still positioning Forrest as a hero and the sex consensual. The curiosity of Bell's take relates not so much to this emphasis as to his value-neutral approach to the material. Nonmoral, if not entirely amoral, Bell's depiction of Forrest floats along a chronologically shattered timeline.

Much of the novel revolves around interactions between Forrest and the women in his life: his mother, wife, and Black mistress. He also says the quiet part of the Forrest myth out loud: violence, race, and sexuality animate the general's image. These characteristics, far from outliers, represented fundamental aspects of his appeal (to some) and his offensiveness (to others). Forrest's particular brand of white masculinity attracted and repelled along the same fault lines. More than any other commentator, Bell speaks to the dynamism looped into Forrest's appeal. In *Devil's Dream,* Bell takes the various torn pieces of the Forrest myth and collages them onto a muddled timeline. The effect subverts as Bell brings into focus Forrest, the white southern philanderer. Bell concentrates on the distortions at the edges of the historical record, especially the what-ifs and rumors that swirled just outside of the available archive. A studied and serious novel in some ways, *Devil's Dream* ultimately confounds with its warping of consensual fictions with nonconsensual realities.

Bell's attention to the significance of women in Forrest's life strikes at the grand omission within the general's image, and the novel remains one of the few explicit explorations of this aspect of the general's public memory. Forrest did not exist in a vacuum, and the women who surrounded him in life deserve way more attention than what has been afforded. A look at his connections to women—and how these relationships get portrayed—illustrates the gendered contours of Forrest's image and how they shape his acceptance within white southern society. Forrest's mother, for instance, linked him to the frontier past, his wife linked him to the upward mobility of marriage, and the Black woman he impregnated tied him to the erased lineage of slavery. These women help define Forrest from a different, often oppositional perspective, and a discussion of their role illuminates the gendered tensions inherent to the general's public persona.

What makes Bell's Forrest convincing lies in its believability—the characters feel lived in. With a tone at once archaic and credible, Bell peppers Forrest's dialogue with "ye's," "oncet's," and "cain't's," which catch the ear in a way that Andrew Lytle's "chillans" and "panters" repelled. Lytle plays a significant role in Bell's novel. Bell dedicates the book to Lytle, and strong Lytle-infused elements anchor the story. Bell strips bare Lytle's stories and tales to their primal, discomfiting core. A totemic Lytlesque panther even emerges as a critical image early in the novel. "[W]hat I tried to do," Bell argued, "is imagine how [Forrest] might have really been, warts and all (and he had plenty), and then describe that in action." "Lytle," in contrast, "idealized rather than romanticized him." Uninterested in Lytle's ideological Forrest, Bell uses the general to explore the tangled ways history, memory, race, and sexuality collide in the southern past and present. Only a handful of stories of Forrest's mother survive, but she plays a representative role in many Forrest biographies. Biographers used Forrest's relationship with his mother, seen through the scattered tall tales of his childhood, to situate his moral compass.

The basket-of-chickens story first appeared in John Wyeth's biography. Wyeth frames the incident as a frontier encounter in Mississippi "from which the Indians had but recently been removed." "The sun had gone down," Wyeth intones, as Forrest's mother and aunt returned from a neighbor's house with a gifted basket of chickens. Close to home, the women heard "the yelp and scream of a panther in the dense woods, and only a few yards distant."[22] As her sister cried for her to drop the basket of chickens for the panther, Mariam, Forrest's mother, refused. "There was too much determination and Scotch grit in her," Wyeth noted. The panther caught up to its prey and pounced on Mariam and her horse. As the wounded horse pushed forward, the panther fell back, gouging into her skin and tearing her blouse off in shreds. The screams alerted Forrest, who rushed to their defense with a team of dogs. "Mother," Forrest promised, "I am going to kill that beast if it stays on the earth." Forrest left with his dogs and soon shot and killed the panther. The dutiful son returned with the ears and scalp. But the larger context of Forrest's life and career weighs down this vignette with symbolic foreshadowing. Wyeth emphasizes the Native American claims to the region while stressing the scalping of the panther. Wyeth plays the tableau as allegory: the darkness and the light, the foreboding natural world and the violent harnessing of order and revenge, familial responsibilities, and the solo nature of the hunt. The frontier looms large here, too, as does the color symbolism of Forrest stalking, shooting, and mutilating the black animal. Reduced to its component parts, the story provides a thumbnail sketch of Forrest's childhood as well as the perspective and bias of his biographers. Forrest, thrust into a dangerous world broken down between alleged civilization and assumed barbarianism, slays a panther to avenge his mother and supplant his dead father. The bloody scalp and ears testify to his present place and foreshadow his violent future.

Miriam/Mariam Beck, Forrest's mother, had a family line that stretched back into the Carolinas. Her parents moved to Bedford County, Tennessee, where she married William Forrest. Biographers focused on Beck's height, just as they did her son's stature. "Mentally and physically Marian Beck was a remarkable woman," Wyeth writes.[23] He gives her height as just shy of six feet, though a later biographer notes that her "herculean frame" was a matter of dispute.[24]

She bore eleven children to William, and six sons survived into adulthood. Bedford, her eldest, had a twin named Frances (Fanny) for Miriam's sister, who witnessed the panther attack. The family moved to Mississippi in 1834, and Miriam's husband, William, died three years later. Miriam married Joseph Luxton in 1841 and had four more children with him. In 1867, Miriam died of blood poisoning after stepping on a nail near Navasota, Texas. Andrew Lytle's account of her death portrays a sentimentalized separation scene as Miriam calls for her son in delirium. Her son told her that he had wired Bedford the news and arranged a trip to see her. "In this way," Lytle notes, "he was able to pacify her until she died."[25]

Lytle showed particular interest in her. He begins and ends his biography with Forrest's mother and incorporates her into the story in ways no other biographer had attempted. His book opens with the basket-of-chickens tale as Miriam ("heavy-boned") seems to imply unhappiness with Mississippi and her ability to raise and attend to her "chillurn."[26] Lytle borrows Wyeth's focus on indigenous land and a trail shaped like a "bent arrow." The frontier looms large here, too, and Forrest feels a twinge of Tennessee homesickness among the Mississippi mosquitoes. Forrest locates the "panter" in a tree, the white teeth set off by the surrounding blackness. The teenager shoots, and the animal collapses to the ground with a thud. The scalping and ear-taking mirror Wyeth's account, but Lytle imprints more personality into the characters. Later, Lytle includes an unusual story involving Miriam and her son, Joseph Luxton, Forrest's half-brother. Luxton had returned to Memphis to visit his mother and seemed to find pleasure in his uniform with "gold lace and other fancy trappings." His mother tasked him with corn shucking one morning. He told a "servant" that "he did not intend to go to the mill; she might as well send one of the n——rs with the corn." Mariam thrashed him with a peach-tree switch. Lytle added that Bedford "was as docile in her presence as a child."[27] A rare instance of a family story coming through, Lytle's anecdote reinforces the bond between Bedford and his mother, not to mention the casual racism that defined the characters—and the narrative voice.

In 1952, Aileen Wells Parks published *Bedford Forrest: Boy on Horseback* and crafted Forrest into a frontier role model for children. One of the few women to write on Forrest, Parks focuses primarily on Forrest's childhood and splices fictional events onto a historical timeline to create a patriotic archetype. Miriam plays a prominent role here as "Mrs. Forrest," and she tends to Bedford's childhood playfulness and illnesses. His twin sister, Fanny, plays a role, too, having escaped her historical early death. Much of the book focuses on Forrest's preternatural skills as a horse rider and his desire for a Barlow knife. This Forrest follows the script of a Cold War children's primer. He obeys his mother and attends school. "He had earned too many whippings trying to argue with Ma," young Forrest muses, but "school was more tiresome than plowing with oxen." The penultimate chapter focuses on the basket-of-chickens story. Parks's version parallels earlier accounts, though she fleshes out the story with Bedford tending to his mother's wounds. The story ends as it always did, sans scalping. "Grimly Bedford drew out his hunting knife. He cut off the two furry ears."[28] The book ends many years later with a conversation between a young boy named for Forrest and an elderly Confederate veteran who gives a quick synopsis of the general's life, with several pertinent details omitted. The veteran echoed Forrest's final words to his troops by noting his intention for his men to be "good citizens." "The general," the veteran reminded the young boy, "would expect you to be a good citizen too."[29] Parks's imaginary childhood of Forrest sat comfortably with the mid-century fictions of Davy Crockett (the subject of another young-adult biography by Parks) and much of the western landscape on American television—just one more white frontier boy who honored his mother and country.

In *Devil's Dream,* Forrest's mother appears as a soothing voice for Forrest. Bell writes that she "would lay her hands upon his shoulders and hold his burning eyes with hers."[30] Mariam serves as a double to Mary Ann, Forrest's wife, as both women can pacify the general's rage. One character even muses that "*Mariam* might almost rhyme with *Mary Ann.*"[31] Mary Ann plays a substantial role in the novel, and Bell uses her to develop Forrest's masculinity and sexuality. In an early scene, Forrest tells Mary Ann about the basket of chickens. "The painter is a witchy creature," Forrest tells Mary Ann as he launches into the attack on his mother. The panther "tore off her dress and left stripes on her back like she had been whupped."[32] Bell explicates what earlier writers only inferred as he compares the panther attack to the lash whippings of slavery. "That's a terrible story," Mary Ann responds. Forrest proposed marriage to Mary Ann the following day, and she kissed him, "lingering just long enough that he felt the startling rasp of her tongue's tip along the fine edge of the cut his razor had left there that morning."[33] As his hands caressed her body, Mary Ann said, "hush Bedford. . . . Nobody ever touched me like that."[34] The quiet association of violence and sex (with the allusion to race, which Bell builds on later)—the entwined core of the general's life and identity—defines Forrest and his wife.

Born in 1826, Mary Ann Montgomery grew up the daughter of William and Elizabeth Montgomery from Tennessee. After her husband died, Elizabeth moved the family to Horn Lake, Mississippi, just south of Memphis and a few miles north of Hernando, to live with Mary Ann's uncle and guardian, Samuel Cowan, a Presbyterian minister. Horn Lake also placed Mary Ann directly in the vicinity of Forrest. In 1845, their paths collided as Forrest encountered Mary Ann and her mother in a carriage stuck in a muddy creek. The enslaved Black driver worked alone to wrench the carriage out of the muck as two would-be suitors to Mary Ann sat astride their horses, watching the endeavor. Forrest happened up the scene, splashed into the creek, and carried both women to the shore before helping the Black driver unmoor the carriage. He then confronted the two men with a threat of physical violence as he "castigated them for uselessness."[35] If a "basket of chickens" helped define his mother, Forrest's relationship with his wife is reduced to a river crossing gone awry. Positioned in opposition to the two men unhelpful in their foppishness, Forrest represents the rough-hewn frontier white protector of the distressed women. A few days later, Forrest visited the Montgomery/Cowan home and proposed marriage. Much of this interaction focuses on Forrest's uncouth ways, as Cowan felt he was beneath Mary Ann's status. But, as with so many fragments of the Forrest myth, his imagined weaknesses emerge as strengths, and he wins Mary Ann's hand *because* of his unconventional manner.

The river meeting defines the story's first half; her religiosity and presumed teetotaling delineate the end. Mary Ann appears only sporadically in the general's biographies, but she usually plays a role in contextualizing Forrest's social status and his violent demeanor. Before the war, their marriage solidified Forrest's stake in society. After the war and late in life, Mary Ann pushed Forrest to accept Christianity. Much of the focus on the last days of Forrest relates to his religious conversion at the end of his life. In 1875, Forrest made a rare appearance with his wife at the Court Street Cumberland Presbyterian Church to hear Rev. George T. Stainback preach. According to Stainback, at the general's death two years later, Forrest told him he had placed his "trust in my Redeemer."[36] Mary Ann is at the center of this tale as his influence, the narrative goes, bringing him into the world of faith. Stories of Forrest abstaining from alcohol or gambling or cursing abound, at least in the proximity of his wife. His conversion story plays a significant role in his legacy, as it seems to qualify his earlier actions for his supporters and advocates. At the end of his life, Forrest relied on his wife as he struck out for warm springs and other cures, including his wife's "beef tea."[37] Within this period, he also reached out to Reverend Stainback. This conversion served as the understandable focal point of his eulogies. But deep into the twentieth and early twenty-first centuries, and well beyond the limits of the historical record based on rumor, this conversion story helps establish an exit for Forrest. Whatever his earlier transgressions—which many of his admirers cast doubt on—this proverbial deathbed transformation absolves Forrest. As important as the war is to the Forrest image, these two prewar and postwar moments, a dashing rescue and newfound faith, center on Mary Ann and help place Forrest within reach of respectability. As always, Forrest allows it both ways: the coarse and the refined, the latter helping to smooth over the former and permitting a selective take on a complicated man.

For Bell, Mary Ann serves a different role as he uses her mainly as a foil to Forrest's sexual relationship with Catharine, an enslaved Black woman he had purchased in the 1850s. The interaction between the white wife and the Black mistress motivates much of the action of Bell's novel. Rather than providing a patina of decency, Mary Ann highlights the white southern patriarchy and the vast cruel distance between white and Black women. "You go down there to the pens at night," Bell's Mary Ann tells her husband, "and shoot your seed into her black belly like a boar-hog rutting on a sow. And you think I don't know about it!" Bell posits Catharine as the central character in the tension between Forrest and Mary Ann. In Bell's telling, Catharine is a willing and active participant in a sexual relationship with Forrest. Sliding in and out of dialect, Bell presents a series of erotic couplings between Catharine and Forrest. "Somehow in the dark," Bell writes of Catharine, "she had undone her bodice so that her firm chocolatey breasts caressed his cheek, and had unfastened his trouser buttons too, reaching around to grasp the goat tuft of hair at the base of his spine—*thas you aright* she whispered, *thas old Bedford sho nuff.*" "Bowled over by the warm weight of her," Bell continues, "he felt her slide back down his belly, and as he held the long ropy strands of her hair he felt her take him up into her long warm lips as eagerly as a hungry calf seizing on a milk cow's teat. Something Mary Ann could never have conceived." The oscillation between his wife and Catharine is a crucial element of the novel as the enslaved Black woman provides sexual gratification to Forrest in ways denied him by his white wife. "The piercing memory of his wife helped him hold back from going over the edge too soon," Bell writes, "and she also was measuring his every twitch with her wise tongue's point, withdrawing just before it was too late, cradling and lifting his balls, mocking him in the same husky tone. *Ain't you gone take yo boots off, Ginnal?*" Inverting the power relationship, Forrest accedes to Catharine's needs and desires. "He knew," Forrest says later in the novel, "he would risk everything, for this."[38]

No part of the novel speaks to the coercion, compulsion, and sexual assault that defined the realities of stories such as Catharine's. It is fair to recoil from the tone and content of the scenes between Forrest and Catharine, especially as Bell presents the scenes without historical framing of what these interactions would have looked like in real life. Thus, Bell annotates the story of Catharine with a note stating that, in 1853, Forrest purchased "a Negro woman named Catharine aged seventeen and her Child named Thomas aged four months."[39] This is history. Still, the passage introducing Forrest's relationship with Catharine begins at a Thanksgiving dinner, discussing the independent virtues of dark-meat and white-meat turkey. "'I like the dark,' Forrest said, with a lip-smacking smile."[40] Bell treats this story with the purposefulness of history and the tawdriness of a scandalous rumor framed in winking asides.

Early in the novel, Forrest tells his wife that he "must buy a black gal." "Wait a minute," Forrest says to his wife, "not for me." Alluding to the complicated conflicts between white southern women and Black enslaved women, Bell uses Forrest's Black daughter to drive a wedge between husband and wife. Told by Bell through the tawdry sexual language of plantation pulp novels—"his hot milk burst into her molasses"—this storyline connects to hidden transcripts of Forrest's life. In his biography of Forrest in the 1990s, Jack Hurst detailed a birth record of a son born to Forrest and Catharine. In the late 2010s, a group of university history students in Memphis worked through bills of sale related to Forrest and his slave pens. In the archives they found a name, Narcissa Forrest, daughter of Catharine. "She [Catharine] was bought by Nathan Bedford Forrest," the researcher noted. "She was abused by him. She had a kid with him."[41] "The evidence for his relationship with the slave Catharine is suggestive rather than conclusive," Bell argues, "and there's not much of it." "I'd really have liked to know more about that," Bell concludes; "on the other hand not knowing gave me more freedom to invent."[42]

Throughout *Devil's Dream,* Bell erases the realities of slavery and women like Catharine, a woman omitted by most of Forrest's biographers and yet known, at least in broad strokes, by the northern press during the Civil War. Jack Hurst's biography in the early 1990s represents one of the few extensive passages on Catharine. According to Hurst, Forrest purchased "Catharine aged seventeen and her Child named Thomas aged four months" at some point in the 1850s.[43] The connection between Forrest and Catharine may have been an open secret in Memphis. Few contemporary accounts exist, though a northern newspaper article circulated widely after Fort Pillow.[44] Entitled "The Butcher Forrest and His Family," the article described Forrest in contemptible terms ("mean, vindictive, cruel and unscrupulous"). Within the context of Fort Pillow, the writer worked to define Forrest in terms that would anger a white northern readership. "He had two wives," he wrote, "one white, the other colored (Catharine), by each of which he had two children." "His patriarchal wife, Catharine," he concluded, "and his white wife, had frequent quarrels or domestic jars." The newspaper article inverted the usual southern descriptions of Forrest. The general stood "tall, gaunt, and sallow visaged, with a long nose, deep set black, snaky eyes, full black beard without a mustache, and hair wore long." More recent census research shows that Forrest most likely had a child with Catharine, Narcissa, born in 1857. Forrest's shadow history seeped through the historical record—present but unremarked in the white South and weaponized by an angry white North.

Forrest's relationship with women remains a challenging aspect of his biography and legacy. The historical omissions chasm too widely to compile a densely populated account. Yet, one woman defines a considerable corner of his public memory. A chance encounter in 1863 generated the most indelibly feminine aspect of the Forrest myth. Most of the myth rested on the general's masculinity and the way it shaped perspectives through the changing historical matrix of gender. However, one particular woman, Emma Sansom, came to signify Confederate white womanhood and even had her own memorial landscape of statues and monuments. In the first decades of the twentieth century, Sansom (who died in 1900) played a significant role in the Forrest narrative. As the Lost Cause blurred fact and fiction, it also elevated Sansom, a young teenager during the war, as "a symbol of Southern womanhood—beauty and daring, faithfulness to the cause."[45] Her Forrest-adjacent position provided the general a feminine sense of Lost Cause cachet that usually eluded him. Sansom's story highlights a curious melding of militarism and gender roles that brought into contrast Forrest's relationship with women and how women bent the contours of his public image to refract colliding perspectives on honor and manliness.

Between early April and early May 1863, Union Colonel Abel Streight conducted a series of raids from Nashville, Tennessee, to Rome, Georgia. Streight aimed at disrupting Confederate supply lines and rail connections but had problems with supplies of his own. In addition, Streight regrettably outfitted his troops with mules rather than horses, which hindered transportation. In late April, Forrest had caught up with Streight, and the two forces skirmished across northern Alabama. By this point in the war, Forrest had established a pattern of guerilla-style actions with small groups of soldiers. Add a distinct home-field advantage to this strategy, and Streight's numerical advantage disappeared. Still, the Union soldiers had tricks, too, including destroying a bridge near Gadsden, Alabama, at an opportune moment with Forrest directly on their trail. Hoping to give themselves a respite from the constant fighting, Streight's men burned the bridge across the already flooded Black Creek on May 2. The Confederates stalled out with their path obstructed and took on enemy fire from Streight's rear guard. Forrest then approached a nearby farmhouse to look for an alternative crossing, where he encountered a teenage Emma Sansom and her family. Sansom mentioned their cows would cross the creek at a hidden low spot. Forrest commanded her to climb behind him on his horse (against her mother's wishes) and rode off to find the necessary location. Sansom's knowledge gave Forrest the edge he needed. The crossing afforded Forrest time, and due to Sansom's advantage and Forrest's substantial bluff, Streight surrendered roughly fifteen hundred men to a Confederate force one-third the size.

The Emma Sansom story is a central curiosity within the Forrest myth. Their interaction lasted only a few hours but had a peculiar afterlife. Sansom appears in Forrest's first biography, and writers continued to refine and retransmit her depictions and descriptions across the next century. The earliest description, by Jordan and Pryor, erred in various degrees—they place her age as several years older—but sketched the story with enough particulars to tell the tale.[46] Several decades later, however, John Wyeth reached out directly to Sansom—then known as Mrs. C. B. Johnson of Calloway, Texas—to provide her version of the events. Wyeth seemed quite taken by her and the entire story, even dedicating the book to Sansom: "a woman worthy of being remembered by her countrymen as long as courage is deemed a virtue." More details emerged from Wyeth's work—he asked for a lock of her hair, for example—but the main story followed the same rutted path.[47] Wyeth saw in the story the Lost Cause writ small. The Sansom family, for example, "owned no slaves, nor did at least one-half of the families in the South who gave their life and whatever property they possessed to the Southern cause."[48] The tale played directly into the gallantry myth crafted in the early twentieth century around the Confederacy, and the gendered elements of the story enveloped Forrest as much as Sansom. "He was a man," J. Harvey Mathes wrote in 1901 regarding the exchange, "of tender and sentimental moods."[49] "With tones as tender as those of a woman," another writer quoted a few years later, "Do not be alarmed. I am General Forrest, and I will protect you."[50] We see this contrast throughout the Forrest image, with the general positioned as the paragon of white masculinity only to be feminized in relation to women. The Sansom story illustrates this piece clearly, but it glides across his entire memorial story.

Born in 1847 in Georgia, Emma Sansom moved to the area near Gadsden, Alabama, when she was about five. In 1864, not long after her interaction with Forrest, she married Christopher Johnson. In 1866, they had a daughter named after her famous acquaintance—Mattie Forrest Johnson—who died in 1871.[51] Sansom's life shifted away from the Forrest spotlight until Wyeth tracked her down in the late 1890s as part of his biography. Sansom had other children who lived to adulthood, but she passed away near Gilmer, Texas, in 1890, not long after Wyeth published his biography. Soon after her death, however, her life story caught the attention of various Lost Cause advocates and devotees. Her story served several purposes. First, it tended to humanize and romanticize Forrest in a specific way, allowing him to exist simultaneously as a warrior and a protector. It also gave a name to the uncertain concept of Confederate womanhood. Finally, North Alabama could point directly to Sansom as a vivid example of sacrifice and courage. In 1902, the Alabama chapter of the United Daughters of the Confederacy held a meeting in Demopolis, a small town one hundred miles west of Montgomery, Alabama. One speaker, the director of the Department of History and Archives for Alabama, presented the organization with a bust and painting of Sansom and delivered a detailed address on her life and contributions. "The young Southern girl," he spoke as he reiterated her exploits, "her bright eyes flashing and rosy cheeks glowing," acted with "a maiden's modesty and more than woman's courage." The portrait of her, he concluded, "stands not only in perpetuation of an incident of 1863, but it stands as well for the embodiment of the collective aspiration and appreciation of the women of Alabama of 1902."[52]

The blurring of virginal girlishness and patriotic womanhood lends an edge to the Forrest story. Often presented as a story of an intrepid young girl, with Forrest tending to her as a child (the lock of hair—some iterations have him repeatedly asking for it—the handwritten note, the shared horseback ride), the tale shifts with a closer look at her age. Born in June 1847, Sansom was shy of sixteen when Forrest arrived at their farm. Chroniclers casually blundered her age (as they did the spelling of her name), but she was married (to a Confederate soldier) just a year and a half later, in October 1864, at the age of seventeen. In their "authorized" military chronicle, published in 1868, Jordan and Pryor place her as a "tall, comely girl of about eighteen years of age." Did Forrest see her as older than fifteen? Ambiguity frames much of this scene. Of course, none of his actions relate directly to courtship, but they are not wholly unrelated, either. Decades later, biographers codified the story a bit more clearly with a younger, more girlish portrayal emerging. Still, haziness smears the myths. In the 1990s, during the heyday of Civil War–themed art, John Paul Strain, one of the more prominent artists, centered two paintings on Forrest's relationships with women.

One painting, "Mary Ann," focuses on Forrest meeting his future wife stuck in a bog. Her skirt and petticoat unsullied, Mary Ann looks lovingly at Forrest as he casually carries her to safety. In "To the Lost Ford," Strain crafts a similar image with Emma Sansom astride the rear of Forrest's horse, pointing out the passage across the creek. Barefoot with sunbonnet, Sansom plays both assistant and damsel. Her gloved hand clutched Forrest's arm as Forrest's hand cradled Mary Ann's waist. Separately, the two images operate at face value: courtship and bravery. But together, within the larger Sansom narrative, the dress and posture in both paintings situate both women within classic romantic contexts, with Forrest serving as the composed southern gentleman at the center of each scene. The parallels between courage and courtship play out most likely unintentionally. Still, the various pieces of the account—the torn crinoline, locks of hair, arms clutched around Forrest's waist—allude to something perhaps more complicated. Suggestions and ambiguities obscure well-defined margins as to what this story meant initially or even afterward, but the encounter continues to play a role within the larger Forrest myth.

Unique among Forrest-adjacent noncombatants, Sansom had her own memorial landscape built in the years after her death. In 1907, the city of Gadsden erected a monument to Sansom. Made from Italian marble, the statue cost $3,500, paid for by the local chapter of the United Daughters of the Confederacy.[53] The statue's base featured a relief of Emma clutching a rather anonymous-looking Forrest's arm as she points out the passage across Black Creek. The statue, modeled on the granddaughter of the UDC's chapter president, is noticeably girlish and stands pointing serenely out into the distance. Perhaps as an unintentional response to Forrest's biographers misspelling her name, the marker notes she was helping "Gen. Forest" cross the river.[54] A year before the statue's unveiling, a white mob lynched Bunk Richardson, a Black man unconnected to the rape and murder of a local white woman. In 2016, the Equal Justice Initiative placed a historical marker commemorating Richardson's murder bordering the train tracks where he was killed. The sign stands some four hundred feet from the Emma Sansom statue—a reminder of the invisible distance between racial violence and the Lost Cause.

Gadsden hitched its Lost Cause desires and demands on eternally fifteen-year-old Emma Sansom. In 1929, the city named its high school after her, later reorganized as a middle school in 2016.[55] The statue (and school) stood without much fanfare for most of its existence. A chance encounter in 1863 that prevented a Union attack on a town in the next state over (Rome, Georgia), which in turn led to the creation of a reasonably nondescript statue of a young woman, is the type of historical event that cities trap in amber to remember and forget in equal measure. In the twenty-first century, however, the Sansom statue generated more attention as Confederate monuments fell under increased scrutiny following the Dylann Roof murders in 2015. In 2020, the city empaneled a committee to survey potential actions regarding the statue. Throughout that summer, calls grew to remove the monument, including from Emma Sansom's descendants. In a letter to the city, Preston Rhea, a relative of Sansom's, argued that the "public celebration of Forrest's legacy is shameful, and Emma Sansom's aid to his cause cannot be separated from its consequences." Noting the public funding of the monument, Bunk

Emma Sansom monument, Gadsden, Alabama, twentieth-century postcard.

Richardson's lynching, its Jim Crow context, the fact that it did not even pretend to look like Sansom, and the civic consequences of Confederate commemoration, Rhea excoriated the city for considering keeping it in place. "As Emma Sansom's nieces and nephews," he concluded, " the best first step we can take to abolish the stain of white supremacy in Gadsden is to remove this symbol of the enslaving power that once ruled this land."[56] The city voted to keep the statue in place, though one councilman adamantly disagreed. "We had a chance to move forward and stop looking in the past," Thomas Worthy lamented, "and every Black person that walks past or drives past that monument will feel some type of way."[57] Two years later, a local Black Lives Matter group reignited the controversy over the statue, though the city again chose to keep Sansom on her pedestal.

On the surface, the suggestion of sex appeal or sexuality within the Forrest image might surprise, repulse, or confuse. Yet, throughout the twentieth century, sex swirled around Forrest—sometimes suggested or insinuated and sometimes pronounced and unconcealed. Sex clouded and animated what he meant and signified within white admirers and advocates. By the 1980s and 1990s, Forrest's image became much more complicated as Black activists began to shift his memory. Forrest then served as a signifier of whiteness, violence, and militarism. But in the 1960s, a weird playfulness emerged as various publications used Forrest and Forrest-adjacent images in sexual and sexualized contexts. Some of these uses connect to the easy *Playboy*-esque misogyny of the mid-century men's magazines and cartoons. But these pieces also underscore the tensions within the Forrest image as white daydreams of masculinity collided with standard fictions of pirates, outlaws, and antiheroes. Forrest straddled these archetypes, and his swarthy appearance allowed him to inhabit any of these roles.

In 1961, *Stag* magazine ran a story that featured Forrest in full adventure mode. This men's interest magazine had a popular run in the 1950s and 1960s, its issues crammed with tales of World War II derring-do, escapades in "exotic" locales, pinup models (*Stag*'s likeminded competitor, *Stag Party,* was forced to change its name to *Playboy*), bawdy cartoons, and submarines—lots of submarines. Written by Harry Harrison Kroll, "The Camp Follower in Gen. Forrest's Command Tent" fits directly in this mold of military-themed eroticism. Kroll published hundreds of stories as well as novels, including *Cabin in the Cotton,* later made into a 1932 Bette Davis film, and his Forrest tale represented just one example of his fast-paced, quickly published tales. Kroll based this story on actual historical events late in the Civil War, but the more considerable emphasis lay on the highly sexualized relationship between Forrest and a Black enslaved woman. Kroll gives no introduction to Forrest—he is just one more valiant warrior—but the easy blending of fact and fiction within a highly innuendoed account of sex and espionage underscores the knowledge and demands of the magazine's readership and audience. The expectations of the primarily male readers of *Stag* no doubt dictated the contours of Kroll's story. Still, it also fits directly into the Forrest myth of the mid-twentieth century: unscrupulous white male hero always one step ahead of the enemy with time for arousal and, in an unguarded moment, romance. Emphasizing sex, espionage, slavery, and blowing things up, Kroll brought Forrest into the postwar pulp world of martial masculinity.

Kroll set his story on the Battle of Johnsonville in November 1864, where Forrest attacked a large number of Union gunboats, barges, and transport craft on the Tennessee River. In this iteration, however, the focus falls on Forrest's relationship with an enslaved Black woman named Celia, whom he had owned at one point and then sold to a planter named Van Mason, who lived in the area. The reader is introduced to Celia through her "soft, musical" voice as she carries fried chicken and various baked goods to sell to Union soldiers.[58] Forrest wants Celia to spy on the enemy's location and capabilities as she sells her food and snacks—something he has done before. "The idea of using the attractive slave girl as a spy," Forrest thinks, "was one of his happiest ideas." Much of the middle of the account relates to Forrest using Celia's information to surprise the Union Army resource depot. Celia's guerilla espionage pays off for Forrest as he successfully disrupts and destroys their supply chain. The entire story alludes to Forrest's deep connections to slavery, the relatively hidden element of his success as he used his prewar slave trade networks to outfit his troops and maintain home-ground superiority. Celia then signifies this intricate aspect of Forrest's superiority, valorizing Forrest's military acumen and illustrating how he used other people to get what he needed.

Kroll says little about Celia's Blackness, though her enslavement plays a role in the story. The main two-page illustration of the story, by prolific pulp artist Walter Popp, reaffirms this point by portraying Celia as a smiling white woman of ambiguous ethnicity. Celia cradles a picnic basket of food and reaches up to a train filled with leering Union soldiers. Reminiscent of World War II troop trains rather than Civil War conveyances, the illustration has a western feel as a hatted Forrest crouches next to a tree, his sidearm cocked. The story centers much more strongly on her sexuality and connection to Forrest. Kroll describes Celia as "comely" (that word again) and flirtatious. Forrest had a complex history with Celia, with the insinuation that he sold her after his wife discovered their sexual relationship. "Celia," Kroll writes, "was the type white southern wives did not want around the house." Kroll paints Celia as desperate to return to Forrest—"General, I wish you'd buy me back"—playing into the multiple white male readership fantasies of sex, control, and race. At one point, Forrest visits the Van Mason farm, where Celia lives, and after dinner, he slips into her living quarters, where he caresses her hair. A conversation alludes to Forrest fathering one of her children, and he later asks himself "if his attachment for her ran deeper than the flesh." Kroll keeps the sexuality muted and implied for most of the story. Forrest, for example, overdoes it with the dinner and the rum one time, and she leaves for another tent. But near the end, the two are intimate in a scene quite evocative of *Devil's Dream* as Celia massages Forrest's body as foreplay. After the hints, allegations, and shadowy innuendo, Kroll has Forrest submit his report to his commanders. "The Richmond government would finger this report with pleasure," Kroll writes as Celia helps Forrest mount his horse. "Then he rode away into the night," the story concludes, "just another soldier moving south while the mud and legends gathered him in."

A few weeks after *Stag* ran "The Camp Follower in Gen. Forrest's Command Tent," Monroe Cockrell wrote a letter to the Tennessee state librarian asking him to procure a copy of the magazine. Far from happy, Cockrell wanted the library to seek some sort of legal redress to the contents of the story. "I have never seen in print," Cockrell wrote, "anything that is so disgusting as this where the character of Forrest is pitched into the gutter alongside of the lowest kind of human beings." Always sensitive to how writers and media portrayed Forrest, Cockrell took almost personal offense at Kroll's depiction of the sexual Forrest. "Surely," he pleaded, "there is [some] legal instrumentality by which you all can put this author where he belongs."[59] Something hit a particular nerve with Cockrell. Perhaps the innuendo went too far, or maybe Celia's Blackness was too challenging for the Illinois researcher to comprehend. As provocative as Kroll's account of Forrest was—intentionally so—it was also situated within the historical record and even spoke to the metanarrative of the general's success. What Cockrell would have made of *Devil's Dream* is left to the imagination.

A year after the *Stag piece,* the *Memphis Commercial Appeal* ran a cartoon entitled "Ladies Day." This one-panel cartoon features a beach scene with five men in swim trunks surrounding a curvy brunette in a bikini. Beaming with a big smile and soaking up the attention of the men (two less enthusiastic women stand in a huff off in the background), the busty woman takes center stage. The caption reads: "That Miss Forrest got here fustest with the mostest again."[60] The hometown paper knew their readers would understand the gag without much more than the phrase. No record exists as to Cockrell's response. Somewhere between the Strain paintings and *Stag* magazine and cartoons of buxom beachgoers existed a perplexing combination of imaginings that speak to the near-infinite ways Forrest encompassed invisible threads of sexuality. In addition, the ways artists portrayed Forrest's various relationships with the women in his life underscore the mythic paternalism that shaped (and was shaped by) the Lost Cause. These relationships humanized him in some ways and flattered him in others. However, his history with Catharine, left out of this discourse, alludes to something more sinister shimmering just beneath the surface. Madison Bell understood this bleaker, darker aspect of Forrest and how this story was written out of the public memory. Bell also had the vantage point of writing in the 2000s and could survey a century of mythmaking and posturing. As white sexual icon, Forrest sat just off to the side of the general's lore, but his carnal phosphorescence glowed at the edges. Bell knew the history and the warped ways in which history and fable collided and crushed against each other. His novel places the radioactive waves of Forrest's memory at the center of the story, thus upending the mythic narrative through paradox and irony. It is not that Bell produced an account that exceeds the work of biographers and historians but that he brings the unspoken aspects of the story to the forefront with all of their barbs, spikes, and thorns.

Sexualized descriptions and images of Forrest swerved away from the explicitness of the 1960s. This turn partly relates to the cultural move away from the mainstream misogyny of mid-century men's magazines. More specifically, Black commentators and protesters successfully reframed the public memory of Forrest in the 1970s as a story of race and racism. By the 1980s and 1990s, the sexual overtones thawed into an amorphous slurry of white masculinity—not quite sexual, not quite not. As usual, Shelby Foote plays an important role here. Late in Ken Burns's Civil War documentary, Foote riffed on Forrest in 1864. "You're asking about," Foote says, "the most man in the world, in some ways."[61] Foote returned to this phrase time and again in the years after Burns. He enjoyed the allusive epigram. With whatever twists and turns defined Foote's relationship with civil rights, he maintained a steadfast attraction to Forrest. Foote saw in the general the primal elements of white southern manhood—a white man to be honored, sure, but also to be emulated. An echo of "*fustest with the mostest,*" Foote's "most man in the world" offers a playful elevation of Forrest's status while simultaneously decontextualizing his meaning and cultural worth. But in one interview, Foote took it a bit further and argued that "Forrest is one of the most attractive men who ever walked through the pages of history."[62] Replacing the nebulous "most man," which he rarely expanded on, Foote ups the stakes by labeling Forrest "the most attractive," conjuring magnetism as a leader but also as his masculine desirability. Foote connects this directly with Fort Pillow by admonishing the interviewer to "better read back again on the Fort Pillow massacre instead of some piece of propaganda about it." "Fort Pillow was a beautiful operation," Foote argues, "tactically speaking." "Forrest did everything he could to stop the killing of those people who were in the act of surrendering," Foote defensively contends, "and did stop it." Regardless of the logical mess of the sentence, the pairing of "attractive" and "beautiful" catches the eye. Slavery, Fort Pillow, and the Klan all collapse into meaninglessness as Foote condenses Forrest to a representation of manliness.

In April of 2009, amid the growing clatter of the "Tea Parties," then Texas governor Rick Perry flirted with talk of secession in reaction to perceived attacks on state sovereignty by the Obama administration. "There's a lot of different scenarios," Perry said. "We've got a great union. There's absolutely no reason to dissolve it. But if Washington continues to thumb their nose at the American people, you know, who knows what might come out of that. But Texas is a very unique place, and we're a pretty independent lot to boot."[63] A group of scholars at the Abbeville Institute echoed Perry's statement. This group of professors, self-consciously modeled on the Southern Agrarians, sought, in Donald Livingston's words, a "simpler time" with more overt politeness and a more genial culture, albeit one dominated by the whispers of secession if not white supremacy. "Anyone raised in the South," Livingston maintained, "has a certain dissonance in his imagination because he receives a history of his own identity and country that he knows is not quite right."[64] This Andrew Lytle–haunted neo-Agrarianism reflected deep concerns over southern identity and its continuance and corruption. These fears, however imagined, set the scene for Bell's novel, which played against this defensiveness and provided a practical and updated symbol to amalgamate these suspicions and worries.

In June 2009, during Barack Obama's first presidential summer, Ta-Nehisi Coates wrote a provocative essay for *The Atlantic* entitled "Nathan Bedford

Forrest Has Beautiful Eyes." A Black writer and journalist, Coates devoted much of his blog to this rehabilitated take on the old white southern victimhood and defensiveness narrative. Coates examines the magnetic pull of Forrest in terms of history and southern culture and summarizes Forrest's myth succinctly: "Forrest is the model of Southern chivalry—too much so." The victimhood piece emerges at the end as Coates (referencing the then-current Supreme Court confirmation battles surrounding Sonia Sotomayor) places this discussion into a broader context. "The temptation to continue to lie, to see yourself as the victim in a grand play is formidable," Coates writes; "consider Lindsay Graham chafing at the constraints of whiteness, while Sonia Sotomayor evidently swims in a free world of color." "No, I can't be sure (were I white) that I would not have wanted to roll with Forrest," Coates responds to one of the commenters on his site. "In fact, I even suspect the opposite. That's the point. But there comes a time of reckoning with the past. I think we're past that time."[65] The myth has power, Coates recognizes, but so does historical consciousness.

But in a more interesting turn, he imagines Forrest's hold on the southern *male* population. "I imagine for a kid coming up in these times, in certain sectors of the South," he writes, "it's painful to face up to Nathan Forrest, to the notion that the pomp and glamour, all the talk of honor and independence was, at the end of the day, dependent on slavery. The Lost Cause isn't just 'lost,' it's barely a cause."[66] Coates's empathy here is striking, but he goes further. "Nathan Bedford Forrest is beautiful," he writes; "again, dig those steely eyes, that dead serious countenance, the warrior's beard." Returning to the idea of victimization, Coates argues that race would play a role in developing defensiveness out of the white South. "Sooner or later," Coates writes, "I think the South will understand that the ideology of noble victimhood' is a luxury it too can ill-afford." "But sooner or later," he concludes, "I think most of the South will be black like me." This constant echoing of the past leads us back to Madison Bell's novel. "Was it the future that hadn't happened yet?" time-lost Henri asks, "Or was it the past?"[67] When dealing with race, memory, and Nathan Bedford Forrest, sometimes it can be difficult to tell.

5

REMOVAL(S)

> They shifted the statues for harboring ghosts.
>
> —MICHAEL STIPE, 1984

> You are stuck here forever,
> General Forrest,
> without so much as a ghost to talk to.
> Memphis
> is sick and tired of the past.
>
> —DON SHARE, 2013

In the late 1990s, Nathan Bedford Forrest materialized once again astride his horse on a spit of private land south of Nashville. Two stories tall and bulletproof, or at least graffiti-proof as the artist doused his creation with a paint-repellant varnish, the statue towered over I-65 with Forrest waving a saber and a pistol. Part question mark, part exclamation point, this polystyrene abstraction in brash pewter and bronze reframed Forrest as a mythic form pressed into molded synthetic polymer. Jack Kershaw, the sculptor, understood and adored the fabled elements of Forrest, but he also understood the contemporary moment. As he bashed out the statue's form with a butcher knife, he knew, too, that he had created a target. Private art on private property, Kershaw's statue filled public space in ways distinct from other monuments. Forrest—his robot-like face contorted into a distressed open mouth with craft-store crystal blue eyes twinkling in the sun—loomed over suburban Tennessee.[1] "He's crying 'Follow me!'" Kershaw noted at the unveiling in 1998. A local newspaper writer countered by describing the statue as "the ugliest piece of overblown yard art imaginable."[2]

Unloved, perhaps unlovable, the Nashville statue worked more as a punchline than as a point of academic discussion. Still, the story of this statue, in all its weirdness, refracts the expansiveness of the Forrest myth. The sculptor's past, the landowner's comments, the denunciations, the attacks, and the winking op-eds all pressed into a discernable shape, a postmodern Forrest for a postmodern moment. The Forrest fictions of the twentieth century had coalesced into something at once tangible and mysterious, a cryptic suburban riddle. If the 1905 Memphis monument represented the civic reaction of white history-making and unmaking, the 1998 Nashville statue originated in a very different space. Tennessee held both in tension, with two Forrests representing competing sides of the yawning twentieth century. The Memphis cast bronze weighted with the white needs of a city runs directly counter to the Nashville synthetic resin untethered to much beyond the white supremacist visions of the sculptor. The Memphis statue maintained more gravitas and civic importance, making it a more complex symbol and issue. But the Nashville statue captured the headlines. More than Forrest, the Nashville statue seemed to represent for many pundits the lunacy of memorializing the Confederacy writ large. The complexity of Memphis bolted to the superficiality of Nashville, though, underscores the position of Forrest in the twentieth century.[3] Forrest mattered more to more people at the end of the century than at any other time, yet the Kershaw statue stood as the high-water mark of notoriety and the beginning of the end. Within two decades, construction crews would wrench both statues from their pedestals, and the public memory of Forrest would drift into disarray and ambiguity.

To grasp the meaning and significance of the Nashville statue, one must confront Jack Kershaw in all his contrarianism and fury. Artist, activist, advocate, attorney, agitator—Kershaw traipsed through postwar Nashville straddling careers in painting and sculpture as well as white supremacy and anti–civil rights crusading. Born in 1913, he was in his eighties when he constructed the Forrest statue, and Kershaw slips and slides along the Forrest-memory narrative of the twentieth century. He connects to Andrew Lytle and the Agrarians. He shapes the slanted genteel racism of Nashville's anti–civil rights movement. He touches the blood-soaked legacy of white Memphis. He refracts the irritation underneath Shelby Foote's conviviality. More than an outsider crank tinkering away at a discomforting effigy for his hero, Kershaw represents a significant aspect of the modern history of white Tennessee: elusive, hard to pin down, and yet a vociferous supporter of segregation, racism, and white

Forrest statue outside of Nashville, Tennessee, 2015.
Photo by Eric England for the *Nashville Scene.*

supremacy. Often dismissed as an aberration, Kershaw serves as a conduit of all of the different fragments of the Forrest myth, stretching back to the nineteenth century. By extension, more than an accidental chaos sculpture in suburban Nashville, the Kershaw sculpture encompasses the Forrest myth in all its complexity. Equal parts offensive and defensive, provocative and corny, the Kershaw statue stood as a plastic signifier of Forrest in the 1990s. Kershaw's background melts into his work, forcing a multidirectional look back to Forrest and the Ku Klux Klan, Andrew Lytle and the Agrarians, and Shelby Foote and his larger audience. Memphis might lay claim to Forrest's depth, but Nashville, via Kershaw, laid claim to Forrest's breadth.

As espoused by Andrew Lytle and others, white southern agrarianism encodes Kershaw's Forrest. As an undergraduate at Vanderbilt, Kershaw encountered the key Agrarians and developed lasting relationships with Lytle and Donald Davidson.[4] These relationships extended past his university days. Kershaw would marry Lytle's first cousin, Mary Noel, for example, and his Forrest matched in spirit and vibe Lytle's Forrest. In its broadest form, agrarianism most likely appealed to Kershaw with its cultural obstinance before any detailed ideological platform. Kershaw may not have built a coherent political philosophy throughout his life and career—something that would connect his early dabbling in college to the Forrest statue six decades later—but a line emerges out of regional defensiveness and outsider rage. In 1955, the *Chattanooga Daily Times* quoted Kershaw about the post–*Brown v. Board* storm slinking across Tennessee.[5] Here, Kershaw defined a stance that he would return to again and again: desegregation harmed Black students by removing them from Black culture. "It is a cruel injustice to the minority Negro group," Kershaw intoned, "to bury its cultural potential by forcing him to go to school with people outside his own cultural group." Fifty years later, Kershaw argued that, if "you don't know the difference between black and white, you're insulting your black brother, because he's different and he's proud of it and he wants to develop that way."[6] He liked the way that argument sounded even as the n-word slipped easily into interviews and conversations. The artist devoted much of his public energies in the 1950s to an organization called the Tennessee Federation for Constitutional Government (TFCG), a group cofounded by Donald Davidson. Kershaw may have married into the Lytle lineage, but Davidson was the Agrarian most associated with the artist. Davidson's racism—he was the one who sent Lytle the handmade Christmas card featuring mocking dialect and a Black child in the field—forms an essential backstory to the activities of the TFCG.

The TFCG found a white Nashville audience as it seemed to suggest an anti-desegregation movement less horrific than the Klan. However, hints of violence encircled the group after a local elementary school was dynamited following their admitting of a six-year-old Black student. Kershaw denied involvement but also provided aid to the primary suspect, John Kaspar, though authorities never charged anyone with the bombing. Fifty years later, Kershaw argued that he wanted to keep Kaspar out of Nashville because he saw him as a rabble-rouser. Kershaw argued that Kaspar "performed a certain service by arousing the citizens of Clinton [the location of a series of anti-desegregation riots] to make a noise, and the rank-and-file is oftentimes very useful in that field."[7] This late-life ambivalence notwithstanding, Kershaw's career as a pro-segregation activist rode a wave of public proclamations and photo opportunities. The TFCG failed in its goals, but Kershaw continued with a quieter role over the next few years. In the mid-1960s, Kershaw worked to obtain a law degree through the Nashville YMCA Night Law School, an institution cofounded incidentally by Robert Selph Henry, the author of *"First with the*

Most": Nathan Bedford Forrest. This newfound legal career would soon define Kershaw's public life in the 1970s.

In 1968, James Earl Ray, a career criminal who had served prison sentences for mail fraud and various robberies, had been on the lam for almost a year, having escaped the Missouri State Penitentiary. That March, Ray traveled from Los Angeles, where he had worked on George Wallace's campaign, to Atlanta and then to Birmingham. Along the way, Ray purchased a rifle, scope, and ammunition using various aliases and excuses. Finally, on April 2, Ray drove to Memphis, where he followed Martin Luther King Jr.'s movements. Two days later, Ray, perched in a boarding room across from the Lorraine Motel, shot and killed King as he stood on a balcony with friends and associates. Fleeing to Canada and then to Europe, Ray was arrested in London in March 1969. Over the next few years, Ray would confess, recant, accept a plea deal to avoid a jury trial (and, in his mind, the death penalty), fire lawyers, and eventually fight to withdraw the guilty plea. In 1977, Ray escaped from a state penitentiary in Petros, Tennessee—northwest of Knoxville. This escape—which would inspire the Barkley Marathons, an infamous trail race run near where Ray fled—would lead Ray to hire a new lawyer: Jack Kershaw. With a new legal team in tow, Ray began circulating a series of new conspiracies involving a mysterious Cuban named Raul/Raoul. In other words, Ray was a patsy for a dark scheme to murder King. Kershaw trotted out this defense and had Ray sit for a polygraph test to prove his innocence for *Playboy* magazine.[8] Ray failed the test.

Kershaw would not last long as Ray's attorney. Ray fired him after discovering he had accepted $11,000 from *Playboy* for the interview. Yet, a weird footnote emerges in this heady moment of Cuban intrigue, prison escapes, and men's magazine meetings. Kershaw's wife, Mary (his Lytle connection and attorney), conspired with Gary Revel, who had assisted in the investigation to clear Ray, to compose "They Slew the Dreamer." This song, released on Rebel Records in 1977, uses the Raul story to show how a conspiratorial "they," not Ray, killed King. "They turned the courtroom into a costume ball," Revel sings. "The dreamer fell to die," the song continues, "Raul slipped into hiding." The sleeve of the single was a stark red-and-black painting of a city on fire. The B-side? A recording of "Take My Hand, Precious Lord," the hymn King asked to hear in the moments before he was murdered. A new mix appeared in 2020, which added Memphis police dispatch recordings from the night of King's murder. Directly below the video clip sits a looped GIF of the Zapruder kill shot.[9]

Mary Noel Kershaw died in 1989, and later, Jack Kershaw established the Mary Noel Kershaw Foundation, a nonprofit organization brought under the umbrella of the "League of the South," the white nationalist, neo-Confederate group cofounded by Kershaw in the 1990s. This organization, designated a hate group by the Southern Poverty Law Center in 2000, became more radical in the 2000s and 2010s, and worked with other like-minded groups to promote the "Unite the Right" rally in Charlottesville in 2017, ostensibly to protest the proposed removal of a Robert E. Lee statue. That same year, a Tennessee minister faced public pressure after a news team uncovered that he had shifted money from his conservative Christian home-schooling organization through the Mary Noel Kershaw Foundation. He denied the accusations, but the foundation also appeared to have used its funds to support self-defense training for League of the South members. On one level, the League of the South offered Kershaw one more organizational soapbox for his brand of southern white nationalism. However, the political sides had shifted, and what was once perceived as cranky defiance, regardless of his intent, now openly reflected the white supremacy only hinted at earlier. Kershaw talked about race so abstractly that the idea almost floated away in a cloud of white southern doublespeak. Throughout his life, though, Kershaw spoke consistently on the dangers inherent to desegregation and the impact of Black liberation on Nashville and the South. By the 2000s, the hazy blur of winking justifications gave way to much firmer proclamations of white supremacy. By the 2000s, for example, he openly talked of secession, and speaking on the history of desegregation in 2008, Kershaw noted, "we can see that it has not exactly borne fine fruit."[10] At times, Kershaw seemed to troll the regional culture wars of the time. A reporter asked Kershaw if the League of the South was racist. He responded with verve: "absolutely not. We have Negro members."[11] A month later, Kershaw argued that Black people deserved reparations, which would have raised eyebrows if he had not immediately followed it by including white southerners due not to slavery but to Sherman's march through Georgia.[12]

Kershaw argued throughout this period that Black people wanted to live separately from white people. In a 2003 interview, Kershaw argued (in response to being called a racist—and moments after using the n-word), "I can tell a difference between black and white. If you are such a racist that you don't know the difference between black and white, you're insulting your black brother, because he's different and he's proud of it and he wants to develop that way."[13] In 2005, Kershaw spoke on slavery in a public forum at Austin Peay University. To an audience comprised primarily of Black students, Kershaw argued that the mistreatment of enslaved people had been distorted and exaggerated. "Some slaves," a writer quoted Kershaw, "probably did receive a few 'bops on the head.'" Still, "slaves were treated well and received three square meals a day, medical care and the Christian religion." "He spoke these words," the writer noted, "without blinking, flinching or embarrassment."[14] Kershaw enjoyed puncturing serious debate or academic discourse with an arched eyebrow or a deflating humorous comment. Whether or not he sincerely held these beliefs, and it is impossible to gauge where the earnestness ended and the trolling began, Kershaw relished the attention and the notoriety. Throughout his life, civil rights and desegregation served as unserious punchlines for Kershaw, who instead aimed to win on technicalities or exhaustion, whether it was school boards or the assassination of Martin Luther King Jr.

The Forrest statue of the 1990s emerges from this morass of opinionated racism and pointed white activism. Kershaw's turn to build the massive sculpture seems spontaneous. After years of painting large-scale paintings of Joan of Arc and nude portraits of his friends' wives—always the provocateur—Kershaw procured "bath-fixture material" and a cherry picker and started in on his Forrest.[15] Kershaw's use of butcher knives, polyurethane blocks, and plastic eyes places the piece charitably in the realm of outsider art, though he saw the process as part of a larger conversation of art history. In a newspaper column in the weeks after the unveiling, Kershaw laid out reasons behind the statue, which served as a rationalization of his methods and intent. Equal parts defensive and delighted, Kershaw positioned himself as a present-minded futurist. "The statue of Forrest that I built," Kershaw argued, "is thoroughly appropriate to its time and place." At the same time, he rejected claims that his art was traditional. "The statue," Kershaw wrote, "built like a racing yacht from polyester resin and fiberglass, it is much lighter and much stronger than 'classical' bronze strangely demanded by some of our modern young critics who in the same breath fault us for 'living in the past.'" Never far from his mind, race informed his plastic ode to Forrest. He consistently argued, regardless of sincerity, that his statue would "create a climate for civilized conversation," and he often spoke of using Forrest as a way to talk openly about race (from his perspective). "I have talked to informed blacks," Kershaw wrote, "that he dissolved the Klan, protected and encouraged blacks in Memphis, conducted no massacres, and had seven black bodyguards." "Forrest," he argued, "is an ideal role model for every young American of whatever race." Curiously, Kershaw intended to use the Nashville statue as a model for nine other Forrests to be placed across the South. "After the ninth casting," Kershaw noted, "the mold will be destroyed (unless Massachusetts wants one)."[16]

Kershaw's Forrest was a mascot for any racial issues, whether connected to desegregated schools, local politics, or larger questions of inclusion and erasure. This new iteration of Forrest refracted the past into the present: a dead-eyed killer remade with plastic Hobby Lobby eyes functioning as a hulking polyurethane metaphor for everything and nothing. Kershaw had high hopes for his piece. "I think it will promote an attitude of respect for southern culture," he said in one of the many interviews after the statue's unveiling.[17] Still, the subject of his scraping and gouging refused some value-neutral patina of neutrality. Forrest spoke to Kershaw in direct terms, and the artist worked to portray those values. No staid representation of corporate leadership, Forrest sat astride a rearing horse with a pistol and saber hoisted into the air. Kershaw condensed Forrest to pure action. "Forrest is unjustly maligned," Kershaw said years later. "Is this the villain?" Kershaw asked rhetorically, "is this a n——er-hater? No. He was a great leader and he was a great leader because he did understand that these black men were men, [and] the white men he had were men too."[18] If Kershaw meant to avoid controversy, he meant it only facetiously. Michael Hill, a cocreator of the League of the South, which he referred to as an "ethno-nationalist movement," spoke at the unveiling and echoed much of what Kershaw said in interviews.[19] "There can be no peace until we are a separate and free people again," Hill argued, and the "day of apologizing for the conduct of our Confederate ancestors is over."[20] For his part, Kershaw went straight to the point. "Somebody needs to say a good word for slavery," he told a reporter. "Where in the world," he maintained, "are the Negroes better off than today in America?"[21]

An interesting dichotomy emerges from the statue. On the one hand, it stands for most people as the only known work of Kershaw's—and thus represents to most pundits the embarrassing and amateurish output of an untrained nonartist. On the other hand, Kershaw felt inexplicably rushed to finish the project on whatever personal timetable he had concocted. Writer Connor Townes O'Neill saw in this urgency a more significant symbol of Forrest's meaning. "Standing there at the foot of the statue," O'Neill notes, "I started to pick up on a strange kind of honesty in it—the fever-dream impressionism somehow offers, to my mind, a more accurate view of Confederate history than, say, [other Forrest statues].' Forrest should look this ugly, this preposterous, in our remembrances."[22] The choppy condition of the statue and the multiple targeted attacks on it led William Dorris, who owned the property on which it stood, to spend, to his reckoning, tens of thousands of dollars to fund repairs and upkeep.[23] Dorris also maintained the Confederate flags surrounding the sculpture, which disappeared in 2004 during a dispute with the local Sons of Confederate Veterans. Dorris replaced them after the falling-out concluded, but the flags punctuated the meaning of the entire display.[24] However, the provenance of the new flags bothered Dorris, and he complained to the local press that the "last ones came from a Southern manufacturer but were built in China, and that didn't sit too well with me."[25]

Kershaw and his creation offered a spiked ball of Forrest's myth of one degree of separation: the Agrarians, Andrew Lytle, Robert Selph Henry, James Earl Ray, and Madison Smartt Bell. Bell, for his part, drew various boundaries around his connection to Kershaw. Kershaw was a "reptilian white supremacist," Bell once argued, but he "was still drawn to some of his art."[26] The early public life of Kershaw centered on his art. In early 1950, the *Nashville Tennessean* ran a piece on his burgeoning art career featuring a dramatic photograph taken by his wife.[27] The photo, in all its chiaroscuro spectacle, portrays Kershaw as if Carl Van Vechten snapped a portrait of a Thomas Hart Benton painting. A few months later, the newspaper ran a piece on his local one-artist show. The writer summarized the positive comments of the art-world critics present and claimed Kershaw had "brilliant technique" though "more gifted in sculpture than painting." There was one real criticism that catches the modern eye, given the mocking comments later aimed at Kershaw's Forrest statue. "His outstanding problem," the writer notes, "seems to be a lack of congruity between his heads and the bodies beneath them."[28]

But what of Kershaw the artist? Most commentators on the statue tend toward the shock (this is *terrible*), and it reinforces a media point made again and again that Kershaw was a crank, trolling suburban Nashville with a mind-blowingly odd eyesore. And yet, to look back at the totality of his career underscores that art, certainly early on, played as prominent a role in his life as did white national activism later. Overall, Kershaw played a major role in Nashville's art scene; he gave public lectures, curated art shows, and reviewed an exhibition of Egyptian art for the local press. An alternative trajectory materializes when looking at these old newspaper sketches as one could squint and catch a blurry glimpse of an artist on the edge of respectable culture working toward an audience. Perhaps within this narrative, Kershaw found less interest in white supremacist rabble-rousing and more interest and luck in the art world. Looking backward from the chaos sculpture of Forrest is to survey Kershaw as a workaday artist who somehow tumbled into a different arc. Instead, right as his art career seemed to be emerging, he devoted most of his public life to states' rights politics. Kershaw probably had no teetering moment between art and politics—his public statements show consistency over the decades. However, as his public art career faded, it remains helpful to understand the larger context of the Forrest statue.[29]

Despite a rancorous national reception, Kershaw had local friends. In the mid-2000s, a local columnist for the *Nashville Tennessean,* Frank Ritter, wrote a series of defensive pieces about the artist. Ritter used his column to rebut the attacks made following the Forrest unveiling.[30] Ritter described Kershaw so often as "gentle" that it took on a Homeric vibe: "very gentle, genial," "gentle and spry," "gentle-spoken," "a gentle smile," and "gentle gray-green eyes."[31] To Ritter, Kershaw represented a gentleman artist "of the old school" who never spoke of racial prejudice; he just wanted separate legal associations based on race.[32] Using the indefinite "they," Ritter later noted that "they insulted Jack's piece of art as low-brow kitsch. They labeled Jack a racist and a nut." "Well, he certainly is a fanatic about the Civil War. But this unassuming widower," Ritter countered, "is not a racist."[33] These defensive columns peaked in 2005 as Ritter wrote more openly about Kershaw's benign existence. "Does," Ritter asked, "a gentle smile and soft, gray-green eyes camouflage and hide a malevolent inner core that holds African Americans in scornful disdain?" Ritter implied that these descriptors were flat-out falsehoods and that Kershaw once worked as a building contractor who "directed an all-black crew of workers."[34]

Ritter's cheerleading did not go unnoticed by his colleagues. Dwight Lewis, a Black newspaper writer at the *Nashville Tennessean,* chided the praise heaped on Kershaw (without mentioning Ritter by name). "I wonder if Kershaw understands," Lewis pondered, "how many people feel every time they drive past that awful looking Confederate Park off Interstate 65 that features his statue as well as a display of Confederate flags."[35] Lewis had long made similar statements. Before the statue even went up, Lewis argued that Black people needed to "educate people about what the Confederacy was all about."[36] He also took aim at Kershaw and thought that the press coverage covered up his segregationist career. "People," Lewis wrote in 1998, "are letting him get away looking like an angel."[37] One canard that emerged during the removal of Confederate monuments in the twenty-first century signified that no one protested when they went up. But Black people protested Kershaw in the 1990s as they did the Nashville bust in the 1970s and most likely in the decades before, too. The cultural erasure of these objections laid the foundation for a narrative of unity and cohesion—these monuments reflected a consensus disrupted by their politicized removal, a forged civic harmony made believable through expurgation to act as a bulwark against more realistic local representation.

The decade after the Kershaw statue went up witnessed a renewed, if chaotic, wave of Forrestmania, this time with a more pronounced ambivalence if not anger. Media coverage, already primed from the Shelby Foote flush times of the early 1990s, picked up story after story of Forrest-related controversy. Some of these stories related to hidden-in-plain-sight issues, such as Middle Tennessee State University's continued use of Forrest iconography for decades. The school removed Forrest's silhouette from its logo in the 1960s, but the university ROTC building maintained the general's name into the 2000s.[38] Another flurry of stories followed the tale of a bust of Forrest, placed in Selma, Alabama. Irony defined Selma's connection to Forrest as the Union Army overwhelmed his attempt to save the town. Still, the town moved in the early 2000s to contract a monument in his honor. The mayor who approved of the monument, Joseph Smitherman, had served in the position off-and-on for thirty-five years. One of his earliest actions as mayor in 1965 was the order to use police force against Martin Luther King Jr.'s march to Montgomery, which Alabama state troopers blocked at the Edmund Pettus bridge. One of his last actions as mayor, after losing to James Perkins Jr.—who, in a 2000 run-off election, became Selma's first Black mayor—was to support the Forrest monument. Depicting a grim and steely Forrest, the Selma bust sat atop a granite base with an embedded full-color Confederate flag with the phrases "Wizard of the Saddle," "Untutored Genius," and "The First with the Most" carved into the stone—a Forrest greatest hits of sorts. Soon after its creation, the city relocated the bust away from its original location behind a historic home and to a Confederate memorial area in a local cemetery. The bust thus sat near the grave of Edmund Pettus.[39]

In 2012, unknown perpetrators stole the bust, which led to reward offers and fretting over the meaning of the act. In 2015, however, the Daughters of the Confederacy replaced the bust with a replica.[40] Together, the MTSU controversy and the Selma theft underscore the developing din that started to define Forrest's memory in the 2010s as the anti-Forrest protests grew, as did the pro-Forrest backlash to these protests, as did the pro-Forrest defensive activism to counteract changes to the monument landscape, as did the anti-Forrest protests against such moves. With Forrest, time and past collapsed into the present as anger (from all sides) toward representations of perceived actions—and in the case of Selma, actual defeat—became the story itself. The Selma monument story serves as a particularly unforgiving example of the closeness of the past as Bloody Sunday in 1965 and a 2000 Forrest bust both fell under the governing purview of a single man. As a result, Forrest of the 1860s and 1870s drifted further away from the shore of historical significance as his shadow form, with radiant spokes of self-generating narratives, created history and myth simultaneously.

In the early 2000s, the annual birthday celebration for Forrest in Memphis coincided with the one-hundredth anniversary of the Charles Niehaus statue. From blackface minstrel shows set to coincide with Forrest's birthday—a promotional email noted "you'll be rolling in the aisle"—to threats of a full-regalia Ku Klux Klan protest in Elmwood Cemetery in Memphis, race sat at the center of these proceedings.[41] Racialized language defined the Forrest image as anti-Forrest voices grew in volume and force during this period. "Forrest," the *Tri-State Defender* quoted a director of a civil rights nonprofit, "was a traitor to the United States, a racist to the core of his soul, and a slave trader."[42] A week later, the *Memphis Commercial Appeal* ran a story with a Black descendent of Forrest who argued strongly that the Niehaus statue should be removed. "Put his grave where it belongs," he maintained, "back in the woods . . . or wherever he came from."[43]

None of this sentiment was new, but the increased volume spoke to an uptick in the rage driving the Forrest conversation in the early 2000s. Since Forrest's death, his image had been driven primarily by white groups and individuals who worked to construct and preserve a manicured version of the general. Forrest's history could be explored and broadened, but the basic outlines had to be defended. Provocative and contested since his first forays into public life in the 1850s, Forrest cast a sunbaked shadow across Memphis and the South. Flurries of dissent pushed against the white narratives of Forrest's life and significance, but proponents of the general could write off much of this conflict as a form of historical ignorance—the Lost Cause of "if they only knew the real Forrest, they would celebrate him, too." As Black Memphians pushed against normative visions of Forrest, the image would shift to silence any new questioning of what he represented. No part of the Forrest image remained static, and as much as defenders wanted to believe in a consistent vision of manhood and virtue, the Forrest image mutated throughout the twentieth century. For instance, no white admirer of Forrest in the 1890s would have publicly said that an important component of the Forrest myth related to his progressive stance on civil rights. His connection to the slave trade required finessing through fictions and distortions (*he never divided families*). Still, this defensiveness emerged from irritation at northern attacks on his character rather than any real sense of humanity toward Blacks.

This revisionism worked as the public face of the general because it gradually consumed most criticism and debate. The strength of the Forrest image was precisely what most defenders of the general denied even existed: a continual shifting and reorienting of what Forrest meant culturally, politically, or historically. At the same time, the image always refracted the race and racism of the moment, whether the overt white supremacy of the early twentieth century, the whispered defensive whiteness of mid-century Memphis, or the contested space of the post–civil rights South. As Black protests gained visibility in the second half of the twentieth century, the patchwork of rationalizations that defined the Forrest image began to fracture. Black critics of Forrest found an increasingly louder voice by the 1970s, and protests against the general became public, such as with the move to add a bust of Forrest to the Tennessee capitol. The reaction was twofold: remake Forrest as a supporter of Black rights (with a growing emphasis on the Pole-Bearers speech after the war) and a subtle erasure of the anti-Forrest activism from the public narrative. But cracks around the base always existed—an acknowledgment that Forrest represented more than just heroism. The removal of the Confederate flags in Forrest Park after the assassination of Martin Luther King Jr., for example, hints at an understanding of the racial volatility that buttressed the Forrest statue.[44] This raw combination of the relativity of meaning, cynical defensiveness, and public erasure of Black counter-voices made the pro-Forrest discourse difficult to challenge as it served as the ersatz culture of contentment. Thus, throughout the early 2000s, as the general came under more regular attack, the pro-Forrest reaction tended toward some version of "this is new, no one complained in the past about these monuments." Silencing led to a false history of consensus—a vaporous narrative built out of its own fabrications.

The story of Forrest Park reflects these changes. An alternative plotline developed adjacent to the Forrest statue in Memphis, where the ownership of the park opened up new ways to talk about the statue without intentionally talking about the statue. Between 1988 and the early 2010s, the University of Tennessee Medical Center played a large role in redefining the conversation surrounding the park. In the 1980s, the university's move to add exercise equipment sparked a backlash in the Black community out of fear that the revitalized park would generate renewed attention to the statue. The ambiguous nature of who owned the property, something unknown to the vast percentage of people driving past or walking through the park, would continue until the early 2010s. The tensions between a university looking to address a cluttered piece of public land abutting their campus and a city increasingly wary as to what role it should play in a consistently explosive situation had little to do directly with the Forrest statue and, of course, had everything to do with the Forrest statue. As the *Commercial Appeal* argued in 2008, the "modern university's close proximity to the symbol of the Old South illustrates the contrast between the area's past of racial unrest" and any modified expectations the public might have of the space.[45] After years of debate, the city rechristened Forrest Park as the blandly innocuous "Health Sciences Park" in 2013.[46] In explaining its decision, the City Council noted that "the names evoked a racist past."[47] The move had an immediate impact, as the Ku Klux Klan demonstrated, the most violent since the late 1990s when Kershaw erected his statue.[48]

As Memphis changed the name of the park (all Confederate-themed parks in the city underwent similar redesignations), a revitalized push to remove the Forrest statue began to emerge. The complexity of "Forrest Park"—hosting both a monument and a gravesite—made the Memphis removal story much more convoluted than in other places. A series of legislative back-and-forths further muddied the waters. In 2015, the City Council voted to exhume and rebury the bodies of Forrest and his wife.[49] A following vote a month later approved the removal of the statue, but an act passed in 2013 and subsequently amended made it nearly impossible to make any substantial changes to the park.[50] Several competing threads emerged during this period, illustrating the difficulty of crafting a consensus. The intentional invisibility placed on Black protestors and the casual visibility of the statue and the park, regardless of name, provided a fake history of imbalanced perspectives. In reality, Black voices had opposed the existing and newly installed monuments for decades. From a pro-general angle, the advantage of the Forrest image was its adaptability and disinterest in yesterday. The Forrest image always faced the present moment. Couched in historical terms and ideology, the monument only ever said something about the Now instead of the infinitely corruptible and changeable Then. But malleability had limits, and by the 2010s, a breaking point emerged as too many fissures and too few galvanizing storylines obliterated cohesion. Name changes, legislative maneuvering, and pivoting from statue to gravesite, these shifts only cluttered directions toward saving the statue.[51]

During the late twentieth century, the question of Confederate iconography, especially the use of the battle flag, had struck at the heart of the significance of Civil War memory. Weaponized throughout the civil rights movement, which corresponded to a general resurgence of the banner due to the Civil War Centennial, the Confederate battle flag had a long history of tension and division. An occasional public building or high school would remove the flag, which might spark local or regional discussion, but widespread removal seemed unlikely. A critical mass of dissent failed to materialize in the 1990s and early 2000s, even as Georgia removed the "stars and bars" from the state flag in 2001. The Confederate flag and the many Confederate memorials that dotted the South's landscape benefited from the hegemony of complacency: removal seemed too jarring, radical, and dramatic. The culture wars of the 1990s placed more emphasis on Civil War memorials, especially in terms of their racial connotations, but a certain false historicism tended to keep them in place. Opponents of removal argued convincingly that these monuments, most of them only seventy to eighty years old, represented forever signposts of the ancient South. As for the flag, the "heritage not hate" mantra diluted the discussion enough to kick the removal can down the road for another generation. As with the monuments and iconography, the Confederate flag seemed forever part of the public arena; the needle would move a bit one way or another, but a solid center held everything in stasis.

On the evening of June 17, 2015, Dylann Roof, a white supremacist in his early twenties, interrupted a church study group at the Emanuel African Methodist Episcopal Church in Charleston, South Carolina. Founded in the 1810s, the church, known as Mother Emanuel, stood as the oldest African Methodist Episcopal church in the South. Roof entered the church and joined a bible study in progress with twelve Black congregation members. Then, as the group turned to pray, Roof started firing a semiautomatic pistol he had tucked into a fanny pack. Across six minutes, Roof berated the group with racist language as he shot and killed nine churchgoers, including Susie Jackson, an eighty-seven-year-old choir member. Roof allegedly planned to kill himself after the attack but ran out of ammunition. The next morning, after a brief manhunt and a tip from a woman who spotted his car, police arrested Roof after a traffic stop over two hundred miles away and just across the North Carolina border.

The brazen brutality of Roof's actions inevitably led to scrutiny of his Internet and social media presence. Roof's white supremacist views came into focus as his racist manifesto and various online associations mirrored the racial outbursts made in the church. The survivors of the shooting spoke of the racist invective shouted by Roof as he aimed at the Black men and women in the church that evening. Photographs of Roof soon emerged that visually corroborated these views. A series of images—one with him crouching in a Gold's Gym tank top and bucket hat while holding out a Confederate flag, another with him holding the flag and a semiautomatic handgun looking down at the lens through mirrored sunglasses, another featuring the flag and a neo-Nazi shirt, and a fourth with Roof standing gripping an American flag lit on fire—went viral, moving the conversation toward what to do with these symbols. The overtness of Roof's muddle of Nazism, white supremacy, and Confederate iconography was far from new. Still, its correlation to the mass killing at Mother Emanuel forced a dialogue that had long simmered without any resolution. After decades of intermittent attention to the Confederate flag and its twentieth-century history of anti-Black demonstrations—as the state ordered the police to meet the marchers with force in Selma in 1965, for instance, many of the officers held Confederate flags along with their batons)—the Roof murders made it impossible for the media to ignore the optics, if not the complete history, of the Confederate symbol.

In the days after the Mother Emanuel mass shooting, the most striking visual came from the South Carolina state capitol building one hundred miles away in Columbia. There, two flags, the United States and South Carolina banners, had been lowered to half-staff in honor of the deceased. A third flag, however, the stars and bars, still waved at full staff. The Confederate flag remained high over the state capitol through legislative decree (only the governor could order it lowered) and pragmatic construction (it could not be physically set at half-staff).[52] On the Sunday following the murders (which took place on a Wednesday), South Carolina governor Nikki Haley, a Republican, attended memorial services at Mother Emanuel. The day before, over a thousand people showed up at the capitol to protest the flag's continued presence, and whether or not this weighed on Haley, the governor called for a press conference for the following Monday. "We," Haley told the press, "are not going to allow this symbol [the Confederate flag] to divide us any longer."[53] Haley thus called for the flag's removal and signed legislation to that effect in early July. Just two decades earlier, the vast majority of Republicans in the state opposed any action against the Confederate flag—and ousted a Republican governor who dared broach the subject. June 17 changed the narrative. Haley's actions gave cover to Republicans to come out against the prominent display of the flag near the capitol (the state Senate voted in favor of removal thirty-seven to three, and the state House voted ninety-four to twenty). "I just didn't have the balls for five years to do it," Rep. Doug Brannon noted after the vote, "but when my friend [the senior pastor, Clementa C. Pinkney, who had served in the statehouse with Brannon] was assassinated for being nothing more than a black man, I decided it was time for that thing to be off the Statehouse grounds." "It's not just a symbol of hate," Brannon argued, "it's actually a symbol of pride in one's hatred."[54]

Haley's actions garnered bipartisan support and applause. In his widely seen eulogy to the victims, President Obama noted that Haley's "recent eloquence" was "worthy of praise."[55] However, as the years passed and Donald Trump used Confederate removals as political kindling, Haley seemed to backtrack. In 2019, promoting her recent book, Haley implied that Roof ruined a perfectly good symbol. "The evil act [Roof] had committed," Haley wrote, "had robbed the good-intentioned South Carolinians who supported the flag of this symbol of heritage and service." During interviews on her book tour, she argued that Roof "hijacked" the symbolism and meaning of the Confederate flag.[56] Whatever consensus existed in the aftermath of the horrors perpetuated at Mother Emanuel dissipated during the Trump years as the culture wars surrounding Confederate memory reached a fever point. With presidential ambitions for 2024, Haley attempted to thread the needle, arguing for its removal while amplifying the idea that people could simply disagree about it representing slavery and secession. The speed at which the flag came down from the South Carolina state capitol presaged as much of the changes over the next few years as did the hesitating politicking that followed. Still, Roof's murderous actions in 2015 redrew the map of Civil War commemoration. Roof's violent racism brought into tragic relief how Confederate symbols sat intimately with Nazi and white power emblems. Charleston ended the interminable Confederate stalemate, but the reverberations across dozens of southern cities had no clear endpoint.

Roof's actions may have stirred new thinking in some observers, but the murders also accelerated other politicians to act on an issue they had already started to question. Mitch Landrieu, mayor of New Orleans, had drifted into the choppy waters of removal in the months preceding the Roof shooting. The memorial landscape of New Orleans featured several high- and low-profile Confederate markers, most of which the city erected between the 1880s and 1910s. The most visible symbol, however, stood atop a sixty-foot column in the middle of a central city traffic circle, once known as Tivoli Circle, that linked Uptown to downtown. In 1870, right after Lee's death, a city group fundraised for a statue honoring the general, who had only wisps of a connection to New Orleans. In 1877 (just a few months before Forrest's death), the city rechristened the intersection as Lee Place, though the traffic circle remained officially Tivoli Circle. Seven years later, the city placed a sixteen-and-a-half-foot bronze sculpture by Alexander Doyle on the column. Doyle, an artist from Ohio, lived in New Orleans in the 1880s and designed several Confederate monuments for the city, including a statue celebrating General P. G. T. Beauregard (who actually had strong connections to the city). Central to the fundraising and creation of the Lee statue stood Charles E. Fenner, a Louisiana lawyer and Civil War veteran who fought in several campaigns, including the Battle of Nashville. After the war, Fenner played a role in the White League, a white nationalist terrorist organization in New Orleans similar to the Ku Klux Klan.[57] He also served on the Supreme Court of Louisiana, where he wrote the state's decision in *Ex Parte Plessy,* establishing the core idea of "separate but equal," later adopted by the U.S. Supreme Court in its radical segregation decision in 1896. If Robert E. Lee maintained little connection to the city, Fenner reflected the most virulent white supremacist attitudes of late nineteenth-century New Orleans. Overall, Lee Place represents the ideologies of Fenner and his associates more deliberately than anything Lee may have meant spiritually to the city.

The Lee monument loomed over the New Orleans Central Business District throughout the twentieth century. However, as the debates over Confederate monuments grew in the early twenty-first century, the Lee statue generated more discussion. In 2010, Mitch Landrieu became mayor of New Orleans and was the first white mayor since 1978, when his father, Moon Landrieu, left office. Landrieu won reelection in 2014, and in his second term, he shifted to coming up with a solution to the Confederate markers dotting the city's public spaces. Wynton Marsalis, jazz musician and family friend, asked Landrieu to consider the Lee statue. "What does he represent?" Marsalis asked Landrieu, "and in that most prominent space in the city of New Orleans, does that space reflect who we were, who we want to be or who we are?"[58] This conversation predated the Roof murders, but it primed the actions to follow. In his memoir, Landrieu noted that Roof's actions forced him to "double down" and confront his city's memorials to white supremacy. "We cannot change the past," he writes, "but we are not obligated to cave in to some nostalgia-coated idea that a statue is good because it's old. Symbols matter."[59] Six months after the Mother Emanuel shooting, the New Orleans City Council voted to remove the Lee statue and three others, including the Battle of Liberty Place monument, which had long been the target of scorn as it celebrated the anti-government actions of the White League (and served as a meeting place for the Ku Klux Klan in the 1970s). On May 19, 2017, as Landrieu gave an impassioned speech on the context and history of the statue, work crews used a crane to remove Lee from its pedestal, leaving the column unadorned.[60]

The removal of Lee in New Orleans spawned a rancorous response, with one Republican lawmaker in Mississippi, who represented the district where Emmett Till was murdered, calling for the lynching of those responsible.[61] Anger roared through the summer of 2017 as southern cities tackled their own memorial landscapes. Although the public needle tilted toward removal, at least for many of the higher-profile monuments, a furious backlash arose from Confederate-affiliated organizations and many white supremacist groups. These groups, sometimes in unison, sometimes separately, argued that these removals represented an attack on southern history, generally, and often more explicitly white culture. Landrieu's push to remove Lee exposed the raw underpinnings of what these monuments long represented. For scholars of memory and history, these findings signified nothing new as fragments of this discourse dated back decades, but the prominent nature of the removals, not to mention an uptick in the anxiety and fear related to police violence and mass shootings, provided a spikier, thornier context for these actions and reactions. The lengthy stalemate over Confederate flags and monuments had taken on its own lifespan, too, as the controversy seemed to take on a historic weight more than the monuments themselves. After decades of chatter, it seemed as if the different vectors of Civil War memory would exist in an infinite reaction loop of nonaction. Once statues started to come down, however, the stakes had changed, and the old warhorses of "heritage not hate" and statues representing immutable pillars of the past no longer worked as endpoints to the discourse. The imagined fears of memorial erasure had, by the 2010s, real uncertainties as removal reshaped the silhouette of southern parks, public buildings, and streets. This fury came to a head with another Robert E. Lee one thousand miles away from New Orleans.

Three months before the Lee Place removal, the City Council of Charlottesville, Virginia, voted to remove the equestrian statue of Robert E. Lee, which had stood in Lee Park in the city's historic district since 1924. Dedicated in 1924, the statue was commissioned by a wealthy Charlottesville stockbroker named Paul Goodloe McIntire, who concocted a series of public parks and sculptures throughout the city. Similar to the New Orleans statue—though Lee had infinitely more connections to the area—the monument fell under attack in the months after the Roof shootings. Once the city decided to remove the statue (and rename the park), the Sons of Confederate Veterans and other groups filed a lawsuit seeking to block the proposal. A complex web of legal maneuvering, state laws, and injunctions kept the Lee statue on its pedestal, but the removal attempts had unleashed a torrent of resentment. To the opponents of removal, the idea of taking down Lee hit nerves far removed from the Civil War. The push to remove Confederate flags and memorials from public spaces symbolized a larger battle of political correctness and, to them, "historical vandalism."[62] A particular strain of conservative ideology, then, rather than just a specific interest in Lee, served to incite the response. Richard Spencer, a white nationalist, organized a rally in mid-May 2017 to protest the Lee removal. This rally, lit by the protestors carrying burning tiki torches, centered on the phrases "you will not replace us" and "Jews will not replace us." Charlottesville's move to take down Lee had unintentionally helped coalesce an assembly fueled by white nationalism, racism, and antisemitism.[63]

These uglier ideologies had long worked on the public fringe of the Confederate memory discourse, with the obvious exception of the Ku Klux Klan, but by the 2010s, defenders of Civil War monuments and protectors of civic displays honoring white southern heroes seemed to take second billing. No longer hiding intentions under legalese or the fictions of historical preservation, these anti-removal groups openly argued in racial and antisemitic terms. These statues held special meaning for white supremacists because of the white supremacy embedded in their creation and symbolism. Removing these monuments, at least as argued by the groups beginning to gather in the 2010s, represented a public blow to the continuation of white dominance. Lee (and the others) had to be protected. Donald Trump's electoral victory in 2016 played a role, as many right-wing activist groups saw their values and visions amplified by the new administration as it came into power right as Charlottesville took up the Lee statue matter. Spencer's opening tiki-torch foray further politicized the memorial space, which had also been recently used as a campaign backdrop for a Republican gubernatorial candidate. No longer an issue tethered to hoary disagreements over Civil War memory, the ideological arena established in the summer of 2017 spoke to the outrage of the "alt-right," a term credited to Spencer, and the growing confluence of young white nationalists angry at what they saw as the ominous expansion of multiculturalism, immigration, and diversity initiatives. The Lee statue merely offered a magnetic pole where different groups could congregate.

As the Lee statue impasse persisted throughout the summer, small rallies and demonstrations rattled through Charlottesville. These groups included neo-Nazis, neo-fascists, the Ku Klux Klan, and multiple smaller alt-right organizations. In August, a larger, more formidable gathering came together under the title "Unite the Right." This rally assembled representatives from the many fragments of the white nationalist Venn diagram, including militias and the League of the South—Jack Kershaw's old organization. The openly planned nature of this rally drew in a number of counter-protesters, mainly from the area, but also outsider groups angered by the rise of the alt-right. Throughout the weekend, both the alt-right protestors and the counter-protestors had armed individuals present at the rally as Virginia allowed open-carry of firearms. Tensions, already high due to the white nationalist rally, crested with the individual conflicts between the various groups. On the evening of August 11, an unsanctioned march snaked through the University of Virginia campus as alt-right groups (again with lit tiki torches) shouted antisemitic, racist, and neo-Nazi slogans such as "you will not replace us," "white lives matter," and "Blood and Soil."[64] Violence broke out between the groups, forcing the Virginia State Police to intervene. The next day, hours before the planned (and permitted) start time of noon, violence again erupted, compelling the city to declare a state of emergency. Assaults and arrests coursed through Charlottesville, culminating in the death of Heather Heyer, a white counter-protestor, killed by a speeding car driven directly into the crowd. Police later arrested the driver, a twenty-year-old neo-Nazi, who was eventually charged with over two dozen federal hate crimes. A Virginia judge sentenced the driver to two life terms without parole.[65]

The messy spiraling of violence stemming from the alt-right defense of the Robert E. Lee statue roiled the already murky removal proposition. A week after the "Unite the Right" rally, the City Council, in response to Heyer's murder, voted to cover the Lee statue (and a nearby statue honoring Stonewall Jackson) with black shrouds.[66] The judge who earlier allowed the injunction to prevent removal later ordered these shrouds removed in February 2018. Still, in the weeks and months (and years) following the rally, pro-removal activists routinely tagged the statues with graffiti, including anti-Trump slogans. After mainly staying silent on Twitter the afternoon of the rally, Trump released a statement: "We condemn in the strongest possible terms this egregious display of hatred, bigotry and violence on many sides. On many sides."[67] Trump's role in Charlottesville gave legs to the alt-right, many of whom already felt Trump reflected their general perspectives and goals. The "many sides" part of Trump's response sparked derision as it equated the actions and reactions of the two groups, seemingly conflating fascism with anti-fascism while denying any moral response to the violence and death caused by the rally. In an apparent attempt to clarify his infamous comments, Trump noted that there were "very fine people on both sides." Asked to explain this comment two years later, Trump replied, "if you look at what I said, you will see that that question was answered perfectly." "And," he continued, "I was talking about people that went because they felt very strongly about the monument to Robert E. Lee, a great general."[68]

Trump's comments also gave energy to the white nationalist context for the Lee removal. The elimination of Confederate monuments, in other words, struck directly at the stated fears of cultural erasure by white nationalists. Trump's purposeful ambiguity thus emboldened exactly the individuals and groups who had reoriented the fight over Civil War memory as a fight to preserve white supremacy. To be fair, these arguments had existed in some form or another since the 1950s when anti-segregationists used the monuments as a backdrop to espouse their beliefs, but the barefaced turn to antisemitism and neo-Nazism by more public-facing organizations—not to mention the implied agreement or at least the lack of denouncement by the president—emboldened the more radical factions within the discourse. No longer couched in the language of heritage or family histories, however imprecise and loaded those designations ever were, the argument over the continued presence of Confederate monuments now was shaped openly by the desires and interests of white supremacists.

As a narrative began to emerge that seemed to connect the Roof killings directly to the removal of Confederate monuments, an alternative network of connectors started to converge in Memphis. As in New Orleans and Charlottesville—and dozens of other southern cities and towns—the calls to remove Confederate monuments grew in volume in the mid-2010s. The Memphis connection to its Civil War past, generally, and Forrest, specifically, meant that the trajectory of removal played out in unique ways. Unlike Lee, Forrest had always provoked a more barbed response. Freed of the niceties that shaped Lee's memory and allowed for a wider middle path between the two poles of preserving or eliminating statues, Forrest's image cast cut a jagged outline that rebuked any easy way down the center of public opinion. Race had forever defined significant aspects of the Forrest story, too. As defenders of Lee could obfuscate and complicate his connection to slavery and secession, Forrest struck a different tone since much of his appeal derived expressly from his actions before, during, and after the war. As much as the Mother Emanuel mass shooting framed the general shift to removal, the violent death of a young Black man far removed from the South had as large an impact on the Forrest story. The road to removal in Memphis thus came through a city seven hundred miles away: Cleveland, Ohio.

On the afternoon of November 22, 2014, police officer Timothy Loehmann shot and killed Tamir Rice, a twelve-year-old boy, outside a recreational center in Cleveland. Police responded following a 911 call made by a man who witnessed Rice, who was Black, brandishing what appeared to be a gun. The caller noted that he believed the weapon to be fake, though he admitted being frightened by the boy's actions. The police soon arrived on the scene with Loehmann exiting the car and firing shots at Rice within two seconds of approaching him (and before his partner, Frank Garmback, had time to stop and exit the vehicle). Ninety seconds later, officers tackled and detained Rice's fourteen-year-old sister, who ran toward her brother. The weapon turned out to be an Airsoft replica that a friend had given Rice right before the emergency call. Rice died the next day.

Throughout 2015, the city of Cleveland investigated the killing and subsequently delivered its report to the county prosecutor. The police-shooting death of Rice came two and a half years after the killing of Trayvon Martin in 2012, which ended in a murder acquittal and the eventual organizing of Black Lives Matter. This protest movement grew throughout 2014 after a series of high-profile Black deaths by police officers. Tamir Rice's death occurred at the apex of a nationwide conversation about Black murders and deaths at the hands of police officers. Two days after the shooting, a grand jury declined to indict a white police officer in another high-profile shooting in Ferguson, Missouri. Amid much public scrutiny and a rapidly growing Black Lives Matter movement, the Rice case struck a national chord, especially as video surfaced both of Rice playing with the gun and the rapidity of Loehmann's actions to shoot the young man. In December 2015, a grand jury decided not to indict the two officers, effectively ending the criminal case involving Rice's death.

The grand jury's dismissal resonated loudly across the nation. In Memphis, Tami Sawyer, a Black civil rights activist and a leader in the local Black Lives Matter movement, felt an immediate impulse: "meet at Forrest." Sawyer used the raw moment to bring a group of Memphis activists together to form a prayer circle in front of the 1905 statue. Her symbolic act connected Nathan Bedford Forrest directly to the contemporary anger over police brutality and the killing of unarmed Black Americans. Over seven hundred miles separated Cleveland from Memphis, but the killing of Rice directly affected various entwined Black protest movements in Memphis. Through Sawyer, the grand jury's decision in Ohio served as a galvanizing moment of dissent and action. The Forrest image had long encompassed anger and violence towards Black men and women. Tamir Rice's death inspired Sawyer to convene in the park. Tamir Rice's death motivated activist groups in Memphis to begin to converge behind a common goal. Tamir Rice's death eventually led to an upheaval of the Memphis landscape. Two years, almost to the day, after the Rice grand jury refused to indict the police officers, a crane wrenched the Forrest statue from its base. The media generally linked the toppling of the Forrest statue to the growing wave of removals of Confederate monuments across the United States in the 2010s. But at its heart, the removal of Forrest connected to the tragic death of a young Black preteen near a gazebo in Cleveland. *Meet at Forrest.*[69]

For decades, the Forrest statue had served as a site for protests, small and large. As cities began to grapple with their Confederate monuments in the aftermath of Charleston, Memphis had long encountered challenges to Forrest Park and the 1905 statue. The city met most of these trials with a mixture of legislative kick-the-can-down-the-road and confidence that a tradition of public centrism would prevail, disallowing any civic action. Crowds would gather, crowds would disperse, and the statue would recede into the shadows once more—seen but ignored, present but disregarded. The politics of Forrest refused easy legislative recourse, especially in a city with a complex overlay of demographic interests and desires. If anything preserved the Forrest statue for over its century-plus lifespan, it related to a casual acceptance of white supremacy, on the one hand, and a more fraught conservationist posture of waiting it out, on the other. By the 2010s, however, neither tack worked. External pressures and, more importantly, internal activism pushed Memphis to a crossroads. Inaction could no longer be sustained.

Tami Sawyer's impulsive call to meet at Forrest linked two critical threads. In one move, she took the growing furor over police brutality and its cruel impact on Black communities and connected it directly and forcefully to the local involvement and history of Memphis. Sawyer's activism led her to cofound #TakeEmDown901, an organization focused on removing the Confederate monuments in Memphis, whose area code provided a numeric identifier for the group.[70] The organization helped unite groups affiliated with Black Lives Matter and individuals enraged by the growing visibility of the Confederate flags. In Virginia, Spencer and others on the alt-right had appropriated Lee and the Confederate battle flag to give historical resonance to their desire to bring about a white supremacist resurgence. By bridging the debate over Confederate monuments to the issues central to Black Lives Matter, Sawyer and others had responded, consciously or otherwise, by elevating the removal of Forrest to a symbol of civic righteousness. "These are monuments," Sawyer contended, "to symbols of racism and hatred and nothing more."[71] Charlottesville raised the stakes, and at a rally at Health Sciences Park, Sawyer argued, "What these statues do is give power to a white supremacist movement that is reemerging and growing as we speak every day."[72] Though broadly present-minded and future-oriented, these protests also sought to democratize the past by expanding historical narratives and including voices previously erased or omitted. The Civil War monuments played a major role in these tensions of the 2010s because their vectors of memory crashed through time and space, collapsing past, present, and future into a bronze statement of historical falsity and distortion.

The death of Tamir Rice set the Memphis wheels in motion in 2015, and the death of Heather Heyer galvanized large parts of the city to make good on the promises of removal and renewal. Death, violent and blood-spattered death, long defined Forrest's life and memory. From the cruelty of his Memphis slave pens to the bluffs at Fort Pillow to the violence threatened and insinuated by the Ku Klux Klan, Forrest represented the racial brutalities of the white South. His statue, unveiled in 1905, reoriented these actions into a memorial script of honor and white male integrity—violence silently rewritten as an attribute. Nevertheless, Forrest, in 1864, say, or 1905, or 1998, or 2017 continued to signify the core elements of his life and career, no matter how redefined for any contemporary audience. By the late 2010s, the bonds linking the imagined past and an ideological present stretched to the point of snapping, and the Forrest image sat at the center of this tension. Charlottesville served as the hinge and impetus for the final chapter of the Forrest statue. After a century and a half of the general's devotees wanting Forrest to stand next to Lee in the historical imagining of the Civil War, it happened, but in ways far removed from the expectation of his advocates.

Lee Millar stood as a local foil to Sawyer's activism. Millar, who claimed Forrest as a distant relative, was a prominent voice in the debate. A member of the Sons of Confederate Veterans, Millar often spoke about the importance of the Forrest statue and Forrest's image to Memphis. Millar was a steadfast proponent that the monument speaks to the valor and honor of Forrest, the general and man. His argument bounced between two poles: removal represented a historical wrong, and Forrest signified an honorable part of Memphis's history. "You should never tear down history," Millar said in an interview. "You should always add to it."[73] Millar rarely spoke of the meta-narrative of white supremacy that shaped so much of the discourse in Virginia. Instead, Millar tended to focus on portraying Forrest through the lens of his historical perspective. The statue, Millar argued, "had nothing to do with white supremacy, it had nothing to do with Jim Crow laws, it had nothing to do with racism."[74] "The citizens back then [in 1905]," Millar said in another interview, "were erecting these statues to those veterans." "It had nothing to do with race," he maintained, "nothing to do with slavery."[75] Instead, Millar saw the removal as an affront to a hero that had not been adequately understood. Millar's view of Forrest incorporated slavery, but he remained steadfast in his conviction that, if only people knew more about the realities of Forrest's life and career, they would see the general in a similar light. This angle had existed in various forms for generations, but Millar worked to reenvision a Shelby Foote–styled argument for a contemporary audience.

As Sawyer and Millar developed into the spokespeople of the two primary sides of the public debate, less open maneuverings kept Forrest on Union Avenue. Decades of legislative choreographies made it nearly impossible to imagine Forrest leaving his pedestal. Tennessee, for example, had passed state laws such as the oft-amended Tennessee Heritage Protection Act forbidding the removal of Confederate monuments without state approval. The gravesite aspect of the memorial, too, created even more obstacles to removal. For most of the 1990s and 2000s, even if the city had wanted to make a move, it would have required legalistic finagling of a high order to bring any action to bear.[76] The growing chorus of grassroots opposition led by Sawyer and others represented a new and real threat to the frayed removal centrism that abetted state laws, freezing any shift toward change. Then, in a swift and unexpected move in December 2017, the Memphis city government sold the park—as well as the rechristened Fourth Bluff Park, where a statue of Jefferson Davis stood—to a nonprofit organization called Memphis Greenspace. Run by Van Turner Jr., Memphis Greenspace sought to control the two parks. In a unanimous vote, the city of Memphis sold the public spaces to Turner's company for $1,000 per park. Memphis mayor Jim Strickland said that the deal had been worked out for months, and Turner had found the necessary, if legally gray, loophole to remove the Forrest statue. The speed and covert nature provided cover to the city from protests, and as soon as the City Council ratified the contract, construction crews entered Health Science Park.[77]

On the evening of December 20, 2017, one hundred or so spectators (and perhaps twice as many police officers) gathered to witness the removal of the Forrest statue. Earlier that day, at 5:30 p.m., the Memphis City Council voted unanimously to remove Forrest and a statue honoring Jefferson Davis. Four hours later, Forrest was gone. The crane that pulled the statue off its base, first erected in 1905, left an empty pedestal as a useful metaphor for the city's uneasy relationship with its past. Now, the city could project onto this nondescript marble base infinite new representations of Memphis's new meanings. As heavy machinery carried off Forrest, they also capped off a 112-year saga that came to define (sometimes raucously, sometimes silently) the city's relationship to the Civil War, to the past, and to itself. This moment unleashed endless questions about what would come next, the meaning of the past in the present, and the past's power over the present. After 112 years, a seemingly unmovable monument, which had weathered public storm after public storm, collapsed under the pressure of growing Black anger and resentment. "I looked Nathan Bedford in the eyes," Sawyer told the *New York Times*, "and shed a tear for my ancestors."[78] "The park has always been a park of death," Van Turner asserted in 2022. "Now it's become a park of life and vibrancy," he continued, "of new beginnings."[79]

The Mother Emanuel murders in 2015 and the George Floyd murder in 2020 served as the cruel bookends to a sea change in how Americans viewed Confederate monuments and iconography. After decades of cultural seesawing, the racially motivated violence of the 2010s and the overt use of Confederate flags by the perpetrators and advocates for these attacks led to a national reckoning about these symbols. Of the many monuments removed during this period—one hundred came down in the aftermath of Floyd's death—most were simply whisked away from public view. Some of these monuments returned to private Confederate memorial groups, and others were placed in storage—removed, to be sure, but temporarily.[80] The impermanent nature of these removals—not to mention the potential of long-term court cases—gave some people hope that the statues could return.[81] In a 2018 interview with NPR, Millar stated clearly that the statues need to return. "The statues," Millar argued, "deserve to be in the public sphere because they were meant to honor military service."[82] Still, the empty pedestals slowly cast their own foreshortened shadows in Memphis. Just as the statues invoked an immutable feeling that they had always existed, so too did their crane-altered marble bases. The statues still sat in warehouses, but the landscape had changed. Opponents of removal often argued that the statues represented lessons in history and that eliminating Confederate monuments served to erase the past. "But," as one scholar notes, "monuments aren't history lessons—they're pledges of allegiance."[83]

On September 7, 2010, Jack Kershaw died at the age of ninety-six. Friends kept the news of his death out of the press until after a memorial service, presumably over privacy concerns. His obituary referred to him as a "gold-plated eccentric." The notice designates the Forrest statue as his "most notable art piece." Born only a handful of years after the construction of the 1905 statue, Kershaw died just as the final wave of protests and demonstrations brought it down. In 2017, amid the fight in Memphis, someone doused the Kershaw statue with a thick coat of pink paint. William Dorris, the landowner, decided to keep the statue in its newly smeared condition, which added a cartoonish dimension to the already peculiar vision in polystyrene south of Nashville. Dorris died a few years afterward, in 2020, draping Kershaw's Forrest with a series of unanswered questions. In a final splash of media attention, Dorris's will stipulated that five million dollars of his estate (a comically exaggerated figure) would go to his Border Collie, Lulu. The property and statue itself went to the Battle of Nashville Trust. The owners of the trust released a statement disputing Dorris's account of the land, noting both the lack of historical significance of the space to the battle and the fact that "the statue is ugly . . . even Forrest would think it is ugly."[84] On December 7, 2021, the executor of Dorris's will (with the support of the Battle of Nashville Trust) ordered Kershaw's Forrest to be dismantled. The removal process severely damaged the sculpture, breaking it into pieces. Forrest lay on his side, his face forever frozen into an open-mouthed howl—a pink-spattered plastic ruin serving as the final image of a contentious and battered sculpture.

Base of Nashville statue after removal in 2022.
Photo by Carla Ciuffo.

CONCLUSION

RECONSTRUCTION OF THE FABLES

> The past is obdurate.
>
> —STEPHEN KING, 2011

Nathan Bedford Forrest—ingloriously pitched into the dumpster of history, or at least sitting tarped and silent in a secret Tennessee warehouse—still casts a slanted shadow across modern-day Memphis. Even with Forrest Park renamed and unoccupied by bronze, the city features near-infinite historic overlays that allow irony, in its cruelest and most callous sense, to leech into the soil. The rich and complex history of Memphis creates a jumble of memorials as its indigenous history collapses into the Civil War, the civil rights movement, and the postwar music scene. For example, Forrest's most infamous slave pens on Adams Street now sit beneath a church parking lot on B. B. King Boulevard (as the city designated a stretch of Third Street). A comprehensive historical marker highlighting Forrest's role in the slave trade now abuts a mid-century sign noting only the location of the general's home.[1] The historical erasure was embodied in the original marker with its emphasis on Forrest's home and prosperity—"his business enterprises made him wealthy"—without once revealing the brutal reality concealed by the expression "business enterprises." During the period of Confederate monument removal following the Dylann Roof killings, opponents to the removals spoke often of how the process erased history. Yet, these monuments and heritage signs, often with the official imprint of state historical societies, represented their own erasures and fictions that help civic power. The city's dense network of palimpsests softened facts and fictions into a deconstructed muddle of ghost narratives serving various ideological interests and none.

Forrest Park sat at the crossroads of Memphis. Pinched between Sun Studio, just a few hundred yards west, and the former site of John Gaston Hospital, where Martin Luther King Jr. was taken after his assassination, to the east. Sam Phillips's Sun Studio, in its most favorable light, helped redefine the varied musical identity of the city and sat across from the historic Black hospital of the city (redefined out of existence into the Health Sciences portion of Health Sciences Park). Two vectors of memory, complicated in their race-defined legacies, lay separated by a monument merging so much of the city's history into a pillar obliterating the past as much as it served any historical perspective. Of these three markers of Memphis history, only Sun Studio remains since the city demolished John Gaston and redefined Forrest Park into emptiness. Still, a brief walk of only a few hundred yards connects the present to the past, underlining the closeness of history as well as its forever infinite distance. Fort Pillow, too, sits nearby, just a ninety-minute indirect drive from the park. No longer overlooking the river, the fort represents a critical look at how the chaotic waves of forgetting and (mis)remembering work to reshape and reclaim the past. The site concedes only the scarcest of secrets today as an attempted facsimile of the structure borders hollows and indentations that speak to the mass graves lining the area. Go at certain times of the year and you would be hard-pressed to orient even the basics of what happened in 1864. The shift of the river left the fort landlocked, further weirding the space as if nature, too, wished to silently vacate the blood-soaked bluff, leaving its radioactive horrors to drift across a forgotten landscape.

A blood thread runs through the myth of Nathan Bedford Forrest—at once spectral and physical. More than an exercise in public history, these sites, monuments, and markers give shape to the distortions of both the past and the contemporary moment. The Forrest image helps calculate and document these misrepresentations by accentuating these changes through the lens of the general's myth and memory. Trauma circumscribes much of this narrative, and in many ways, this trauma remains the central defining feature of the Forrest myth. From the destruction of Black bodies through the violence of slavery, war, or the Ku Klux Klan during his lifetime to the lynchings, threats of violence, and racial invective advocated later in his name, Forrest's image encapsulates and compresses the harshest aspects of the southern past. The destruction of the Black body plays heavily here, too, for often, it was not indiscriminate viciousness that defined Forrest's struggle in life and after but a targeted ferocity aimed at controlling and subduing Blackness. From the brutal downtown slave pens of antebellum Memphis onward, the brutalization and death of Black Americans defined Forrest's life and legacy. The specter of this violence drove the protests against his image throughout the late twentieth and early twenty-first centuries. After the cranes had dismantled the Forrest statue, Van Turner, whose actions led directly to the removal, spoke to the meaning of the action as he recalled his father's stories of having to contend with Forrest on his walks to and from work.[2] These generational stories, some public, most private, give voice to the protracted trauma links binding the present to the past.

This layering of memory and trauma inspired Ekundayo Bandele to create a play based on the creation and destruction of the Forrest statue. In his play, *Tumbling Down,* presented in Memphis in the spring of 2022, Bandele crafted a stage meditation on the memory strata that scaffolded the Forrest image. The bifurcated play featured two pairs of actors portraying Black Memphians divided between the period immediately prior to the unveiling of the 1905 statue and the action surrounding the removal of Forrest in 2017. Bandele's play bridged the work of Ida B. Wells (alluded to in the earlier storyline) and Tami Sawyer (alluded to in the later one) to underscore the connections that informed both historical moments. As general or as statue, Forrest plays only a small, implied role in the play as the action centers primarily on the Black men and women affected by his spectral presence. The play's soundtrack emphasized the link between the two eras as well as the power of music to reflect Black history and protest. Bandele incorporated two different recordings of the "Joshua Fit de Battle of Jericho" (one by Sidney Bechet and one by Paul Robeson) to highlight the association between Joshua destroying the walls of Jericho—*the walls came tumbling down*—and the Forrest removal in the 2010s. Later, the play incorporated "I Can't Breathe," a song by H.E.R. released in 2020 in reaction to the George Floyd murder, as a coda underscoring the nearness of the past. By inverting the focus of the removal narrative, Bandele helped emphasize the impact of Forrest's actions on Black Memphis long after his death and (first) burial.

Death gives us Forrest. The bodies of the unfree, the bodies of the massacred, even his own bones (and the bones of his wife), which long rested below the stone pedestal in Memphis, demarcate the hazy limits of the general's image. In 2021, after years of consideration and debate, the bodies of Forrest and his wife were exhumed once more and interred at a Confederate museum in Columbia, Tennessee.[3] As with the bodies of the Black soldiers killed at Fort Pillow—who had been moved from mass grave to mass grave to anonymous, if marked, graves in the Memphis National Cemetery—Forrest's remains endured impermanent resting places. Restless in death as in life, Forrest gives an agitated and anxious image defined more by violence and bloodshed than by any patina of civic righteousness. Without this death, quantifiable in some ways, hopelessly incalculable in others, Forrest would not have the power he continues to wield. The story of Forrest shows how this meaning was created, who invested in it, and how that meaning continued to shift and mutate over time. Forrest's memory rests on the intersection of racism, violence, masculinity, and a specific reverberation of white southern culture. Forrest would cease to have power without the destructive impulse, without the specter of racism, without the masculine signifiers; it is precisely this nexus of brutality and ferocity that fueled his appeal. Almost a century and a half after his death, he resonates today more than at any other moment. Today, Forrest's public image represents an exceptionally bloodied example of the harshness of the southern past and the American present. No doubt, his image, however defined and symbolized, will continue to affect future discussions about the implication of history and the ways race and memory unmake and remake a stubborn past.

NOTES

INTRODUCTION

1. See Wills, *A Battle from the Start,* 4–23; Hurst, *Nathan Bedford Forrest,* 16–42; Davison and Foxx, *Nathan Bedford Forrest,* 15–26.

2. Hurst, *Nathan Bedford Forrest,* 258.

3. Hurst, *Nathan Bedford Forrest,* 284–87.

4. Hurst, *Nathan Bedford Forrest,* 360.

5. Carney, "The Contested Image of Nathan Bedford Forrest."

6. "Confederate monuments," Karen Cox writes, "can no longer be debated solely as objects of history, when they have become rallying points for a violent movement" ("What Changed in Charlottesville," *New York Times,* August 11, 2019).

1. THE BUTCHER

1. See, for example, Browning, *Forrest,* 10.

2. Wyeth, *That Devil Forrest,* 113, 564–65.

3. Wills, *A Battle from the Start,* 122–27; Hurst, *Nathan Bedford Forrest,* 130.

4. For Forrest's conflict with Bragg, see: Lawrence Lee Hewitt, "Did Furious Forrest Really Threaten Bragg's Life after Chickamauga?" August 13, 2019, www.historynet.com/did-forrest-really-threaten-braggs-life/. See also Powell, *Failure in the Saddle,* 318–27.

5. For the early history of the fort, see Strickland and Huebner, *From Civil War Fort to State Park,* 2–5.

6. Fuchs, *An Unerring Fire,* 55; *The War of the Rebellion: A Compilation of the Official Records of the Union and Confederate Armies* (hereafter *OR*), vol. 32, ser. 1, pt. 1: 621.

7. *OR* 32, ser. 1, pt. 1: 596.

8. *OR* 32, ser. 1, pt. 1: 610.

9. *OR* 32, ser. 1, pt. 1: 610.

10. Hurst, *Nathan Bedford Forrest,* 178.

11. *Chicago Tribune,* May 4, 1864. See also Hurst, *Nathan Bedford Forrest,* 178–79.

12. Hurst, *Nathan Bedford Forrest,* 198.

13. *The Home Journal* (Winchester, TN), January 20, 1859. See also Parsons, "We Don't Have Enough Contempt for Nathan Bedford Forrest."

14. Hurst, *Nathan Bedford Forrest,* 117.

15. See also Ashdown and Caudill, *The Myth of Nathan Bedford Forrest,* 71–102.

16. Hurst, *Nathan Bedford Forrest,* 74–75, 94–95.

17. Bergeron, ed., *The Papers of Andrew Johnson* 8: 331. See also Liulevicius, *Rebel Salvation,* 129–32.

18. Blair wrote to his brother, Montgomery Blair, who had served as postmaster general under Lincoln. See Hurst, *Nathan Bedford Forrest,* 280–81.

19. Bergeron, eds., *The Papers of Andrew Johnson 11:* 484. See also Hurst, *Nathan Bedford Forrest,* 282–84.

20. Hurst, *Nathan Bedford Forrest,* 287; Davison and Foxx, *Nathan Bedford Forrest,* 439.

21. Hurst, *Nathan Bedford Forrest,* 298–99.

22. Hurst, *Nathan Bedford Forrest,* 299–300.

23. Hurst, *Nathan Bedford Forrest,* 301.

24. Wills, *A Battle from the Start,* 347.

25. Hurst, *Nathan Bedford Forrest,* 302.

26. *Harper's Weekly,* July 11, 1868, p. 444.

27. Duke, *Reminiscences,* 348.

28. Duke, *Reminiscences,* 348.

29. Lytle, *Bedford Forrest and His Critter Company,* 381.

30. Morton, *The Artillery of Nathan Bedford Forrest's Cavalry,* 342.

31. Morton, *The Artillery of Nathan Bedford Forrest's Cavalry,* 337. For a good overview of the origins of the Ku Klux Klan, see Parsons, *Ku-Klux: The Birth of the Klan in Reconstruction.*

32. Hurst, *Nathan Bedford Forrest,* 284.

33. Davison and Foxx, *Nathan Bedford Forrest,* 446–47.

34. Henry, *"First with the Most" Forrest,* 449–50.

35. Davison and Foxx, *Nathan Bedford Forrest,* 457.

36. *Report of the Joint Select Committee to Inquire into the Condition of Affairs in the Late Insurrectionary States,* 6–7 (hereafter *RJSC*).

37. *RJSC,* 7.

38. Wills, *A Battle from the Start,* 364.

39. *RJSC,* 9.

40. *RJSC,* 12.

41. Moore, ed., *Rebellion Record* 8.

2. MEMPHIS, 1905

1. *Memphis News-Scimitar,* May 17, 1905.

2. Ash, *A Massacre in Memphis,* 33.

3. This section is based on the research of Stephen Ash and his monograph, *A Massacre in Memphis.* See also Golightly and Judaken, eds., *Memphis: 200 Years Together,* 30.

4. "The Memphis Riot of 1866" has long been a politicized misnomer for the actions of that spring. "The Memphis Massacre" perhaps gets closer to the truth by alluding to the violence to-

ward Black Memphians, though the word "massacre" still tends to obscure what occurred. In many ways, the actions in Memphis were riots, but the rioting was driven by white Memphians against Black people and businesses. Recently, Gregory Downs has referred to the riots more specifically as a "three-day pogrom" ("Foreword: Remembering Memphis, Remembering Reconstruction," Bond and O'Donovan, eds., *Remembering the Memphis Massacre,* ix). See also David Waters, "Time to Tell the Truth: It Was a Massacre Not Just a Riot," *Memphis Commercial Appeal,* March 5, 2016; Andrew L. Slap, "On Duty in Memphis: Fort Pickering's African American Soldiers," in Bond and O'Donovan, eds., *Remembering the Memphis Massacre,* 120–31.

5. Wills, *A Battle from the Start,* 325. See also Hurst, *Nathan Bedford Forrest,* 272–75; Davison and Foxx, *Nathan Bedford Forrest,* 416–23.

6. Davison and Foxx, *Nathan Bedford Forrest,* 417; Wills, *A Battle from the Start,* 328.

7. *Memphis Daily Appeal,* April 13, 1870 (first quote); August 25, 1870 (second quote). *Memphis Public Ledger,* July 11, 1873 (third quote).

8. *Memphis Daily Appeal,* May 31, 1874 (first quote); *Memphis Public Ledger,* June 1, 1874 (second quote); *Memphis Public Ledger,* June 5, 1874 (third quote). See also *Memphis Public Ledger,* June 8, 1874.

9. *Nashville Union and American,* July 3, 1875 (first quote); *Memphis Daily Appeal,* July 1, 1875 (second quote).

10. "Go to work," Forrest advised, "be industrious, live honestly and act truly, and when you are oppressed[,] I'll come to your relief." *Memphis Daily Appeal,* July 6, 1875.

11. *Memphis Public Ledger,* July 13, 1875 (first quote); "Death of General Forrest," *New York Times,* October 30, 1877 (second quote); *Augusta* (GA) *Chronicle,* July 31, 1874, 4 (third quote). "Why we would rather have sent him a car filled with the rarest exotics plucked from the dizziest peaks of the Himalayas or the perilous fastnesses of the Andes than he should have thus befouled the fair home of one of the Confederacy's most daring general officers." *Augusta Chronicle,* July 31, 1874, 4.

12. For contemporary commentary on his image as civil rights advocate, see Andy Holt, "Nathan B. Forrest, one of South's first civil rights leaders," *Jackson Sun,* July 17, 2015, www.jacksonsun.com/story/opinion/2015/07/16/rep-holt-nathan-forrest-one-souths-first-civil-rights-leaders/30246083/.

13. Wrenn, *Crisis and Commission Government in Memphis,* 16–19. "[B]y 1878, as a result of higher rates of white out-migration and high death rates, blacks comprised a two-thirds majority of the 20,000 people who remained in the city" (Rushing, *Memphis and the Paradox of Place,* 14). See also Blum, "The Crucible of Disease: Trauma, Memory, and National Reconciliation during the Yellow Fever Epidemic of 1878," 791–820. "In a reversal of Civil War outcomes, no southern city suffered as much from yellow fever as Memphis" (Rushing, *Memphis and the Paradox of Place,* 14). See also Capers, *The Biography of a River Town,* 210; Wrenn, *Crisis and Commission Government in Memphis,* xi–xii; Pohlmann and Kirby, *Racial Politics at the Crossroads,* 3, 6–8; Lauterbach, *Beale Street Dynasty,* 48–50.

14. Preston Lauterbach pointed out that Forrest's slave mart created a geographic space of whiteness and Blackness through forced encounters. "Those corners at Beale and Hernando would form a nexus of black culture and power for the ensuing century," Lauterbach writes, also noting that "Forrest had unwittingly placed the cornerstone for one of the outstanding black

communities in the country" (*Beale Street Dynasty,* 42). For a look at the diversity of Black presence in Memphis politics in the last half of the nineteenth century, see Gritter, *River of Hope,* 236n13.

15. "They circled their wagons, tightening their geography and concentrating their homes and institutions close together" (Lauterbach, *Beale Street Dynasty,* 29). See also Gritter, *River of Hope,* 16. The *Memphis Evening Scimitar* referred to Church as a "firm believer in Memphis" (qtd. in Gritter, *River of Hope,* 19).

16. Lauterbach, *Beale Street Dynasty,* 50, 63–65. Wells, Lauterbach writes, "looked up to Bob Church's family" (*Beale Street Dynasty,* 62).

17. See also Goings and Smith, "'Unhidden' Transcripts,'" 380–81; Wells-Barnett, *On Lynchings,* 16–19. Moss's final quote has also been transcribed as "tell my people to go west, there is no justice here." See Giddings, *Ida,* 183. This more poetic version would serve as a rallying cry for Wells and others. See, Tucker, "Ida B. Wells and Memphis Lynching," 116.

18. This aggregate account appeared in the *St. Paul Appeal,* March 26, 1892, 1 and 4. "[A]s many as two thousand black Memphians," one historian writes, "may have fled the city not only in search of freedom for their children, but with the vague hope that depopulating the area would cause the whites to regret their violent oppression of black people" (Tucker, "Ida B. Wells and Memphis Lynching," 117). Wells saw lynching, Tucker argues, "as the latest attempt to preserve white supremacy at any cost" ("Ida B. Wells and Memphis Lynching," 117–18).

19. "Paradoxically, the city lacking Old South traditions and aristocratic pretensions, as well as New South achievements, found itself at the turn of the century being governed by white political leaders who drew on selective 'memory' of a glorious southern past to bolster their authority, advance their own self-interests, and create new identities for themselves" (Rushing, *Memphis and The Paradox of Place,* 36). See also Gritter, *River of Hope,* 19–20. "In the decades that followed [the Civil War]," Timothy Huebner writes, "White Memphians reasserted control over the Black population" (Timothy Huebner, "The Civil War and its Legacy in Memphis," in Golightly and Judaken, eds., *Memphis: 200 Years Together,* 30). *Memphis News-Scimitar,* May 17, 1905 (second quote).

20. "It was thought and suggested by many at that time," Samuel T. Carnes later wrote of the early attempt at fundraising, "that the occasion was not just ripe for the accomplishment of this work, so it was suspended for a while" (*The Forrest Monument: Its History and Dedication: A Memorial in Art, Oratory and Literature,* 23–24).

21. See "Tributes to Gen. George W. Gordon," 499; Harkins, *Metropolis of the American Nile,* 103; Weeks, *Memphis,* 137–39. One-third of leadership committee of the FMA were too young to have served in the Civil War (Forrest Monument Association Cash Ledger Book).

22. *Forrest Monument,* 24–25.

23. Rushing, *Memphis and the Paradox of Place,* 37–38. "Planning for Forrest Park and the equestrian statue," Rushing writes, "took place during a period in European and American history described as 'statuemania—the rage for commemorative statues'" (*Memphis and the Paradox of Place,* 39). U.S. Department of the Interior—National Park Service, "National Register of Historic Places Continuation Sheet," hereafter NRHPCS (first quote on p. 6); McFarland, *Memoirs and Addresses,* 128 (second quote); Dulaney, *Memphis Park Commission Books,* 2014, 22. Minute Book One, 82–83, June 7, 1905 (third quote).

24. The Confederate Reunion also led to some provocative fundraising as Robert Church "ran

into controversy" stemming from a $1,000 donation to the "entertainment fund"—which may have been part of the fundraising for Confederate Hall. "I feel it my duty," Church responded, "to aid in entertaining those men who fought bravely for the Lost Cause" (Gritter, *River of Hope*, 26). No record of Church donating to, or commenting on, the Forrest statue yet exists. *Minutes of the Eleventh Annual Meeting and Reunion of the United Confederate Veterans* (hereafter *UCV Minutes*), 19 (first quote); *UCV Minutes*, 18 (second quote).

25. *UCV Minutes*, 23, 53; *Memphis Commercial Appeal*, May 30, 1901; *UCV Minutes*, 37.

26. "Monument to Gen. N. B. Forrest," 390. See also *Memphis Commercial Appeal*, May 30, 1901; May 28, 1901; May 29, 1901; *Memphis News-Scimitar*, May 7, 1905.

27. NRHPCS, 15. *UCV Minutes*, 23 (dated September 26, 1901). This document is typed and adhered to the Minutes book. Note: "fully" was penciled in before "accomplished." See also *Forrest Monument*, 26; *Memphis Commercial Appeal*, May 31, 1901.

28. *Forrest Monument*, 25–26. See also NRHPCS, 15. The contract between the FMA and Niehaus stipulated a final sculpture comprised of "standard bronze, 90% copper," and "to be one and one-fourth (1–1/4) life size." Niehaus was to receive $25,000 in installments: one-fourth of the sum after the creation of the model, one-fourth of the sum after a clay model was completed, one-fourth of the sum after the statue was completed in bronze, and the final one-fourth of the sum after the finished statue was erected and accepted by the FMA ("Forrest Monument Addendum—Niehaus Contract," Digital Archive of Memphis Public Libraries, memphislibrary.contentdm.oclc.org/digital/collection/p13039coll5/id/1541/rec/16).

29. "I am more than willing," Niehaus wrote the FMA, "to make concessions to have it larger, and to that end it may be so, I would agree to make it [one- and one-half] size for $25,000; twice life size for $30,000. This does not provide for the pedestal, which could be made from $5000 up" (Forrest Monument Association Minutes Book, 39, letter dated June 8, 1902, CHN to committee [Judge Young]). See also letter dated June 28, 1902, in Clipping File, Memphis Room: October 8, 1902 ("colossal size" quote). Forrest Monument Association Minutes Book, 46, letter dated May 20, 1903 (CHN to Judge Young). He also quietly pushed the FMA to reconsider certain choices such as their desire to build the base out of brick; they acquiesced to his adoption of marble (Forrest Monument Association Minutes Book, October 4, 1904, 237).

30. *Forrest Monument*, 31 (first quote); 55 (second quote); 60 (third quote); 63 (fourth quote); 61 (fifth quote); 62 (sixth quote).

31. *Forrest Monument*, 65 (first quote); 66 (second quote); 68 (third quote); 69 (fourth quote). *Memphis Press-Scimitar*, May 14, 1905 (fifth quote). *Forrest Monument*, 78 (sixth quote).

32. *Forrest Monument*, 30 (first quote); 35 (second quote); 62 (third quote); 82 (fourth quote). The remains of the Forrests were reinterred in Forrest Park in 1904 (Finger, "Forrest Park").

33. See *Forrest Monument*, 12. FMA Minutes, May 13, 1905, 156 ("grateful subject" quote). The entire statue, with pedestal and terrace, stood over twenty-one-feet.

34. As historian Bill Black notes in his discussion of the 1905 unveiling: "Forrest specifically was a symbol of what would happen if black people tried to get too much power: they would be stamped underfoot" ("Celebrating Nathan Bedford Forrest Is Celebrating White Supremacy"). Three years later, at a stage performance of Thomas Dixon's *The Clansman*, Forrest's son suffered a stroke at the entrance of an actor representing his father (*Memphis News-Scimitar*, February 8, 1908).

3. FORREST AS HISTORY, FORREST AS FICTION

1. *Memphis Press-Scimitar,* April 2, 1974.

2. John Morton, an artillery captain under Forrest, published a memoir in 1902. The Forrest material fails to rise to the level of biography, though Morton includes significant fragments, such as the general's connection to the Ku Klux Klan.

3. "Biography" is a bit of a stretch for the Jordan and Pryor book, and in fairness the title denotes a study of Forrest campaigns. Forrest's involvement, however, elevated the book's importance. Of the first four full-length books on Forrest, Jordan and Pryor's devotes, in percentage of total coverage, less time on Forrest's nonmilitary life than all others. It also covers nothing past Forrest's surrender in 1865. Wyeth's book, published in 1899, represents the first full-scale biography of the general and the first book to give any coverage to his postwar life and death (fewer than 10 pages out of a 550-plus-page book). Mathes and Lytle expanded on his nonmilitary life with both authors devoting roughly 10 percent of their respective books to Forrest before and after the war.

4. J. P. Pryor Letter, University of Tennessee, SCOUT, scout.lib.utk.edu/repositories/2/resources/142.

5. Jordan and Pryor, *Campaigns of Lieut.-Gen. N. B. Forrest,* vii.

6. Jordan and Pryor, *Campaigns of Lieut.-Gen. N. B. Forrest,* xiv.

7. Jordan and Pryor, *Campaigns of Lieut.-Gen. N. B. Forrest,* 18.

8. Jordan and Pryor, *Campaigns of Lieut.-Gen. N. B. Forrest,* 25.

9. Jordan and Pryor, *Campaigns of Lieut.-Gen. N. B. Forrest,* 26.

10. One of Wyeth's sons, Marion Sims Wyeth, would go on to be the architect for the Mar-a-Lago mansion in Palm Springs, Florida, in the 1920s.

11. "General Jordan had for a considerable period after the war been intimately associated with Forrest, and from him I received much that was of service to me in the work I had in hand" (Wyeth, *That Devil Forrest,* xxxvii).

12. Wyeth, *That Devil Forrest,* 11.

13. Wyeth, *That Devil Forrest,* 18.

14. Wyeth, *That Devil Forrest,* 18.

15. Mathes, *General Forrest,* 18.

16. Mathes, *General Forrest,* 18.

17. Mathes, *General Forrest,* 21.

18. Mathes, *General Forrest,* 338.

19. Mathes, *General Forrest,* 344.

20. *Memphis Commercial Appeal,* December 23, 2017.

21. Jordan and Pryor, *Campaigns of Lieut.-Gen. N. B. Forrest,* 424–53.

22. Wyeth, *That Devil Forrest,* 327.

23. Lytle, *Bedford Forrest and His Critter Company,* xxvi, 36.

24. Lytle, *Bedford Forrest and His Critter Company,* xxvi–xxvii, 388.

25. Lytle, *Bedford Forrest and His Critter Company,* xix.

26. Lucas, *The Southern Vision of Andrew Lytle,* 1–2, 6–7.

27. Andrew Nelson Lytle Papers (MSS 267), box 9, folder 4. His undated outline also includes a rough "Table of Contents," which comes close to the finished project.

28. On the back of one draft of "The Vine and the Fig Tree," Lytle inscribed: "At Yorktown the colonies broke the physical ties with their [parent], at Appomattox, the cultural [the last hope of rebirth] was stifled with the Reconstruction" (Lytle Papers, box 9, folder 6).

29. Lytle Papers, box 11, folder 23.

30. Lytle Papers, box 11, folder 23.

31. Lytle, *Bedford Forrest and His Critter Company,* 27.

32. Lytle, *Bedford Forrest and His Critter Company,* 28.

33. Smith, "Introduction," in *Life and Labor in the Old South,* by Phillips. See also Smith, "Ulrich Bonnell Phillips."

34. Lytle, *Bedford Forrest and His Critter Company,* 385.

35. Lytle Papers, box 11, folder 23.

36. Lytle, *Bedford Forrest and His Critter Company,* 390.

37. *New York Herald Tribune,* June 28, 1931.

38. *New York Herald Tribune,* June 28, 1931.

39. *New York Herald Tribune,* June 28, 1931.

40. *Memphis Press-Scimitar,* July 13, 1937.

41. *Memphis Commercial Appeal,* July 13, 1940.

42. Henry, *"First with the Most" Forrest,* 18–21; *New York Tribune,* May 27, 1918.

43. *New York Times,* May 28, 1918; Henry, *"First with the Most" Forrest,* 18–21.

44. *Memphis Commercial Appeal,* January 20, 1941; July 13, 1940.

45. *Memphis Press-Scimitar,* November 20, 1942.

46. *Memphis Press-Scimitar,* June 25, 1943.

47. Letter from Manfred Rommel to H. P. Andrews, April 10, 1996. Rpt. in undated and unpublished paper, H. P. Andrews, "The Rommel Myth," Tennessee State Library Archives.

48. Shelby Foote was cited in the *Memphis Commercial Appeal* on this subject. "Rommel never came to America, . . . but [Rommel] and other German military leaders had studied Forrest's tactics carefully. . . . The German blitzkrieg was nothing more than a Forrest cavalry charge on tanks instead of horses" (July 13, 1985).

49. *Chicago Daily News,* September 26, 1946.

50. *Eastern State News,* September 28, 1949.

51. *Yachting,* August 1948.

52. *Broadcasting,* January 12, 1948; *Traffic World,* March 27, 1948.

53. *Chess Review,* February 1948.

54. *Chicago Tribune,* February 5, 1948.

55. *Milk Plant Monthly,* May 1948. See also a 1952 story in the *Memphis Commercial Appeal,* "Dixie Dairies Stick to Claim—Fustest with Mostest Milk," June 14, 1952.

56. Letter from Monroe Cockrell to David Weisbart (February 3, 1952), Tennessee State Library and Archives.

57. Letter from David Weisbart to Monroe Cockrell (February 6, 1952), Tennessee State Library and Archives.

58. *Memphis Press-Scimitar,* July 14, 1958.

59. Tate, "On Nathan Bedford Forrest (& the Death of Heroes)," 13; Tennessee State Code 55-204 (1969).

60. "[M]embers of a group called Black Tennesseans for Action gathered at the Capitol to protest against alleged recism [*sic*] on the part of Gov. Lamar Alexander's administration" (*Nashville Tennessean,* February 19, 1979).

61. An Associated Press piece noted that, because of the slave trade, Fort Pillow, and the Klan, "the coalition of black and religious leaders takes a dim view of having Forrest's bust, unveiled last fall, in an honored place in the state Capitol" (January 28, 1979).

62. Tate, "On Nathan Bedford Forrest (& the Death of Heroes)," 13; Davis, "Behind the Lines," 50.

63. *Memphis Commercial Appeal,* November 3, 1979.

64. *Memphis Tri-State Defender,* August 10, 1985.

65. Park commission chairman: "I don't know if we have the right to rename it or to remove the statue" (*Memphis Commercial Appeal,* May 7, 12, 1988).

66. *Memphis Commercial Appeal,* May 8, 1988.

67. *Memphis Commercial Appeal,* May 12, 1988.

68. Stainchak, "Behind the Lines," 18; Dawson, "Another Skirmish for N. B. Forrest," 16; *Memphis Commercial Appeal,* May 7, 12, 1988.

69. *Memphis Commercial Appeal,* July 14, 1969.

70. *Memphis Tri-State Defender,* May 28, 1988.

71. *Memphis Tri-State Defender,* June 11, 1988.

72. Landess, "Tilting at Statues," 6.

73. *Memphis Commercial Appeal,* July 13, 1985.

74. *Memphis Commercial Appeal,* August 21, 1966.

75. Mathes, *General Forrest,* 61.

76. See Huebner and McGrady, "Shelby Foote, Memphis, and the Civil War in American Memory."

77. "My book falls between two stools—academic historians are upset because there are no footnotes and novel readers don't want to study history" (Foote, "Shelby Foote, The Art of Fiction").

78. Carter, *Conversations with Shelby Foote,* 119.

79. *Memphis Commercial Appeal,* June 27, 2004.

80. *Memphis Commercial Appeal,* November 18, 1982.

81. Foote on Elvis: "I heard him in Memphis and thought he had it" (Carter, *Conversations with Shelby Foote,* 65).

82. Carter, *Conversations with Shelby Foote,* 44.

83. Carter, *Conversations with Shelby Foote,* 46.

84. Carter, *Conversations with Shelby Foote,* 46.

85. Chapman, *Shelby Foote: A Writer's Life,* 226.

86. Carter, *Conversations with Shelby Foote,* 86.

87. Carter, *Conversations with Shelby Foote,* 264.

88. *Los Angeles Times,* June 29, 2005.

89. Wills, *A Battle from the Start,* 2.

90. Longacre, "Review," 193–95.

91. *Kirkus Reviews,* June 6, 1993. www.kirkusreviews.com/book-reviews/jack-hurst/nathan-bedford-forrest/. Wills reviewed Hurst's book for the *Journal of American History,* where he argued

that, despite a few caveats, "Hurst has produced a worthy biography of a remarkable and controversial man. . . . Hurst's efforts will continue properly to ensure Nathan Bedford Forrest a place in Civil War scholarship and debate" (Wills, "Review," 1320–21).

92. *New York Times,* July 5, 1992.

93. *New York Times,* August 23, 1992.

94. Foote, "Shelby Foote, The Art of Fiction."

95. Foote, "Shelby Foote, The Art of Fiction."

96. Sharrett, "Reconciliation and the Politics of Forgetting," 28; Horwitz, *Confederates in the Attic.*

97. He also blamed white southern women: "The women of the South just would not allow somebody to stay home and sulk while the war was going on. It didn't take conscription to grab him. The women made him go" (Foote, "Shelby Foote, The Art of Fiction").

98. Zeitz, "Rebel Redemption Redux."

99. "Many among the finest people this country has ever produced died in that war. To take [the Confederate flag] and call it a symbol of evil is a misrepresentation" (Reed, "The Banner That Won't Stay Furled," 88).

100. *Los Angeles Times,* June 29, 2005.

4. THE MOST MAN IN THE WORLD

1. Wyeth, *That Devil Forrest,* 556.

2. Johnson, *The Partisan Rangers of the Confederate States Army,* 39.

3. Wyeth, *That Devil Forrest,* 556–57.

4. Wyeth, *That Devil Forrest,* 557.

5. Wyeth, *That Devil Forrest,* 548. "Even his admirers were alarmed by what came over Bedford in battle: A glandular or cardiovascular surge that caused him visibly to darken and swell, like a serpent mustering its poisons" (Ward, *River Run Red,* 13).

6. Jordan and Pryor, *Campaigns of Lieut.-Gen. N. B. Forrest,* 35.

7. Mathes, *General Forrest,* 23–24. An earlier writer noted that Forrest's "face flushed till it bore a striking resemblance to a painted Indian warrior" (Wyeth, *That Devil Forrest,* xv).

8. Henry, *"First with the Most" Forrest,* 13.

9. Hurst, *Nathan Bedford Forrest,* 7.

10. *Memphis Commercial Appeal,* July 13, 1940.

11. *Memphis Commercial Appeal,* March 28, 1954.

12. Jordan and Pryor, *Campaigns of Lieut.-Gen. N. B. Forrest,* 35.

13. Stephenson, *Civil War Memoir,* 268. "He was a man to catch the look and hold the attention of the most casual observer, and as we gazed on each other I felt that he was a born leader and one that I would be willing to follow" (Johnson, *The Partisan Rangers of the Confederate States Army,* 39).

14. Ashdown and Caudill, *The Myth of Nathan Bedford Forrest,* 10.

15. "The Attractiveness of a Beard."

16. Johnson, *The Partisan Rangers of the Confederate States Army,* 39.

17. Jordan and Pryor, *Campaigns of Lieut.-Gen. N. B. Forrest,* 35.

18. Wyeth, *That Devil Forrest,* 555.

19. Mathes, *General Forrest,* 22.

20. Wyeth, *That Devil Forrest,* 556.

21. "Civil War Hairstyles II."

22. Wyeth, *That Devil Forrest,* 6–8.

23. Wyeth, *That Devil Forrest,* 4.

24. Mathes, *General Forrest,* 13.

25. Lytle, *Bedford Forrest and His Critter Company,* 388.

26. Lytle, *Bedford Forrest and His Critter Company,* 3.

27. Lytle, *Bedford Forrest and His Critter Company,* 34–35.

28. Parks, *Bedford Forrest,* 181.

29. Parks, *Bedford Forrest,* 182–92.

30. Bell, *Devil's Dream,* 136.

31. Bell, *Devil's Dream,* 136.

32. Bell, *Devil's Dream,* 20.

33. Bell, *Devil's Dream,* 22.

34. Bell, *Devil's Dream,* 23.

35. Hurst, *Nathan Bedford Forrest,* 15.

36. Hurst, *Nathan Bedford Forrest,* 370.

37. Davison and Foxx, *Nathan Bedford Forrest,* 479.

38. Bell, *Devil's Dream,* 291.

39. Bell, *Devil's Dream,* 310.

40. Bell, *Devil's Dream,* 55.

41. Baldwin, "Naming the Enslaved, Reconciling the Past in Memphis."

42. To this point, Bell argues explicitly that he would "have liked to know more about his wife, Mary Ann, and also about his siblings" (Browning, "In His New Novel, Madison Smartt Bell Tackles the Confederacy's Most Controversial Son, Nathan Bedford Forrest").

43. Hurst, *Nathan Bedford Forrest,* 36.

44. "The Butcher Forrest and His Family," *Chicago Tribune,* May 4, 1864. See Eiland, "The Unspoken Demands of Slavery."

45. Ashdown and Caudill, *The Myth of Nathan Bedford Forrest,* 22.

46. Jordan and Pryor, *Campaigns of Lieut.-Gen. N. B. Forrest,* 267.

47. "My highest regardes to Miss Ema Sanson for hir gallant conduct while my forse was Skirmishing with the Federals across Black Creek near Gadisden, Allabama" (Davison and Foxx, *Nathan Bedford Forrest,* 149).

48. "They fought no war for slavery" (Wyeth, *That Devil Forrest,* 187).

49. Mathes, *General Forrest,* 118. "Unlettered though he was, Forrest instinctively had the gallant manner of all Southern cavalrymen" (Davison and Foxx, *Nathan Bedford Forrest,* 149).

50. Atkins, "Alabama Confederate Heroine, Emma Sansom."

51. The intrepid investigator Monroe Cockrell tracked down many of the facts of Emma Sansom's life in the early 1950s. As ever, he was most interested in spelling variances as well as genealogical data. See Monroe Cockrell Collection, University of Alabama Special Collections.

52. Owen, "Emma Sansom, an Alabama Heroine."

53. "Emma Sansom Monument Gadsden, AL"; Crownover, "The Vagabond—109 Years Ago Unveiling of the Emma Sansom Statue."

54. "Emma Sansom Monument."

55. In 1964, the Texas Division of the United Daughters of the Confederacy raised money to place a memorial marker inscribed: "Texas, honored as the chosen home and last resting place of the Confederate heroine of Alabama, pays tribute to her memory" on her gravesite in Texas (www.findagrave.com/memorial/10788038/emma-johnson).

56. Khalil, "Descendants of Emma Sansom Call for Removal of Statue in Gadsden."

57. Rodgers, "In Gadsden, Officials Take No Action against Monument to Confederate Sympathizer Emma Sansom." Historian Camille Agricola Bowman: "Emma can be a local young girl heroine, with a school named after her, that's taught us more about our history than what her statue symbolizes underneath her" ("Historian Has Suggestion to Resolve Alabama Confederate Monument Controversy").

58. All quotes from Kroll, "The Camp Follower in Gen. Forrest's Command Tent."

59. Cockrell collection.

60. *Memphis Commercial Appeal,* July 16, 1962.

61. Burns, *The Civil War,* episode 7.

62. Coates, "The Convenient Suspension of Disbelief."

63. Shannon, "Perry Fires Up Anti-Tax Crowd."

64. Terris, "Scholars Nostalgic for the Old South Study the Virtues of Secession, Quietly."

65. Coates, "Nathan Bedford Forrest Has Beautiful Eyes."

66. Coates, "Nathan Bedford Forrest Has Beautiful Eyes."

67. Bell, *Devil's Dream,* 192.

5. REMOVAL(S)

1. Stephen Colbert noted that the figure of Forrest looked more like a figurine of the Nutcracker (Dessem, "Watch Stephen Colbert's Impression of the Confederacy's Dumbest Monument").

2. "Forrest's Cavalry Rides Again," *Nashville Tennessean,* July 12, 1998; "Forrest Statue Is Simply Hideous," *Nashville Tennessean,* July 14, 1998.

3. "Seeing the statue up close like this I also started to pick up on a strange kind of honesty in it—the fever-dream impressionism somehow offers a more accurate view of Confederate history than, say, the stately equestrian statue under which Forrest is buried in Memphis or the bust, inconspicuous and modest, in the Tennessee Capitol" (O'Neill, "America's Ugliest Confederate Statue Isn't Coming Down Anytime Soon").

4. "On Saturday evenings, the aspiring painter attended salons hosted by the Agrarians, a group of 12 poets and writers who had recently published I'll Take My Stand, a semi-fascistic tome arguing for the restoration of a distinctive white, rural, Southern identity. I'll Take My Stand reads like the Ur-text of the Make America Great Again platform, rife with racism posing as rural, white industrial discontent" (O'Neill, "America's Ugliest Confederate Statue Isn't Coming Down Anytime Soon").

5. *Chattanooga Daily Times,* August 8, 1955.

6. Kershaw interview.

7. Kershaw interview. See also Betsy Phillips, "Nashville Desegregation and the Bombing of Hattie Cotton Elementary," *Nashville Scene,* September 7, 2017.

8. O'Neill, "America's Ugliest Confederate Statue Isn't Coming Down Anytime Soon."

9. "MLK: The Gary Revel Story."

10. *Nashville Tennessean,* January 21, 2008.

11. *Nashville Tennessean,* September 10, 2000.

12. *Nashville Tennessean,* October 6, 2000.

13. Kershaw interview.

14. Molly Secours, *Nashville Tennessean,* December 10, 2005.

15. O'Neill, "America's Ugliest Confederate Statue Isn't Coming Down Anytime Soon." "One of my wife's friends. Mary approved of the friend posing for me." *Nashville Tennessean,* May 10, 2000.

16. *Nashville Tennessean,* July 26, 1998.

17. *Nashville Tennessean,* June 27, 1998. Forrest "gives us a language in which we can argue about other things—political power-sharing, affirmative action, civil rights, equal opportunity, a host of issues that haven't been settled—while speaking about him" (O'Neill, *Down Along with That Devil's Bones,* 205).

18. Kershaw interview.

19. O'Neill, "America's Ugliest Confederate Statue Isn't Coming Down Anytime Soon."

20. O'Neill, "America's Ugliest Confederate Statue Isn't Coming Down Anytime Soon."

21. Robert Steinback, "Jack Kershaw, Stalwart of White Nationalism, Dies," *Southern Poverty Law Center,* September 24, 2010.

22. O'Neill, *Down Along with That Devil's Bones,* 132.

23. O'Neill, *Down Along with That Devil's Bones,* 131.

24. *Nashville Tennessean,* January 9, May 14, 2004.

25. *Nashville Tennessean,* January 6, 2005.

26. O'Neill, *Down Along with That Devil's Bones,* 141. "Mr. Kershaw is an interesting and unusual person, whose political views I do not share—but he is an ingenious and energetic iconoclast, and also a very talented and accomplished outsider artist (he has a very large body of virtually unknown work, most of it far more aesthetically pleasing than the Forrest statue)" (Browning, "In His New Novel, Madison Smartt Bell Tackles the Confederacy's Most Controversial Son, Nathan Bedford Forrest").

27. *Nashville Tennessean,* April 16, 1950.

28. *Nashville Tennessean,* December 15, 1950.

29. *Nashville Scene,* November 5, 2009.

30. *Dickson* (TN) *Herald,* September 24, 2010.

31. *Nashville Tennessean,* March 10, 1999; May 10, 2000; June 21, November 22, 2005; October 12, 2004.

32. *Nashville Tennessean,* May 10, 2000; November 22, 2005.

33. *Nashville Tennessean,* October 12, 2004.

34. *Nashville Tennessean,* November 22, 2005.

35. *Nashville Tennessean,* January 9, 2005.

36. *Nashville Tennessean,* July 18, 1997.

37. *Nashville Tennessean,* July 19, 1998.

38. "Many in Murfreesboro see Forrest as their savior" (O'Neill, *Down Along with That Devil's Bones,* 75). "Middle Tennessee State University Students Seek to Rename a Campus Building That Honors the Founder of the Ku Klux Klan," 41. Howard, "A Confederate on Campus."

39. Thompson, *Smashing Statues,* 167.

40. Cox, *No Common Ground,* 137–41; O'Neill, *Down Along with That Devil's Bones,* 19–69, 179–242.

41. *Memphis Commercial Appeal,* May 15, 2005; *Tri-State Defender,* August 6, 2005.

42. *Tri-State Defender,* August 6, 2005.

43. "To question that Forrest would not impregnate a black woman is offensive to common sense. . . . its almost like were going to look back at slavery and say they [the slave masters] had honor and morals and ethics" (*Memphis Commercial Appeal,* August 14, 2005).

44. Stokes-Casey, "Richard Lou's ReCovering Memphis," 329.

45. *Memphis Commercial Appeal,* July 6, 2008.

46. Stokes-Casey, "Richard Lou's ReCovering Memphis," 339.

47. "One committee member, Doug Cupples, a history professor at Christian Brothers University here, called for keeping the original names but building more monuments to honor African-American leaders. 'I would like to see us adding to our history, not taking away from it,' he said. 'We have a very expansive history, which includes some saints and some scoundrels'" (Brown, "Memphis Drops Confederate Names from Parks").

48. Stokes-Casey, "Richard Lou's ReCovering Memphis," 329.

49. Stokes-Casey, "Richard Lou's ReCovering Memphis," 322. "Both of Lou's performances directly challenged the controversial monument located in public space and were met with mixed responses." "A palimpsest of untold and underrepresented histories of Memphis residents in the public sphere" (Stokes-Casey, "Richard Lou's ReCovering Memphis," 324).

50. Stokes-Casey, "Richard Lou's ReCovering Memphis," 330, 342; see also Tim Bounds, "Remembering Nathan Bedford Forrest."

51. Brown, "Memphis Drops Confederate Names From Parks." Jim Strickland, a City Council member, said the entire parks debate had become a distraction from Memphis's real problems. The city has a shrinking population and a high unemployment rate, and it is trying to negotiate a complicated merger of the county and city school systems. "We have many, many challenges in this city that are much more important than the names of these parks," Mr. Strickland said. "We ought to compromise and get it behind us" (Brown, "Memphis Drops Confederate Names from Parks").

52. Justin Wm. Moyer, "Why South Carolina's Confederate Flag Isn't at Half-Staff After Church Shooting," *Washington Post,* June 19, 2015; and Ta-Nehisi Coates, "Take Down the Confederate Flag—Now," *The Atlantic,* June 18, 2015.

53. Aaron Blake, "The Story of Nikki Haley and the Confederate Flag," *Washington Post,* February 15, 2023.

54. Seanna Adcox, "SC Legislator: Take Down Confederate Flag," *Greenville News,* June 20, 2015.

55. Obama, "Remarks by the President in Eulogy for the Honorable Reverend Clementa Pinckney," June 26, 2015.

56. Colby Itkowitz, "Nikki Haley: Mass Murderer Dylann Roof 'Hijacked' Meaning of Confederate Flag," *Washington Post,* December 6, 2019.

57. John Reeves, "Robert E. Lee and the Redemption of White New Orleans," *Medium,* August 18, 2017.

58. Angelique Yack, "Landrieu defends removing Confederate monuments on 'Powerhouse Politics,'" *ABC News,* March 21, 2018.

59. Yack, "Landrieu defends removing Confederate monuments on 'Powerhouse Politics.'"

60. Jeff Adelson and Jessica Williams, "New Orleans completes removal of Confederate monuments with take down of Robert E. Lee statue," *New Orleans Advocate,* May 19, 2017.

61. Ed Pilkington, "Mississippi lawmaker calls for lynchings after removal of Confederate symbols," *The Guardian,* May 22, 2017.

62. Laura Vozzella, "White nationalist Richard Spencer leads torch-bearing protesters defending Lee statue," *Washington Post,* May 14, 2017.

63. Sarah Wildman, "'You will not replace us': a French philosopher explains the Charlottesville chant," *Vox,* August 15, 2017.

64. Matt Pearce, "Chanting 'blood and soil!' white nationalists with torches march on University of Virginia," *Los Angeles Times,* August 11, 2017.

65. Sasha Ingber, "Neo-Nazi James Fields Gets 2nd Life Sentence for Charlottesville Attack," *NPR,* July 15, 2019.

66. Sarah Rankin and Steve Helber, "Charlottesville's Confederate Statues Shrouded in Black," *Fox 5 News,* August 23, 2017.

67. Jenna Johnson and John Wagner, "Trump condemns Charlottesville violence but doesn't single out white nationalists," *Washington Post,* August 12, 2017.

68. Jordyn Phelps, "Trump defends 2017 'very fine people' comments, calls Robert E. Lee 'a great general,'" *ABC News,* April 26, 2019.

69. See also O'Neill, *Down Along with That Devil's Bones,* 182. Sawyer refers to the impromptu protest as a "healing circle."

70. The name also echoed an earlier group organized in New Orleans: "Take 'Em Down NOLA."

71. "Threats against the bodies of black people who fight for change are by no means new. For example, last summer, a white man threatened to throw me in the Mississippi River for speaking in support of the Memphis Bridge Protest," wrote Tami Sawyer, *MLK50,* May 22, 2017.

72. O'Neill, *Down Along with That Devil's Bones,* 180.

73. O'Neill, *Down Along with That Devil's Bones,* 223.

74. O'Neill, *Down Along with That Devil's Bones,* 223.

75. Noah Caldwell and Audie Cornish, "Where Do Confederate Monuments Go After They Come Down?" *NPR,* August 5, 2018.

76. "These preemption laws are part of a broader battle between conservative state governments, often dominated by white conservatives, and more liberal cities, often with large African American populations" (David A. Graham, "Memphis's Novel Strategy for Tearing Down Confederate Statues," *The Atlantic,* December 21, 2017).

77. Graham, "Memphis's Novel Strategy for Tearing Down Confederate Statues."

78. Daniel Connolly and Vivian Wang, "Confederate Statues in Memphis Are Removed after City Council Vote," *New York Times,* December 20, 2017.

79. Wiley Henry, "Turner, Franklin Partner to Restore Life to 'Death' Park," *Tennessee Tribune,* June 30, 2022.

80. "Shuffling statues around our cities is like moving an abusive priest to another parish" (Erin L. Thompson, *Smashing Statues,* 170).

81. Cari Wade Gervin, "House Cuts Memphis Bicentennial Funds," *Nashville Post,* April 18, 2018; Caldwell and Cornish, "Where Do Confederate Monuments Go After They Come Down?"

82. Caldwell and Cornish, "Where Do Confederate Monuments Go After They Come Down?"

83. Erin L. Thompson, *Smashing Statues,* xviii.

84. Nick Beres, "Nathan Bedford Forrest statue along I-65 removed after more than 2 decades," Nashville *NewsChannelFive,* December 7, 2021; William Williams, "Forrest statue property offered for $1.85M," *Nashville Post,* June 23, 2022.

CONCLUSION

1. "Forrest and the Memphis Slave Trade." See also O'Neill, *Down Along with That Devil's Bones,* 229–30.

2. O'Neill, *Down Along with That Devil's Bones,* 215–20.

3. *Memphis Commercial Appeal,* June 15, 2021; *Washington Post,* June 2, 2021.

BIBLIOGRAPHY

ARCHIVES

Monroe Cockrell Collection, University of Alabama Special Collections.
Elmwood Cemetery, Memphis.
Filson Historical Center.
Library of Congress.
Andrew Nelson Lytle Papers, Vanderbilt University.
Memphis and Shelby County Public Library.
Memphis National Cemetery.
National Archives.
Tennessee State Library and Archives, Nashville.
University of Memphis.
University of Tennessee, Special Collections Online at UT (SCOUT).
Virginia Tech.

PUBLISHED RECORDS AND PAPERS

Bergeron, Paul, ed. *The Papers of Andrew Johnson. Vol. 8, May–August 1965.* Knoxville: University of Tennessee Press, 1990.

———. *The Papers of Andrew Johnson. Vol. 11, August 1866–January 1867.* Knoxville: University of Tennessee Press, 1994.

Minutes of the Eleventh Annual Meeting and Reunion of the United Confederate Veterans. New Orleans: Schumert & Warfield, 1901.

Report of the Joint Select Committee to Inquire into the Condition of Affairs in the Late Insurrectionary States. Washington, DC: Government Printing Office, 1872.

Reports of the Committee on the Conduct of War: Fort Pillow Massacre. House Report No. 65. 38th Cong., 1st sess., Washington, D.C.: U.S. Government Printing Office, 1864.

U.S. Department of the Interior—National Park Service. "National Register of Historic

Places Continuation Sheet." archive.org/stream/memoirsaddressesoomcfa/memoirsaddressesoomcfa_djvu.txt.

The War of the Rebellion: A Compilation of the Official Records of the Union and Confederate Armies. 70 vols. in 127 and index. Washington, DC: Government Printing Office, 1880–1901.

UNPUBLISHED RECORDS AND PAPERS

Forrest Monument Association Cash Ledger Book. Memphis and Shelby County Public Library.

Forrest Monument Association Minutes Book. Memphis and Shelby County Public Library.

PERIODICALS AND WEBSITES

ABC News.
AL.com.
The Atlantic.
Chattanooga Daily Times.
Dickson Herald.
Gadsden Messenger.
Greenville News.
The Guardian.
Harper's Weekly.
Historynet.com.
Intelligencer.
Kirkus Reviews.
Los Angeles Times.
Medium.
Memphis Commercial Appeal.
Memphis Daily Appeal.
Memphis Evening Herald.
Memphis News-Scimitar.
Memphis Press-Scimitar.
MLK50.
Montgomery Advertiser.
Nashville NewsChannelFive.
Nashville Post.

Nashville Scene.
Nashville Tennessean.
New Orleans Advocate.
New Orleans Democrat.
NPR.
Slate.
St. Paul Appeal.
Tennessee Tribune.
Vox.
Washington Post.

BOOKS

Ash, Steven F. *A Massacre in Memphis: The Race Riot That Shook the Nation One Year After the Civil War.* New York: Hill and Wang, 2013.

Ashdown, Paul, and Edward Caudill. *The Myth of Nathan Bedford Forrest.* Washington, DC: Rowman & Littlefield, 2004.

Bearss, Edwin C. *Forrest at Brice's Cross Roads and in North Mississippi in 1864.* Dayton, OH: Press of Morningside Bookshop, 1979.

Beifuss, Joan Turner. *At the River I Stand.* Memphis: St. Lukes Press, 1990.

Bell, Madison Smartt. *Devil's Dream: A Novel.* New York: Pantheon Books, 2009.

Biles, Roger. *Memphis in the Great Depression.* Knoxville: University of Tennessee Press, 1986.

Bloom, Khaled J. *The Mississippi Valley's Great Yellow Fever Epidemic of 1878.* Baton Rouge: Louisiana State University Press, 1993.

Bodnar, John. *Remaking America: Public Memory, Commemoration, and Patriotism in the Twentieth Century.* Princeton, NJ: Princeton University Press, 1992.

Bond, Beverly Greene, and Susan Eva O'Donovan, eds. *Remembering the Memphis Massacre: An American Story.* Athens: University of Georgia Press, 2020.

Bordewich, Fergus M. *Klan War: Ulysses S. Grant and the Battle to Save Reconstruction.* New York: Knopf, 2023.

Browning, Robert M. *Forrest: The Confederacy's Relentless Warrior.* Sterling, VA: Potomac Books, 2004.

Capers, Gerald. *Biography of a River Town: Memphis, Its Heroic Age.* Chapel Hill: University of North Carolina Press, 1939.

Carter, William C. *Conversations with Shelby Foote.* Jackson: University Press of Mississippi, 1989.

Cartwright, Joseph H. *The Triumph of Jim Crow: Tennessee Race Relations in the 1880s.* Knoxville: University of Tennessee Press, 1976.

Chapman, C. Stuart. *Shelby Foote: A Writer's Life.* Jackson: University Press of Mississippi, 2006.

Cimprich, John. *Fort Pillow, a Civil War Massacre, and Public Memory.* Baton Rouge: Louisiana State University Press, 2005.

Connelly, Thomas L., and Barbara L. Bellows. *God and General Longstreet: The Lost Cause and the Southern Mind.* Baton Rouge: Louisiana State University Press, 1982.

Coppock, Paul R. *Memphis Memoirs.* Memphis: Memphis State University Press, 1980.

Cox, Karen L. *No Common Ground: Confederate Monuments and the Ongoing Fight for Racial Justice.* Chapel Hill: University of North Carolina Press, 2021.

Davison, Eddy W., and Daniel Foxx. *Nathan Bedford Forrest: In Search of the Enigma.* New Orleans: Pelican Press, 2007.

Domby, Adam H. *The False Cause: Fraud, Fabrication, and White Supremacy in Confederate Memory.* Charlottesville: University of Virginia Press, 2020.

Duke, Basil W. *The Civil War Reminiscences of General Basil W. Duke, C.S.A.* New York: Cooper Square Press, 2001.

Foote, Shelby. *The Civil War: A Narrative.* 3 vols. New York: Vintage Books, 1958–74.

———. *Shiloh: A Novel.* New York: Dial Press, 1952.

Forrest Monument Association. *The Forrest Monument: Its History and Dedication; A Memorial in Art, Oratory, and Literature.* Memphis, 1905.

Foster, Gaines M. *Ghosts of the Confederacy: Defeat, the Lost Cause, and the Emergence of the New South.* Oxford, UK: Oxford University Press, 1987.

Fuchs, Richard. *An Unerring Fire: The Massacre at Fort Pillow.* Rutherford, NJ: Fairleigh Dickinson University Press, 1997.

Giddings, Paula J. *Ida: A Sword Among Lions: Ida B. Wells and the Campaign Against Lynching.* New York: Amistad, 2009.

Glatthaar, Joseph T. *Forged in Battle: The Civil War Alliance of Black Soldiers and White Officers.* New York: Free Press, 1990.

Goldfield, David R. *Cotton Fields and Skyscrapers: Southern City and Region, 1607–1980.* Baton Rouge: Louisiana State University Press, 1982.

Golightly, Karen, and Jonathan Judaken, eds. *Memphis: 200 Years Together, An Anthology.* Nashville: Susan Schadt Press, 2019.

Gordon, Caroline. *None Shall Look Back.* New York: Charles Scribner's Sons, 1937.

Gordon, Robert. *It Came from Memphis.* Boston: Faber and Faber, 1995.

Gritter, Elizabeth. *River of Hope: Black Politics and the Memphis Freedom Movement, 1865–1954.* Lexington: University Press of Kentucky, 2014.

Harkins, John E. *Metropolis of the American Nile: Memphis and Shelby County.* 2nd ed. Oxford, MS: Guild Bindery Press, 1991.

Hearn, Lafcadio. *Occidental Gleanings.* New York: Dodd, Mead and Co., 1925.

Henry, Robert Selph. *"First with the Most" Forrest.* 1944. Rpt. New York: Konecky and Konecky, 1992.

Horwitz, Tony. *Confederates in the Attic: Dispatches from the Unfinished Civil War.* New York: Pantheon Books, 1998.

Hurst, Jack. *Nathan Bedford Forrest: A Biography.* New York: Vintage Books, 1993.

Johnson, Adam Rankin. *The Partisan Rangers of the Confederate States Army.* Kerrville, TX: State House Press, 1995.

Jordan, Thomas, and J. P. Pryor. *The Campaigns of Lieut.-Gen. N. B. Forrest, and of Forrest's Cavalry.* New Orleans: Blelock & Co., 1868.

Keller, Morton. *The Art and Politics of Thomas Nast.* New York: Oxford University Press, 1968.

Lamon, Lester C. *Blacks in Tennessee, 1791–1970.* Knoxville: University of Tennessee Press, 1981.

Lauterbach, Preston. *Beale Street Dynasty: Sex, Song, and the Struggle for the Soul of Memphis.* New York: W. W. Norton & Co., 2015.

Litwack, Leon F. *Trouble in Mind: Black Southerners in the Age of Jim Crow.* New York: Alfred A. Knopf, 1998.

Liulevicius, Kathleen Zebley. *Rebel Salvation: Pardon and Amnesty of Confederates in Tennessee.* Baton Rouge: Louisiana State University Press, 2021.

Lucas, Mark. *The Southern Vision of Andrew Lytle.* Baton Rouge: Louisiana State University Press, 1986.

Lytle, Andrew Nelson. *Bedford Forrest and His Critter Company.* 1931. Rpt. Nashville: J. S. Sanders and Co., 1984.

Macaluso, Gregory J. *The Fort Pillow Massacre: The Reasons Why.* New York: Vantage Press, 1989.

Mathes, J. Harvey. *General Forrest.* New York: D. Appleton and Co., 1902.

Mayo, James M. *War Memorials as Political Landscape: The American Experience and Beyond.* New York: Praeger Publishers, 1988.

McFarland, Louis Burchett. *Memoirs and Addresses.* London: Forgotten Books, 2018.

McIlwaine, Shields. *Memphis: Down in Dixie.* New York: E. P. Dutton and Co., 1948.

Miller, William D. *Memphis During the Progressive Era, 1900–1917.* Memphis: Memphis State University Press, 1957.

Moore, C. Moffett, ed. *Nathan Bedford Forrest and the Civil War in Memphis: A Subject Bibliography of Books and Other References.* Memphis: Memphis Public Library, 1961.

Moore, Frank, ed., *The Rebellion Record, vol. 8: A Diary of American Events, With Documents, Narratives, Illustrative Incidents, Poetry, Etc.* London: Forgotten Books, 2017. www.perseus.tufts.edu/hopper/text?doc=Perseus%3Atext%3A2001.05.0092%3Achapter%3D144.

Morton, John Watson. *The Artillery of Nathan Bedford Forrest's Cavalry, "The Wizard of the Saddle." Nashville: M. E. Church, South, 1909.*

O'Neill, Connor Towne. *Down Along with That Devil's Bones: A Reckoning with Mon-*

uments, Memory, and the Legacy of White Supremacy. Chapel Hill, NC: Algonquin Books, 2020.

Parks, Aileen Wells. *Bedford Forrest: Boy on Horseback.* New York: Bobbs-Merrill Co., 1952.

Parsons, Elaine Frantz. *Ku-Klux: The Birth of the Klan in Reconstruction.* Chapel Hill: University of North Carolina Press, 2016.

Peterson, Merrill D. *Lincoln in American Memory.* New York: Oxford University Press, 1994.

Phillips, Robert L. *Shelby Foote: Novelist and Historian.* Jackson: University Press of Mississippi, 1992.

Phillips, Ulrich B. *American Negro Slavery.* New York: Appleton, 1918.

———. *Life and Labor in the Old South.* Boston: Little Brown and Co., 1929.

Piehlar, G. Kurt. *Remembering War the American Way.* Washington DC: Smithsonian Institution Press, 1995.

Pohlmann, Marcus D., and Michael Kirby. *Racial Politics at the Crossroads: Memphis Elects Dr. W. W. Herenton.* Knoxville: University of Tennessee Press, 1996.

Powell, David A. *Failure in the Saddle: Nathan Bedford Forrest, Joe Wheeler, and the Confederate Cavalry in the Chickamauga Campaign.* El Dorado Hills, CA: Savas Beatie, 2010.

Rabinowitz, Howard. *Race Relations in the Urban South: 1865–1900.* New York: Oxford University Press, 1978.

Rushing, Wanda. *Memphis and the Paradox of Place: Globalization in the American South.* Chapel Hill: University of North Carolina Press, 2009.

Savage, Kirk. *Standing Soldiers, Kneeling Slaves: Race, War, Monument in Nineteenth-Century America.* Princeton, NJ: Princeton University Press, 1997.

Share, Don. *Union.* London: Eyewear Publishing, 2013.

Sigafoos, Robert. *Cotton Row to Beale Street: A Business History of Memphis.* Memphis: Memphis State University Press, 1979.

Silver, Christopher, and John V. Moeser. *The Separate City: Black Communities in the Urban South, 1940–1968.* Lexington: University Press of Kentucky, 1995.

Stephenson, Philip Daingerfield. *Civil War Memoir of Philip Daingerfield Stephenson, D.D.* Baton Rouge: Louisiana State University Press, 1998.

Strickland, Colin A., and Timothy S. Huebner. *From Civil War Fort to State Park: A History of Fort Pillow.* Memphis: Rhodes College, 2006.

Thompson, Erin L. *Smashing Statues: The Rise and Fall of America's Public Monuments.* New York: W. W. Norton, 2022.

Toplin, Robert, ed. *Ken Burns's The Civil War: Historians Respond.* New York: Oxford University Press, 1996.

Tucker, David M. *Memphis Since Crump: Bossism, Blacks, and Civic Reformers, 1948–1968.* Knoxville: University of Tennessee Press, 1980.

Vinson, J. Chal. *Thomas Nast: Political Cartoonist.* Athens: University of Georgia Press, 1967.

Ward, Andrew. *River Run Red: The Fort Pillow Massacre in the American Civil War.* New York: Penguin, 2005.

Ward, Geoffrey, Ric Burns, and Ken Burns. *The Civil War: An Illustrated History.* New York: Knopf, 1990.

Weeks, Linton. *Memphis: A Folk History.* Little Rock, AR: Parkhurst Publishers, 1982.

Wells-Barnett, Ida. *On Lynchings: Southern Horrors, a Red Record, Mob Rule in New Orleans.* New York: Arno Press, 1969.

Widener, Ralph W. *Confederate Monuments: Enduring Symbols of the South and the War Between the States.* Washington, D.C.: Andromeda Associates, 1982.

Williamson, Joel. *William Faulkner and Southern History.* New York: Oxford University Press, 1993.

Wills, Brian Steel. *A Battle from the Start: The Life of Nathan Bedford Forrest.* New York: HarperCollins, 1992.

Wilson, Charles Reagan. *Baptized in Blood: The Religion of the Lost Cause, 1865–1920.* Athens: University of Georgia Press, 1980.

Woodward, C. Vann. *The Strange Career of Jim Crow.* 3d ed. New York: Oxford University Press, 1974.

Wrenn, Lynette Boney. *Crisis and Commission Government in Memphis: Elite Rule in a Gilded Age City.* Knoxville: University of Tennessee Press, 1998.

Wyeth, John Allen. *That Devil Forrest: A Life of General Nathan Bedford Forrest.* New York: Harper & Bros., 1899.

ARTICLES AND WEB PAGES

Alexander, Benjamin B. "Nathan Bedford Forrest and Southern Folkways." *Southern Partisan* 7 (Summer 1987): 27–32.

Atkins, Leah Rawls. "Alabama Confederate Heroine, Emma Sansom." Alabama Department of Archives and History. web.archive.org/web/20051030230042/http:/www.alabamamoments.state.al.us/sec19.html.

"The Attractiveness of a Beard." *Civil War Talk,* September 14, 2009. civilwartalk.com/threads/the-attractiveness-of-a-beard.13824/page-5.

Bailey, Fred Arthur. "Mildred Lewis Rutherford and the Patrician Cult of the Old South." *Georgia Historical Quarterly* 57, no. 3 (Fall 1994): 509–35.

Baldwin, Hannah. "Naming the Enslaved, Reconciling the Past in Memphis." *Southern Poverty Law Center,* October 19, 2018. www.splcenter.org/news/2018/10/19/naming-enslaved-reconciling-past-memphis-0.

Biles, Roger. "Cotton Fields or Skyscrapers? The Case of Memphis, Tennessee." *Historian* 50, no. 2 (February 1988): 210–33.

Black, Bill. "Celebrating Nathan Bedford Forrest Is Celebrating White Supremacy." MLK50, July 12, 2017. mlk50.com/2017/07/12/celebrating-nathan-bedford-forrest-is-celebrating-white-supremacy/.

Bounds, Tim. "Remembering Nathan Bedford Forrest: White Supremacy and the Memphis Monument." dokumen.tips/documents/remembering-forrest-white-supremacy-and-the-memphis-.html.

Brooksher, William R. "Betwixt Wind and Water: A Short Account of Confederate Major General Nathan Bedford Forrest's Attack on Fort Pillow." *Civil War Times Illustrated* 32, no. 5 (November–December 1993): 64–83.

Brown, Robbie. "Memphis Drops Confederate Names from Parks, Sowing New Battles." *New York Times,* March 28, 2013.

Brown, Jane. "Nathan Bedford Forrest: The Hero in Fiction." *Southern Partisan* 16 (Fourth Quarter 1996): 39–41.

Browning, Maria. "In His New Novel, Madison Smartt Bell Tackles the Confederacy's Most Controversial Son, Nathan Bedford Forrest." *Nashville Scene,* November 5, 2009. www.nashvillescene.com/news/in-his-new-novel-madison-smartt-bell-tackles-the-confederacys-most-controversial-son-nathan-bedford/article_48fb6355-7ab8-5156-a8bb-3efd9ea5f415.html.

Burns, Ken. *The Civil War. PBS, 1990.* www.pbs.org/kenburns/the-civil-war/.

Carney, Court. "The Contested Image of Nathan Bedford Forrest." *Journal of Southern History* 67, no. 3 (August 2001): 601–30.

———. "'The Most Man in the World': Nathan Bedford Forrest and the Cult of Masculinity in the South." In Watts, ed., *White Masculinity in the Recent South.* Baton Rouge: Louisiana State University Press, 2008.

Castel, Albert. "The Fort Pillow Massacre: A Fresh Examination of the Evidence." *Civil War History* 4, no. 1 (March 1958): 37–50.

Cimprich, John, and Robert C. Mainfort Jr. "The Fort Pillow Massacre: A Statistical Note." *Journal of American History* 76, no. 3 (December 1989): 830–37.

"Civil War Hairstyles II." *Yesterhair,* February 21, 2010. yesterhair.wordpress.com/tag/nathan-bedford-forrest/.

Coates, Ta-Nehisi. "The Convenient Suspension of Disbelief." *The Atlantic,* June 13, 2011. www.theatlantic.com/national/archive/2011/06/the-convenient-suspension-of-disbelief/240318/.

———. "Nathan Bedford Forrest Has Beautiful Eyes." *The Atlantic,* June 17, 2009. ta-nehisicoates.theatlantic.com/archives/2009/06/of_the_many_reckoning_that.php.

Cox, Karen. "What Changed in Charlottesville." *New York Times,* August 11, 2019.

Crownover, Danny. "The Vagabond—109 Years Ago Unveiling of the Emma Sansom Statue." *Gadsden Messenger,* April 1, 2016.

Davis, William C. "Behind the Lines." *Civil War Times Illustrated* 18, no. 4 (July 1979): 50.

Dawson, David. "Another Skirmish for N. B. Forrest." *Southern Magazine,* August 1988, 16.

Dessem, Matthew. "Watch Stephen Colbert's Impression of the Confederacy's Dumbest Monument." *Slate,* August 19, 2017.

Dowdy, Wayne. "'Something for the Colored People': Memphis Mayor Frank Tobey and the East Olive Bombing." *West Tennessee Historical Society Papers* 51 (December 1997): 108–15.

Dulaney, John T. "Memphis Park Commission Books." Memphis and Shelby County Room, 2014.

Eiland, Sarah W. "The Unspoken Demands of Slavery: The Exploitation of Female Slaves in the Memphis Slave Trade." *The Gettysburg College Journal of the Civil War Era* 10, article 6 (2020).

Ellis, John H. "Disease and the Destiny of a City: The 1878 Yellow Fever Epidemic in Memphis." *West Tennessee Historical Society Papers* 28 (1974): 75–89.

"Emma Sansom Monument." Historical Marker Database. www.hmdb.org/m.asp?m=12297.

"Emma Sansom Monument Gadsden, AL." *Civil War Talk,* March 4, 2021. civilwartalk.com/threads/emma-sansom-monument-gadsden-a1.183128/.

Finger, Michael. "Forrest Park—As It Looked Then, and As It Might Look Soon?" *Memphis Magazine.* October 28, 2015. memphismagazine.com/features/columns/forrest-park--as-it-looked-then-and-as-it-might-look-soon/.

Finkelston, Theodore. "The Apotheosis of St. Louis: Politics, Ego, and High Ideals in the Making of a Civic Symbol." *Gateway Heritage* 9, no. 1 (Summer 1988): 2–11.

Foote, Shelby. "Shelby Foote, The Art of Fiction No. 158." Interviewed by Carter Coleman, Donald Faulkner, William Kennedy. *Paris Review* 151 (Summer 1999). www.theparisreview.org/interviews/931/the-art-of-fiction-no-158-shelby-foote.

"Forrest and the Memphis Slave Trade." Rev. February 7, 2023. *Historical Marker Database.* www.hmdb.org/m.asp?m=117144.

Goings, Kenneth W., and Gerald L. Smith. "'Unhidden' Transcripts: Memphis and African American Agency, 1862–1920." *Journal of Urban History* 21, no. 3 (March 1995): 372–94.

Grimsley, Mark. "The Great Deceiver: The Life of Nathan Bedford Forrest, Part II." *Civil War Times Illustrated* 32, no. 5 (November–December 1993): 32–39, 94–97.

———. "Leader of the Klan: The Life of Nathan Bedford Forrest, Part III." *Civil War Times Illustrated* 32, no. 6 (January–February 1994): 34–38, 41, 63–66, 68–70, 72.

———. "Millionaire Rebel Raider: The Life of Nathan Bedford Forrest, Part I." *Civil War Times Illustrated* 32, no. 4 (September–October 1993): 58–61, 63–70, 72–73.

Harwick, Kevin R. "'Your Old Father Abe Lincoln Is Dead and Damned': Black Soldiers and the Memphis Race Riot of 1866." *Journal of Social History* 27 (Fall 1993): 109–28.

"Historian Has Suggestion to Resolve Alabama Confederate Monument Controversy." AL.com, December 13, 2020. www.al.com/news/2020/12/historian-has-suggestion-to-resolve-alabama-confederate-monument-controversy.html.

Holmes, Jak D. L. "The Underlying Causes of the Memphis Race Riot of 1866." *Tennessee Historical Quarterly* 17 (September 1958): 195–221.

Howard, Josh. "A Confederate on Campus: Nathan Bedford Forrest as MTSU's Mascot." *Sport in American History,* ussporthistory.com/2015/08/24/nathan-bedford-forrest-and-mtsu/.

Howell, Elmo. "William Faulkner and Tennessee." *Tennessee Historical Quarterly* 21, no. 3 (September 1962): 251–62.

———. "William Faulkner's General Forrest and the Uses of History." *Tennessee Historical Quarterly* 29, no. 3 (Fall 1970): 287–94.

Huebner, Timothy S. "Taking Profits, Making Myths: The Slave Trading Career of Nathan Bedford Forrest." *Civil War History* 69, no. 1 (2023).

———, and Madeleine M. McGrady. "Shelby Foote, Memphis, and the Civil War in American Memory." *Southern Cultures* 21, no. 4 (Winter 2015): 13–27.

Jordan, John L. "Was There a Massacre at Fort Pillow?" *Tennessee Historical Quarterly* 6, no. 2 (June 1947): 99–133.

Kershaw, Jack. Interviewed by Ben Houston, June 30, 2003. original-ufdc.uflib.ufl.edu/UF00093233/00001.

Khalil, Byron. "Descendants of Emma Sansom Call for Removal of Statue in Gadsden." ABC 33-40 News, Gadsden, AL, June 30, 2020. abc3340.com/news/local/descendants-of-emma-sansom-family-call-for-removal-of-statue?src=link.

Kroll, H. H. "The Camp Follower in Gen. Forrest's Command Tent." *Stag,* June 1961.

Landess, Tom. "Tilting at Statues." *Southern Partisan* 8 (Summer 1988): 6.

Longacre, Edward G. "Review." *Georgia Historical Quarterly* 77, no. 1 (Spring 1993): 193–95.

Lovett, Bobby L. "Memphis Riots: White Reaction to Blacks in Memphis, May 1865–July 1866." *Tennessee Historical Quarterly* 38 (Spring 1979): 9–31.

Maness, Lonnie E. "The Fort Pillow Massacre: Fact or Fiction." *Tennessee Historical Quarterly* 45, no. 4 (Winter 1986): 287–315.

"Middle Tennessee State University Students Seek to Rename a Campus Building That Honors the Founder of the Ku Klux Klan." *Journal of Blacks in Higher Education* 54 (Winter 2006–7).

"MLK: The Gary Revel Story—They Slew the Dreamer." garyrevel.com/dreamer.html.

"Monument to Gen. N. B. Forrest." *Confederate Veteran* 13 (September 1905): 389–91.

Obama, Barack. "Remarks by the President in Eulogy for the Honorable Reverend Clementa Pinckney." June 26, 2015. obamawhitehouse.archives.gov/the-press-office/2015/06/26/remarks-president-eulogy-honorable-reverend-clementa-pinckney.

O'Neill, Towne Connor. "America's Ugliest Confederate Statue Isn't Coming Down Anytime Soon." *Intelligencer,* September 16, 2017.

Owen, Thomas McAdory. "Emma Sansom, an Alabama Heroine: An Address Delivered before the Sixth Annual Convention of the Alabama Division, United Daughters of the Confederacy," Demopolis, May 14, 1902. Birmingham, AL, 1904. digital.library .upenn.edu/women/owen/sansom/sansom.html

Parsons, Elaine Frantz. "We Don't Have Enough Contempt for Nathan Bedford Forrest." *We're History,* July 13, 2015. werehistory.org/nathan-bedford-forrest/.

"Partisan Conversation." *Southern Partisan* 12 (First Quarter 1992): 34–38.

Pettegrew, John. "'The Soldier's Faith': Turn-of-the-Century Memory of the Civil War and the Emergence of Modern American Nationalism." *Journal of Contemporary History* 31, no. 1 (January 1996): 49–73

Pittman, Walter E. "General Nathan Bedford Forrest and Military Leadership." *West Tennessee Historical Society Papers* 35 (1981): 51–56.

Putzel, Max. "Faulkner's Memphis Stories." *Virginia Quarterly Review* 59, no. 2 (Spring 1983): 254–70.

Radford, John P. "Identity and Tradition in the Post–Civil War South." *Journal of Historical Geography* 18, no. 1 (January 1992): 91–103.

Reed, John Shelton. "The Banner That Won't Stay Furled." *Southern Cultures* 8, no. 1 (Spring 2002): 76–100.

Rodgers, Michael. "In Gadsden, Officials Take No Action against Monument to Confederate Sympathizer Emma Sansom." *Montgomery Advertiser,* July 9, 2020. www.montgomeryadvertiser.com/story/news/2020/07/09/gadsden-no-action-against-monument-to-confederate-sympathizer-emma-sansom-nathan-bedford-forrest/5397407002/

Rousey, Dennis C. "Yellow Fever and Black Policemen in Memphis: A Post-Reconstruction Anomaly." *Journal of Southern History* 51, no. 3 (August 1985): 357–74.

Royster, Charles. "A Battle from the Start: The Life of Nathan Bedford Forrest." *The Atlantic* 271, no. 5 (May 1993): 125.

Shannon, Kelley. "Perry Fires Up Anti-Tax Crowd." Associated Press, April 15, 2009. www.heraldbanner.com/news/local-update-3-15-p-m-wednesday--perry-fires-up-anti-tax-crowd/article_68722527-3a82-5e08-89b4-3fec0234fce3.html.

Sharrett, Christopher. "Reconciliation and the Politics of Forgetting: Notes on Civil War Documentaries." *Cinéaste* 36, no. 4 (2011): 26–31.

Smith, John David. "Ulrich Bonnell Phillips." *New Georgia Encyclopedia.* www.georgiaencyclopedia.org/articles/history-archaeology/ulrich-bonnell-phillips-1877-1934/.

———. "Introduction." In *Life and Labor in the Old South,* by Ulrich Bonnell Phillips. Columbia: University of South Carolina Press, 2007.

Smith, Zadie. "What Do We Want History to Do to Us?" *New York Review of Books* (February 27, 2020).

Stainchak, John. "Behind the Lines." *Civil War Times Illustrated* 32 (January–February 1994): 18.

Stokes-Casey, Judy. "Richard Lou's ReCovering Memphis." *Tennessee Historical Quarterly* 75, no. 4 (December 2016): 322–47.

Tap, Bruce. "'These Devils Are Not Fit to Live on God's Earth': War Crimes and the Committee on the Conduct of War." *Civil War History* 42, no. 2 (June 1996): 116–32.

Tate, J. O. "On Nathan Bedford Forrest (& the Death of Heroes)." *Southern Partisan* 4 (Summer 1984): 13–19.

Terris, Ben. "Scholars Nostalgic for the Old South Study the Virtues of Secession, Quietly." *Chronicle of Higher Education,* December 6, 2009.

Thelen, David. "Memory and American History." *Journal of American History* 75, no. 4 (March 1989): 1117–29.

"Tributes to Gen. George W. Gordon." *Confederate Veteran* 19 (1909): 499.

Tucker, David M. "Miss Ida B. Wells and Memphis Lynching." *Phylon* 32, no. 2 (Summer 1971): 112–22.

Vinh, Alphonse. "Southern Agrarian Warrior Hero." *Southern Partisan* 14 (Fourth Quarter 1994): 42–45.

Weller, Jac. "Nathan Bedford Forrest: An Analysis of Untutored Military Genius." *Tennessee Historical Quarterly* 18, no. 3 (September 1959): 213–51.

Williams, Edward F. "The Johnsonville Raid and Nathan Bedford Forrest State Park." *Tennessee Historical Quarterly* 3 (Fall 1969): 225–51.

Wills, Brian S. "Review." *Journal of American History* 81, no. 3 (December 1994): 1320–21.

Wilson, Charles Reagan. "The Death of Southern Heroes: Historic Funerals of the South." *Southern Cultures* 1, no. 1 (Fall 1994): 3–22.

Winberry, John J. "'Lest We Forget': The Confederate Monument and the Southern Townscape." *Southeastern Geographer* 23, no. 2 (November 1983): 107–21.

———. "Symbols in the Landscape: The Confederate Memorial." *Pioneer America Society Transactions* 5 (1982): 9–15.

"Women's Forrest Statue Association." *Confederate Veteran* 8 (July 1900): 302.

Zeitz, Joshua Michael. "Rebel Redemption Redux." *Dissent,* Winter 2001. www.dissentmagazine.org/article/rebel-redemption-redux/.

DISSERTATION

Wangsvick, Paul David. "The Contested Reputation of Nathan Bedford Forrest: A Case Study in Rhetoric and Regional Identity Formation." PhD diss., University of Memphis, 2011.

INDEX